M TCP/IP Ace It!

PLANNING

▶ Given a scenario, identify valid network configurations. This can involve determining the correct subnet mask to allow for a specific number of hosts per subnet.

▶ When determining the number of host IDs or network IDs, remember to subtract 2 from the total number available for the number of bits. This is because the IDs cannot be all 1s or 0s.

INSTALLATION AND CONFIGURATION

▶ Given a scenario, select the appropriate services to install when using Microsoft TCP/IP on a Microsoft Windows NT Server computer. This includes knowing when to install DNS, WINS, DHCP, LMHOSTS, and HOSTS files.

▶ On a Windows NT Server computer, configure Microsoft TCP/IP to support multiple adapters. This includes configuring IP address information for each adapter locally and creating any necessary WINS or LMHOSTS entries for multihomed computers.

▶ Configure scopes by using DHCP Manager. Remember to create a separate scope for each subnet. DHCP Relay Agents can be installed to allow DHCP requests to be passed between subnets. A router can transmit requests if BOOTP is enabled.

TROUBLESHOOTING

▶ Diagnose and resolve IP addressing problems. These can include incorrect subnet masks, incorrect gateway settings, or incorrect IP addresses.

▶ Use Microsoft TCP/IP utilities to diagnose IP configuration problems. The utilities available to help diagnose such problems include:
  - `ping` — Used to determine whether you are capable of connecting to a specific TCP/IP device on the network.
  - `tracert` — Traces the path of network transmissions between two TCP/IP devices. It displays the IP address of each router it crosses along the way.
  - `nbtstat` — Used to view NetBIOS over IP statistics.
  - `arp` — Used to view the IP-address-to-physical-address cache.
  - `route` — Used to view and manage the static routing table.
  - `netstat` — Used to view various TCP/IP statistics including connected sessions.
  - `ipconfig` — Used to view IP settings on a Windows NT Server computer.
  - `winipcfg` — Used to view IP settings on a Win95 computer.

▶ Diagnose and resolve name resolution problems. This can include verifying that the WINS and DNS settings are correct. The HOSTS and LMHOSTS files should also be examined as possible causes of the problem.

Copyright © 1998 IDG Books Worldwide. All rights reserved.
For more information about IDG Books, call 1-800-762-2974.
ISBN: 0-7645-3258-8

- Install and configure a WINS server:
  - Import LMHOSTS files for WINS.
  - Run WINS on a multihomed computer.
  - Configure WINS replication. Know the difference between push and pull replication.
  - Configure static mappings in the WINS database. Know the different types of static mappings used in the WINS database.

- Configure a Windows NT Server computer to function as an IP router. Windows NT is capable of using either static or dynamic routing. Enabling IP forwarding allows for static routing. Installing RIP allows for dynamic routing.

- Install and configure the Microsoft DNS Server service on a Windows NT Server computer:
  - Integrate DNS with other name servers. When integrating DNS with WINS by allowing WINS to use DNS for name resolution, the administrative burden can be eased. Static entries for non-WINS clients can be created in DNS while WINS clients automatically register names with the WINS server.
  - Connect a DNS server to a DNS root server. The CACHE.DNS file contains the name-to-IP-address mappings for the Internet's root DNS servers.
  - Configure DNS server roles. A primary name server gets the data for its zones from the local DNS database. A secondary DNS server gets the data for its zones from the primary DNS server in that zone through a zone transfer.

- Configure HOSTS and LMHOSTS files. These files contain name-to-IP-address mappings. The IP address is listed first and is followed by the name. The HOSTS file performs hostname resolution, whereas the LMHOSTS file performs NetBIOS name resolution. The `#pre` tag in LMHOSTS files loads the entry into the name cache, whereas the `#dom` tag is used to specify a domain controller.

- Configure a Windows NT Server computer to support TCP/IP printing. The TCP/IP printing service must first be installed on the NT Server. The print device is then configured with a valid IP address. A port on the NT server is then mapped to that IP address. This allows the printer to be shared to other users on the network.

- Configure SNMP. Configure the community and trap settings used by SNMP. Traps can only be sent to members of the sender's community.

CONNECTIVITY

- Given a scenario, identify which utility to use to connect to a TCP/IP-based UNIX host. FTP is used to transfer files, whereas telnet allows programs to be run remotely. LPR is used to send print jobs to a UNIX computer, and LPQ enables monitoring of print jobs on a UNIX computer.
- Configure a RAS server and dial-up networking for use on a TCP/IP network. The RAS service must be installed. Windows NT Server is capable of functioning as a PPP server or client, and it can also function as a SLIP client, but not as a SLIP server.
- Configure and support browsing in a multiple-domain routed network. WINS allows for this. This can also be done using LMHOSTS files by adding entries for domain controllers using the #dom tag.
- WINS Proxies allow non-WINS clients to use WINS servers for name resolution. The proxy forwards the request to the WINS server.

MONITORING AND OPTIMIZATION

- Given a scenario, identify which tool to use to monitor TCP/IP traffic. Network Monitor and NETSTAT both have capabilities for monitoring network traffic. Performance Monitor can be used to monitor TCP/IP traffic once SNMP has been installed on the computer.

MCSE TCP/IP Ace It!

MCSE TCP/IP Ace It!

Jason Nash

IDG Books Worldwide, Inc.
An International Data Group Company
Foster City, CA • Chicago, IL • Indianapolis, IN • New York, NY

MCSE TCP/IP Ace It!
Published by
IDG Books Worldwide, Inc.
An International Data Group Company
919 E. Hillsdale Blvd., Suite 400
Foster City, CA 94404
www.idgbooks.com (IDG Books Worldwide Web site)

Copyright © 1998 IDG Books Worldwide, Inc. All rights reserved. No part of this book, including interior design, cover design, and icons, may be reproduced or transmitted in any form, by any means (electronic, photocopying, recording, or otherwise) without the prior written permission of the publisher.

Library of Congress Catalog Card Number: 98-073336

ISBN: 0-7645-3258-8

Printed in the United States of America

10 9 8 7 6 5 4 3 2 1

1P/RW/QZ/ZY/FC

Distributed in the United States by IDG Books Worldwide, Inc.

Distributed by Macmillan Canada for Canada; by Transworld Publishers Limited in the United Kingdom; by IDG Norge Books for Norway; by IDG Sweden Books for Sweden; by Woodslane Pty. Ltd. for Australia; by Woodslane (NZ) Ltd. for New Zealand; by Addison Wesley Longman Singapore Pte Ltd. for Singapore, Malaysia, Thailand, Indonesia, and Korea; by Norma Comunicaciones S.A. for Colombia; by Intersoft for South Africa; by International Thomson Publishing for Germany, Austria, and Switzerland; by Toppan Company Ltd. for Japan; by Distribuidora Cuspide for Argentina; by Livraria Cultura for Brazil; by Ediciencia S.A. for Ecuador; by Ediciones ZETA S.C.R Ltda. for Peru; by WS Computer Publishing Corporation, Inc., for the Philippines; by Unalis Corporation for Taiwan; by Contemporanea de Ediciones for Venezuela; by Computer Book & Magazine Store for Puerto Rico; by Express Computer Distributors for the Caribbean and West Indies. Authorized Sales Agent: Anthony Rudkin Associates for the Middle East and North Africa.

For general information on IDG Books Worldwide's books in the U.S., please call our Consumer Customer Service department at 800-762-2974. For reseller information, including discounts and premium sales, please call our Reseller Customer Service department at 800-434-3422.

For information on where to purchase IDG Books Worldwide's books outside the U.S., please contact our International Sales department at 650-655-3172 or fax 650-655-3297.

For information on foreign language translations, please contact our Foreign & Subsidiary Rights department at 650-655-3021 or fax 650-655-3281.

For sales inquiries and special prices for bulk quantities, please contact our Sales department at 650-655-3200 or write to the address above.

For information on using IDG Books Worldwide's books in the classroom or for ordering examination copies, please contact our Educational Sales department at 800-434-2086 or fax 317-596-5499.

For press review copies, author interviews, or other publicity information, please contact our Public Relations department at 650-655-3000 or fax 650-655-3299.

For authorization to photocopy items for corporate, personal, or educational use, please contact Copyright Clearance Center, 222 Rosewood Drive, Danvers, MA 01923, or fax 978-750-4470.

LIMIT OF LIABILITY/DISCLAIMER OF WARRANTY: AUTHOR AND PUBLISHER HAVE USED THEIR BEST EFFORTS IN PREPARING THIS BOOK. IDG BOOKS WORLDWIDE, INC., AND AUTHOR MAKE NO REPRESENTATIONS OR WARRANTIES WITH RESPECT TO THE ACCURACY OR COMPLETENESS OF THE CONTENTS OF THIS BOOK AND SPECIFICALLY DISCLAIM ANY IMPLIED WARRANTIES OF MERCHANTABILITY OR FITNESS FOR A PARTICULAR PURPOSE. THERE ARE NO WARRANTIES THAT EXTEND BEYOND THE DESCRIPTIONS CONTAINED IN THIS PARAGRAPH. NO WARRANTY MAY BE CREATED OR EXTENDED BY SALES REPRESENTATIVES OR WRITTEN SALES MATERIALS. THE ACCURACY AND COMPLETENESS OF THE INFORMATION PROVIDED HEREIN AND THE OPINIONS STATED HEREIN ARE NOT GUARANTEED OR WARRANTED TO PRODUCE ANY PARTICULAR RESULTS, AND THE ADVICE AND STRATEGIES CONTAINED HEREIN MAY NOT BE SUITABLE FOR EVERY INDIVIDUAL. NEITHER IDG BOOKS WORLDWIDE, INC., NOR AUTHOR SHALL BE LIABLE FOR ANY LOSS OF PROFIT OR ANY OTHER COMMERCIAL DAMAGES, INCLUDING BUT NOT LIMITED TO SPECIAL, INCIDENTAL, CONSEQUENTIAL, OR OTHER DAMAGES.

Trademarks: All brand names and product names used in this book are trade names, service marks, trademarks, or registered trademarks of their respective owners. IDG Books Worldwide is not associated with any product or vendor mentioned in this book.

IDG is an independent entity from Microsoft Corporation, and not affiliated with Microsoft Corporation in any manner. This publication and CD-ROM may be used in assisting students to prepare for a Microsoft Certified Professional Exam. Neither Microsoft Corporation, its designated review company, nor IDG warrants that use of this publication and CD-ROM will ensure passing the relevant Exam. Microsoft is either a registered trademark or trademark of Microsoft Corporation in the United States and/or other countries.

 is a trademark under exclusive license to IDG Books Worldwide, Inc., from International Data Group, Inc.

ABOUT IDG BOOKS WORLDWIDE

Welcome to the world of IDG Books Worldwide.

IDG Books Worldwide, Inc., is a subsidiary of International Data Group, the world's largest publisher of computer-related information and the leading global provider of information services on information technology. IDG was founded more than 25 years ago and now employs more than 8,500 people worldwide. IDG publishes more than 275 computer publications in over 75 countries (see listing below). More than 90 million people read one or more IDG publications each month.

Launched in 1990, IDG Books Worldwide is today the #1 publisher of best-selling computer books in the United States. We are proud to have received eight awards from the Computer Press Association in recognition of editorial excellence and three from *Computer Currents*' First Annual Readers' Choice Awards. Our best-selling ...For Dummies® series has more than 50 million copies in print with translations in 38 languages. IDG Books Worldwide, through a joint venture with IDG's Hi-Tech Beijing, became the first U.S. publisher to publish a computer book in the People's Republic of China. In record time, IDG Books Worldwide has become the first choice for millions of readers around the world who want to learn how to better manage their businesses.

Our mission is simple: Every one of our books is designed to bring extra value and skill-building instructions to the reader. Our books are written by experts who understand and care about our readers. The knowledge base of our editorial staff comes from years of experience in publishing, education, and journalism — experience we use to produce books for the '90s. In short, we care about books, so we attract the best people. We devote special attention to details such as audience, interior design, use of icons, and illustrations. And because we use an efficient process of authoring, editing, and desktop publishing our books electronically, we can spend more time ensuring superior content and spend less time on the technicalities of making books.

You can count on our commitment to deliver high-quality books at competitive prices on topics you want to read about. At IDG Books Worldwide, we continue in the IDG tradition of delivering quality for more than 25 years. You'll find no better book on a subject than one from IDG Books Worldwide.

John Kilcullen
CEO
IDG Books Worldwide, Inc.

Steven Berkowitz
President and Publisher
IDG Books Worldwide, Inc.

Eighth Annual Computer Press Awards ≥1992

Ninth Annual Computer Press Awards ≥1993

Tenth Annual Computer Press Awards ≥1994

Eleventh Annual Computer Press Awards ≥1995

IDG Books Worldwide, Inc., is a subsidiary of International Data Group, the world's largest publisher of computer-related information and the leading global provider of information services on information technology. International Data Group's publications include over 275 computer publications in over 75 countries. More than 90 million people read one or more International Data Group publications each month. International Data Group's publications include: **ARGENTINA**: Buyer's Guide, Computerworld Argentina, PC World Argentina; **AUSTRALIA**: Australian Macworld, Australian PC World, Australian Reseller News, Computerworld, IT Casebook, Network World, Publish, Webmaster; **AUSTRIA**: Computerwelt Österreich, Networks Austria, PC Tip Austria; **BANGLADESH**: PC World Bangladesh; **BELARUS**: PC World Belarus; **BELGIUM**: Data News; **BRAZIL**: Annuário de Informática, Computerworld, Connections, Macworld, PC Player, PC World, Publish, Reseller News, Supergamepower; **BULGARIA**: Computerworld Bulgaria, Network World Bulgaria, PC & MacWorld Bulgaria; **CANADA**: CIO Canada, Client/Server World, ComputerWorld Canada, InfoWorld Canada, NetworkWorld Canada, WebWorld; **CHILE**: Computerworld Chile, PC World Chile; **COLOMBIA**: Computerworld Colombia, PC World Colombia; **COSTA RICA**: PC World Centro America; **THE CZECH AND SLOVAK REPUBLICS**: Computerworld Czechoslovakia, Macworld Czech Republic, PC World Czechoslovakia; **DENMARK**: Communications World Danmark, Computerworld Danmark, Macworld Danmark, PC World Danmark, Techworld Denmark; **DOMINICAN REPUBLIC**: PC World Republica Dominicana; **ECUADOR**: PC World Ecuador; **EGYPT**: Computerworld Middle East, PC World Middle East; **EL SALVADOR**: PC World Centro America; **FINLAND**: MikroPC, Tietoviikko; **FRANCE**: Distributique, Hebdo, Info PC, Le Monde Informatique, Macworld, Reseaux & Telecoms, WebMaster France; **GERMANY**: Computer Partner, Computerwoche, Computerwoche Extra, Computerwoche FOCUS, Global Online, Macwelt, PC Welt; **GREECE**: Amiga Computing, GamePro Greece, Multimedia World; **GUATEMALA**: PC World Centro America; **HONDURAS**: PC World Centro America; **HONG KONG**: Computerworld Hong Kong, PC World Hong Kong, Publish in Asia; **HUNGARY**: ABCD CD-ROM, Computerworld Szamitastechnika, Internetto online Magazine, PC World Hungary, PC-X Magazin Hungary; **ICELAND**: Tolvuheimur PC World Island; **INDIA**: Information Communications World, Information Systems Computerworld, PC World India, Publish in Asia; **INDONESIA**: InfoKomputer PC World, Komputek Computerworld, Publish in Asia; **IRELAND**: ComputerScope, PC Live!; **ISRAEL**: Macworld Israel, People & Computers/Computerworld; **ITALY**: Computerworld Italia, Macworld Italia, Networking Italia, PC World Italia; **JAPAN**: DTP World, Macworld Japan, Nikkei Personal Computing, OS/2 World Japan, SunWorld Japan, Windows NT World, Windows World Japan; **KENYA**: PC World East African; **KOREA**: Hi-Tech Information, Macworld Korea, PC World Korea; **MACEDONIA**: PC World Macedonia; **MALAYSIA**: Computerworld Malaysia, PC World Malaysia, Publish in Asia; **MALTA**: PC World Malta; **MEXICO**: Computerworld Mexico, PC World Mexico; **MYANMAR**: PC World Myanmar; **NETHERLANDS**: Computer! Totaal, LAN Internetworking Magazine, LAN World Buyers Guide, Macworld Netherlands, Net, WebWereld; **NEW ZEALAND**: Absolute Beginners Guide and Plain & Simple Series, Computer Buyer, Computer Industry Directory, Computerworld New Zealand, MTB, Network World, PC World New Zealand, Publish in Asia; **NICARAGUA**: PC World Centro America; **NORWAY**: Computerworld Norge, CW Rapport, Datamagasinet, Financial Rapport, Kursguide Norge, Macworld Norge, Multimediaworld Norge, PC World Ekspress Norge, PC World Netverk, PC World Norge, PC World ProduktGuide Norge; **PAKISTAN**: Computerworld Pakistan; **PANAMA**: PC World Panama; **PEOPLE'S REPUBLIC OF CHINA**: China Computer Users, China Computerworld, China InfoWorld, China Telecom World Weekly, Computer & Communication, Electronic Design China, Electronics Today, Electronics Weekly, Game Software, PC World China, Popular Computer Week, Software Weekly, Software World, Telecom World; **PERU**: Computerworld Peru, PC World Profesional Peru, PC World SoHo Peru; **PHILIPPINES**: Click!, Computerworld Philippines, PC World Philippines, Publish in Asia; **POLAND**: Computerworld Poland, Computerworld Special Report Poland, Cyber, Macworld Poland, Networld Poland, PC World Komputer; **PORTUGAL**: Cerebro/PC World, Computerworld/Correio Informático, Dealer World Portugal, Mac*In/PC*In Portugal, Multimedia World; **PUERTO RICO**: PC World Puerto Rico; **ROMANIA**: Computerworld Romania, PC World Romania, Telecom Romania; **RUSSIA**: Computerworld Russia, Mir PK, Publish, Seti; **SINGAPORE**: Computerworld Singapore, PC World Singapore, Publish in Asia; **SLOVENIA**: Monitor; **SOUTH AFRICA**: Computing SA, Network World SA, Software World SA; **SPAIN**: Communicaciones World España, Computerworld España, Dealer World España, Macworld España, PC World España; **SRI LANKA**: Infolink PC World; **SWEDEN**: CAP&Design, Computer Sweden, Corporate Computing Sweden, Internetworld Sweden, it.branschen, Macworld Sweden, MaxiData Sweden, MikroDatorn, Nätverk & Kommunikation, PC World Sweden, PCaktiv, Windows World Sweden; **SWITZERLAND**: Computerworld Schweiz, Macworld Schweiz, PCtip; **TAIWAN**: Computerworld Taiwan, Macworld Taiwan, NEW ViSiON/Publish, PC World Taiwan, Windows World Taiwan; **THAILAND**: Publish in Asia, Thai Computerworld; **TURKEY**: Computerworld Turkiye, Macworld Turkiye, Network World Turkiye, PC World Turkiye; **UKRAINE**: Computerworld Kiev, Multimedia World Ukraine, PC World Ukraine; **UNITED KINGDOM**: Acorn User UK, Amiga Action UK, Amiga Computing UK, Apple Talk UK, Computing, Macworld, Parents and Computers UK, PC Advisor, PC Home, PSX Pro, The WEB; **UNITED STATES**: Cable in the Classroom, CIO Magazine, Computerworld, DOS World, Federal Computer Week, GamePro Magazine, InfoWorld, I-Way, Macworld, Network World, PC Games, PC World, Publish, Video Event, THE WEB Magazine, WebMaster; online webzines: JavaWorld, NetscapeWorld, and SunWorld Online; **URUGUAY**: InfoWorld Uruguay; **VENEZUELA**: Computerworld Venezuela, PC World Venezuela; and **VIETNAM**: PC World Vietnam.

5/7/98

Welcome to Ace It!

Looking to get certified? The *Ace It!* series is what you're looking for! The *Ace It!* series has been designed to meet your need for a quick, easy-to-use study tool that helps you save time, prioritize your study, and cram for the exam. *Ace It!* books serve as a supplement to other certification resources, such as our award-winning *Study Guides* and *MCSE...For Dummies* series. With these two series and *Ace It!*, IDG Books offers a full suite of study tools to meet your certification needs, from complete tutorial and reference materials to quick exam prep tools.

Ace It's exam-expert authors give you the ace in the hole: our unique insider's perspective on the exam itself — how it works, what topics are really important, and *how you really need to think* to ace the exam. Our features train your brain to understand not only the essential topics covered on the exam, but how to decipher the exam itself. By demystifying the exam, we give you that extra confidence to know that you're really prepared!

Ace It! books help you study with a wealth of truly valuable features in each chapter:

- **Official Word** lists the official certification exam objectives covered in the chapter.
- **Inside Scoop** immediately follows the Official Word and gives you the author's insight and expertise about the exam content covered in the chapter.
- **Are You Prepared?** is a chapter pretest that lets you check your knowledge beforehand: if you score well on the pretest, you may not need to review the chapter! This helps you focus your study. The questions are immediately followed by answers with cross-references to the information in the chapter, helping you further target your review.

- **Have You Mastered?** is a chapter post-test that includes five to ten multiple-choice questions with answers, analysis, and cross-references to the chapter discussion. The questions help you check your progress and pinpoint what you've learned and what you still need to study.
- **Practice Your Skills** consists of three to five exercises related to specific exam objectives. They provide an opportunity to relate exam concepts to real-world situations by presenting a hypothetical problem or guiding you through a task at the computer. These exercises enable you to take what you've learned for the exam and put it to work.

Within each chapter, icons call your attention to the following features:

Test Tips give hints and strategies for passing the exam to help strengthen your test-taking skills.

Test Traps warn you of pitfalls and loopholes you're likely to see in actual exam questions.

Pop Quizzes offer instant testing of hot exam topics.

Know This provides a quick summary of essential elements of topics you *will* see on the exam.

WELCOME TO ACE IT!

In the front and back of the book, you'll find even more features to give you that extra confidence and prepare you to get certified:

- **Ace Card:** Tear out this quick-review card for a distilled breakdown of essential exam-related terms and concepts to take with you and review before the exam.

- **Insider's Guide:** This helpful certification profile describes the certification process in general, and discusses the specific exam this book covers. It explains the exam development process, provides tips for preparing for and taking the exams, describes the testing process (how to register for an exam, what to expect at the testing center, how to obtain and evaluate test scores, and how to retake the exam if necessary), and tells you where to go for more information about the certification you're after.

- **Practice Exam:** A full-length multiple choice practice exam. Questions and answer selections mimic the certification exam in style, number of questions, and content to give you the closest experience to the real thing.

- **Exam Key** and **Exam Analysis:** These features tell you not only what the right answers are on the Practice Exam, but why they're right, and where to look in the book for the material you need to review.

- **Exam Revealed:** Here's your ace in the hole — the real deal on how the exam works. Our exam-expert authors deconstruct the questions on the Practice Exam, examining their structure, style, and wording to reveal subtleties, loopholes, and pitfalls that can entrap or mislead you when you take the real test. For each question, the author highlights part of the question or answer choices and then, in a sentence or two, identifies the possible problem and explains how to avoid it.

- **Glossary:** Not familiar with a word or concept? Just look it up! The Glossary covers all the essential terminology you need to know.

MCSE TCP/IP ACE IT!

With this wealth of features and the exclusive insider's perspective provided by our authors, you can be sure that *Ace It!* completes your set of certification study tools. No matter what you've got, you still need an *Ace It!*

Credits

Acquisitions Editor
  Tracy Thomsic

Development Editors
  Jennifer Rowe
  Steve Anderson

Copy Editors
  Brian MacDonald
  Carolyn Welch

Project Coordinator
  Ritchie Durdin

Book Designer
  Dan Ziegler

Graphics and Production Specialist
  Stephanie Hollier

Graphics Technicians
  Linda J. Marousek
  Hector Mendosa

Quality Control Specialists
  Mick Arellano
  Mark Schumann

Proofreader
  David Wise

Indexer
  Liz Cunningham

About the Author

Jason Nash currently lives in Raleigh, North Carolina, with his wife and coauthor Angie. He works for Wang Global (www.wang.com). His certifications include MCSE, MCT, Novell CNE, and the Network Professional Association's CNP. Outside of writing and work, he and Angie enjoy playing paintball on the weekends and going to the beach. He welcomes comments from readers; his e-mail address is jnash@intrex.net, and his home page is at www.intrex.net/nash.

To Timmy Franks, thank you for everything.

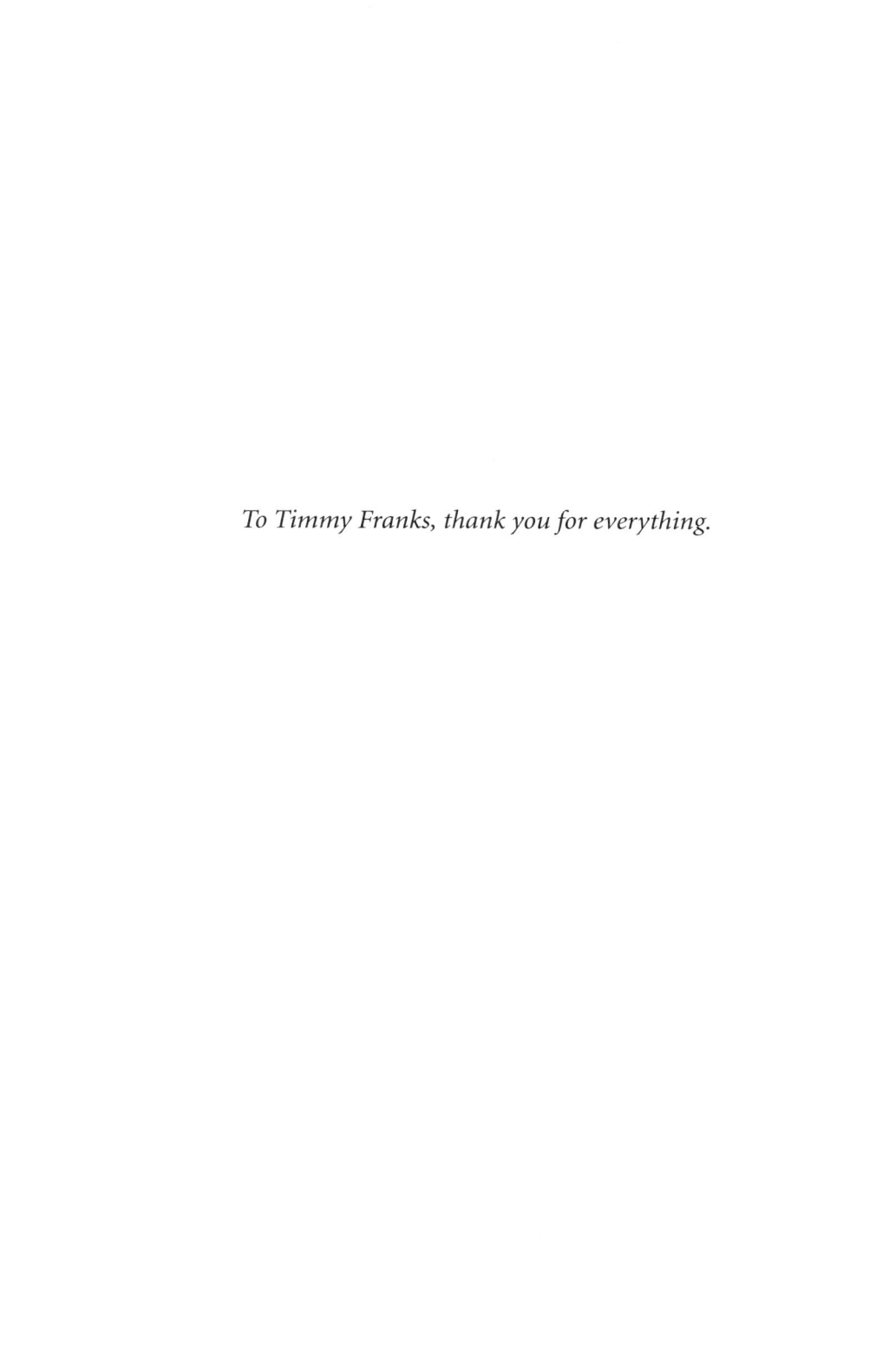

Insider's Guide to MCP Certification

The Microsoft Certified Professional (MCP) exams are *not* easy, and require a great deal of preparation. The exam questions measure real-world skills. Your ability to answer these questions correctly will be greatly enhanced by as much hands-on experience with the product as you can get.

About the Exams

An important aspect of passing the MCP Certification Exams is understanding the big picture. This includes understanding how the exams are developed and scored.

Every job function requires different levels of cognitive skills, from memorization of facts and definitions to the comprehensive ability to analyze scenarios, design solutions, and evaluate options. To make the exams relevant in the real world, exams test the specific cognitive skills needed for the job functions being tested. These exams go beyond testing rote knowledge — you need to *apply* your knowledge, analyze technical solutions, solve problems, and make decisions — just like you would on the job.

Exam Items and Scoring

Microsoft certification exams consist of three types of items: multiple-choice, multiple-rating, and enhanced. The way you indicate your answer and the number of points you receive differ depending on the type of item.

Multiple-choice item

A traditional multiple-choice item presents a problem and asks you to select either the best answer (single response) or the best set of answers (multiple response) to the given item from a list of possible answers.

For a multiple-choice item, your response is scored as either correct or incorrect. A correct answer receives a score of 1 point and an incorrect answer receives a score of 0 points.

In the case of a multiple-choice, multiple-response item (for which the correct response consists of more than one answer), the item is scored as correct only if all the correct answers are selected. No partial credit is given for a response that does not include all the correct answers for the item.

For consistency purposes, the question in a multiple-choice, multiple-response item is always presented in singular form, regardless of how many answers are correct. Always follow the instructions displayed at the bottom of the window.

Multiple-rating item

A multiple-rating item presents a task similar to those presented in multiple-choice items. In a multiple-choice item, you are asked to select the best answer or answers from a selection of several potential answers. In contrast, a multiple-rating item presents a task, along with a proposed solution. Each time the task is presented, a different solution is proposed. In each multiple-rating item, you are asked to choose the answer that best describes the results produced by one proposed solution.

Enhanced item

An enhanced item is similar to a multiple-choice item because it asks you to select your response from a number of possible responses. However, unlike the traditional multiple-choice item that presents you with a list of possible answers from which to choose, an enhanced item may ask you to indicate your answer in one of three ways:
- Type the correct response, such as a command name.
- Review an exhibit (such as a screen shot, a network configuration drawing, or a code sample), and then use

the mouse to select the area of the exhibit that represents the correct response.

- Review an exhibit, and then select the correct response from the list of possible responses.

As with a multiple-choice item, your response to an enhanced item is scored as either correct or incorrect. A correct answer receives full credit of 1 point and an incorrect answer receives a score of 0 points.

Preparing for a Microsoft Certified Professional Exam

The best way to prepare for an exam is to study, learn, and master the job function on which you'll be tested. For any certification exam, you should follow these important preparation steps:

1. Identify the objectives on which you'll be tested.
2. Assess your current mastery of those objectives.
3. Practice tasks and study the areas you haven't mastered.

This section describes tools and techniques that may be helpful as you perform these steps to prepare for the exam.

Exam Preparation Guides

For each certification exam, an Exam Preparation Guide provides important, specific information about what you'll be tested on and how best to prepare. These guides are essential tools for preparing to take certification exams. You'll find the following types of valuable information in the exam preparation guides:

- **Tasks you should master:** Outlines the overall job function tasks you should master
- **Exam objectives:** Lists the specific skills and abilities on which you should expect to be measured

MCSE TCP/IP ACE IT!

- **Product resources:** Tells you the products and technologies with which you should be experienced
- **Suggested reading:** Points you to specific reference materials and other publications that discuss one or more of the exam objectives
- **Suggested curriculum:** Provides a specific list of instructor-led and self-paced courses relating to the job function tasks and topics in the exam

You'll also find pointers to additional information that may help you prepare for the exams, such as *Microsoft TechNet, Microsoft Developer Network* (MSDN), online forums, and other sources.

By paying attention to the verbs used in the "Exam Objectives" section of the Exam Preparation Guide, you can get an idea of the level at which you'll be tested on that objective.

To view the most recent version of the Exam Preparation Guides, which include the exam's objectives, check out Microsoft's Training and Certification Web site at **www.microsoft.com/train_cert/**.

Assessment Exams

When preparing for the exams, take lots of assessment exams. Assessment exams are self-paced exams that you take at your own computer. When you complete an assessment exam, you receive instant score feedback so you can determine areas in which additional study may be helpful before you take the certification exam. Although your score on an assessment exam doesn't necessarily indicate what your score will be on the certification exam, assessment exams give you the opportunity to answer items that are similar to those on the certification exams. And the assessment exams use the same computer-based testing tool as the certification exams, so you don't have to learn the tool on exam day.

An assessment exam exists for almost every certification exam.

INSIDER'S GUIDE TO MCP CERTIFICATION

Taking a Microsoft Certified Professional Exam

This section contains information about registering for and taking an MCP exam, including what to expect when you arrive at the Sylvan Prometric testing center to take the exam.

How to Register for an Exam

Candidates may take exams at any of more than 700 Sylvan Prometric testing centers around the world. For the location of a Sylvan Prometric testing center near you, call (800) 755-EXAM (755-3926). Outside the United States and Canada, contact your local Sylvan Prometric Registration Center.

To register for an MCP exam:

1. Determine which exam you want to take and note the exam number.

2. Register with the Sylvan Prometric Registration Center nearest to you. A part of the registration process is advance payment for the exam.

3. After you receive the registration and payment confirmation letter from Sylvan Prometric, call a Sylvan Prometric testing center to schedule your exam.

When you schedule the exam, you'll be provided instructions regarding the appointment, cancellation procedures, ID requirements, and information about the testing center location.

Exams must be taken within one year of payment. You can schedule exams up to six weeks in advance, or as late as one working day prior to the date of the exam. You can cancel or reschedule your exam if you contact Sylvan Prometric at least two working days prior to the exam.

Although subject to space availability, same-day registration is available in some locations. Where same-day registration is available, you must register a minimum of two hours before test time.

xix

What to Expect at the Testing Center

As you prepare for your certification exam, it may be helpful to know what to expect when you arrive at the testing center on the day of your exam. The following information gives you a preview of the general procedure you'll go through at the testing center:

- You will be asked to sign the log book upon arrival and departure.
- You will be required to show two forms of identification, including one photo ID (such as a driver's license or company security ID), before you may take the exam.
- The test administrator will give you a Testing Center Regulations form that explains the rules you will be expected to comply with during the test. You will be asked to sign the form, indicating that you understand the regulations and will comply.
- The test administrator will show you to your test computer and will handle any preparations necessary to start the testing tool and display the exam on the computer.
- You will be provided a set amount of scratch paper for use during the exam. All scratch paper will be collected from you at the end of the exam.
- The exams are all closed-book. You may not use a laptop computer or have any notes or printed material with you during the exam session.
- Some exams may include additional materials, or exhibits. If any exhibits are required for your exam, the test administrator will provide you with them before you begin the exam and collect them from you at the end of the exam.
- Before you begin the exam, the test administrator will tell you what to do when you complete the exam. If the test administrator doesn't explain this to you, or if you are

unclear about what you should do, ask the administrator before beginning the exam.

- The number of items on each exam varies, as does the amount of time allotted for each exam. Generally, certification exams consist of about 50 to one 100 items and have durations of 60 to 90 minutes. You can verify the number of items and time allotted for your exam when you register.

Because you'll be given a specific amount of time to complete the exam once you begin, if you have any questions or concerns, don't hesitate to ask the test administrator before the exam begins.

As an exam candidate, you are entitled to the best support and environment possible for your exam. In particular, you are entitled to the following:

- A quiet, uncluttered test environment
- Scratch paper
- The tutorial for using the online testing tool, and time to take the tutorial
- A knowledgeable and professional test administrator
- The opportunity to submit comments about the testing center and staff or the test itself

The Certification Development Team will investigate any problems or issues you raise and make every effort to resolve them quickly.

Your Exam Results

Once you have completed an exam, you will be given immediate, online notification of your pass or fail status. You will also receive a printed Examination Score Report indicating your pass or fail status and your exam results by section. (The test administrator will give you the printed score report.) Test scores are automatically forwarded to Microsoft within five working days after you take the test. You do not need to send your score to Microsoft.

If you pass the exam, you will receive confirmation from Microsoft, typically within two to four weeks.

If You Don't Receive a Passing Score

If you do not pass a certification exam, you may call Sylvan Prometric to schedule a time to retake the exam. Before retaking the exam, you should review the appropriate Exam Preparation Guide and focus additional study on the topic areas where your exam results could be improved. Please note that you must pay again for each exam retake.

One way to determine areas where additional study may be helpful is to carefully review your individual section scores. Generally, the section titles in your score report correlate to specific groups of exam objectives listed in the Exam Preparation Guide.

Here are some specific ways you can prepare to retake an exam:

- Go over the section-by-section scores on your exam results, noting objective areas where your score could be improved.
- Review the Exam Preparation Guide for the exam, with a special focus on the tasks and objective areas that correspond to the exam sections where your score could be improved.
- Increase your real-world, hands-on experience and practice performing the listed job tasks with the relevant products and technologies.
- Consider taking or retaking one or more of the suggested courses listed in the Exam Preparation Guide.
- Review the suggested readings listed in the Exam Preparation Guide.
- After you review the materials, retake the corresponding Assessment Exam.

For More Information

To find out more about Microsoft Education and Certification materials and programs, to register with Sylvan Prometric, or to get other useful information, check the following resources. Outside the United

INSIDER'S GUIDE TO MCP CERTIFICATION

States or Canada, contact your local Microsoft office or Sylvan Prometric testing center.

- **Microsoft Certified Professional Program:** (800) 636-7544. Call for information about the Microsoft Certified Professional program and exams, and to order the *Microsoft Certified Professional Program Exam Study Guide* or the Microsoft Train_Cert Offline CD-ROM.

- **Sylvan Prometric Testing Centers: (800) 755-EXAM.** Call to register to take a Microsoft Certified Professional exam at any of more than 700 Sylvan Prometric testing centers around the world, or to order the *Microsoft Certified Professional Program Exam Study Guide*.

- **Microsoft Sales Fax Service: (800) 727-3351.** Call for Microsoft Certified Professional Exam Preparation Guides, Microsoft Official Curriculum course descriptions and schedules, or the *Microsoft Certified Professional Program Exam Study Guide*.

- **Education Program and Course Information: (800) SOLPROV.** Call for information about Microsoft Official Curriculum courses, Microsoft education products, and the Microsoft Solution Provider Authorized Technical Education Center (ATEC) program, where you can attend a Microsoft Official Curriculum course, or to order the *Microsoft Certified Professional Program Exam Study Guide*.

- **Microsoft Certification Development Team: Fax #: (425) 936-1311.** Use this fax number to volunteer for participation in one or more exam development phases or to report a problem with an exam. Address written correspondence to: Certification Development Team, Microsoft Education and Certification, One Microsoft Way, Redmond, WA 98052.

- **Microsoft TechNet Technical Information Network:** (800) 344-2121. Call for support professionals and system administrators. Outside the United States and Canada, call your local Microsoft subsidiary for information.

xxiii

- **Microsoft Developer Network (MSDN): (800) 759-5474.** MSDN is the official source for software development kits, device driver kits, operating systems, and information about developing applications for Microsoft Windows and Windows NT.
- **Online Services: (800) 936-3500.** Call for information about Microsoft Connection on CompuServe, Microsoft Knowledge Base, Microsoft Software Library, Microsoft Download Service, and Internet.

This section contains excerpts from the Microsoft Certified Professional Program Exam Study Guide (Microsoft Corporation, 1998), reprinted with permission.

Preface

Welcome to *MCSE TCP/IP Ace It!* This book is intended to help you hone your existing knowledge and gain a greater understanding of TCP/IP so you have the ability to pass Microsoft Certified Professional Exam No. 70-59: Internetworking with Microsoft TCP/IP on Microsoft Windows NT 4.0.

Consider this book your strategy guide as you prepare for the exam. It supplements any other materials you already have and helps you decide how to make best use of your study time leading up to the exam. Throughout this book I assume you are familiar with TCP/IP concepts, or that you have other study materials to help you understand these concepts. With that in mind, I cover TCP/IP to the depth of the exam objectives, but not beyond that point.

How to Use This Book

The chapters of this book are designed to be studied sequentially. In other words, it would be best if you complete Chapter 1 before you proceed to Chapter 2. A few chapters could probably stand alone, but all in all, I recommend a sequential approach.

For best results (and we both know that the only acceptable result is a passing score on the TCP/IP exam), I recommend the following plan of attack as you use this book. First, take the Are You Prepared? self-test at the beginning of the chapter to see if you've already mastered the topic. Next, if your self-test score tells you that you need more study, read the chapter and the Test Tips and Test Traps highlights, paying particular attention to the Inside Scoop section for pointers on what topics to concentrate on. Then use the Have You Mastered? and Practice Your Skills sections to see if you really have the key concepts under your belt. If you don't, go back and reread the section(s) you're not clear on. If your self-test score indicates you are prepared on this topic, you may want to move on to the next chapter.

After you've completed your study of the chapters, reviewed the Have You Mastered? questions, and done the Practice Your Skills exer-

MCSE TCP/IP ACE IT!

cises, take the Practice Exam included in the back of the book. The Practice Exam will help you assess how much you've learned from your study and will familiarize you with the types of questions you'll face when you take the real exam. Once you identify a weak area, you can use the cross-references to the corresponding chapters (including the Have You Mastered? questions) to improve your knowledge and skills in that area.

Before you take the TCP/TP Exam, tear out the *Ace Card* and use its quick run-down of essential concepts to refresh your memory and focus your review just before the test.

Prerequisites

This book is an exam preparation guide, but it does not start at ground zero. I do assume you have the following knowledge and skills at the outset:

1. Terminology and skills to use a Microsoft Windows NT Server.
2. Networking knowledge or experience equal to the scope required to pass the Microsoft Certified Professional Exam No. 70-67: Implementing and Supporting Microsoft Windows NT Server 4.0.

If you meet these prerequisites, you're ready to begin this book.

If you don't have the basic Windows experience or mouse skills, I recommend you either take a one-day Windows application course or work through a self-study book to acquire these skills *before* you begin this book.

What You Learn

MCSE TCP/IP Ace It! gives you the quickest review of all the essential topics on Exam 70-59. Here's a rundown of what you learn:
- **Introduction to TCP/IP:** fundamentals of TCP/IP networking models and protocols
- **IP addressing:** how TCP/IP locates computers and networks through the Internet

PREFACE

- **Subnet addressing:** what subnets are and how to subdivide a network
- **Dynamic Host Configuration Protocol:** Microsoft's technology for IP address management
- **IP routing:** How IP packets make their way through the Internet and how to configure Windows NT for IP routing
- **Windows Internet Naming Service:** what it is, how it works, installing and configuring it, and managing the WINS server database
- **Domain Name System:** associating names with Internet addresses
- **IP address resolution:** address resolution protocol (ARP), software and hardware; troubleshooting
- **NetBIOS name resolution:** How NetBIOS works for naming users and resources on a Windows network, and how to manage the process
- **Host name resolution:** finding host computers on the Internet
- **TCP/IP internetworking and connectivity:** services provided through TCP/IP and how to configure and manage them through Windows
- **SNMP:** setting up Internet mail
- **Planning, installing and configuring TCP/IP:** how to implement TCP/IP on Windows workstations and servers
- **Performance monitoring and troubleshooting:** keeping TCP/IP working as it should

Let's Get Started!

That concludes the owner's manual on how to operate this book. It's time to get started, and get you on your way to passing the TCP/IP exam. Now, let's get certified!

Acknowledgments

I would like to thank everyone at IDG Books Worldwide for their help with this book. Tracy Thomsic, I would like to thank you for this wonderful opportunity. Jennifer Rowe, I owe you for all of your work helping me to get the material in and making this book the best it can be. Steve Anderson, thanks for all of your help in making this material coherent.

The most important person to thank is my wife. She is the most important thing to me, and as I said in my last book, everything I do, I do for her. She helped me greatly in writing this book and is a wonderful coauthor.

Without the help and support of my mother and stepfather, Peggy and Timmy Franks, and my grandmother Marie Ward, there is no way I would be where I am today. I would also like to thank my sister, Jeanie, my father, Bill Nash, and my grandparents, Homer and Frances Nash.

Finally, all the other people on my list to thank. The people at work: John, Blain, Dave, Chuck, Joe, Mike, Missy, Kris, Tim, and Drew. A few non-work-related friends: Todd Shanaberger, Jacob Hall, Robert Mowlds, Derek Stutsman, Paul Ward, Johannes and Joakim Erdfelt, Yossarian Hulmberg, Andy Scherrer, and Scott Bessler.

Contents at a Glance

Welcome to Ace it!............................ vii

Insider's Guide to MCP Certification xv

Preface....................................... xxv

Acknowledgments......................... xxviii

1   Introduction to TCP/IP..................... 1

2   IP Addressing 29

3   Subnet Addressing........................ 45

4   Dynamic Host Configuration Protocol 69

5   IP Routing 99

6   Windows Internet Naming Service......... 123

7   Domain Name System 153

8   IP Address Resolution 187

9   NetBIOS Name Resolution................ 209

10	**Host Name Resolution** 231
11	**Internetworking and Connectivity** 247
12	**Setting Up the SNMP Service** 275
13	**Installing and Configuring TCP/IP** 297
14	**TCP/IP Performance Monitoring** 321
	Practice Exam 347
	Exam Key 367
	Exam Analysis 369
	Exam Revealed 379
	Glossary 387
	Index 413

Contents

Welcome to Ace it! vii

Insider's Guide MCP Certification xv

Preface xxv

Acknowledgments xxviii

1   Introduction to TCP/IP 1
    Communications Systems and Protocols 4
        Naming and Addressing 4
        Message Segmenting 5
        Flow Control and Synchronization 5
        Error Control 6
        Routing 6
    The OSI Model 7
        The OSI Layered Protocols 8
    The TCP/IP Model 12
        The Network Interface Layer 13
        The Internet Layer 13
        The Transport Layer 14
        The Application Layer 14
    TCP/IP Protocols and Technologies 15
        Dial-up Networking Protocols 16
        Internet Layer Protocols 17
        Transport Layer Protocols 20

Other Networking Components 22
  Network Driver Interface Specification (NDIS) 23
  Transport Driver Interface (TDI) 24
  NetBIOS over TCP/IP (NetBT) 24
  Windows Sockets 24
  Workstation Service 25
  Server Service 26

2 IP Addressing 29
IP Addressing Overview 32
  Physical Addresses 32
  Assigned IP Addresses 33
  IP Address Contents 34
  IP Network Address Classes 35
  Obtaining an Internet IP Address 38
Assigning Host IP Addresses 39
  Assigning Host IDs 39
  Assigning Network IDs 40

3 Subnet Addressing 45
Subnets 48
Subnet Addressing 48
  Partitioning the IP Address 49
  Subnet Masks 50
  Private Internetworks 53
  Supernetting 54
Subdividing a Network 54
  Determining How Many Network IDs Will Be Required 55
  Determining How Many Host IDs Will Be Required 55
  Defining a Custom Subnet Mask 56

Selecting the Appropriate Subnet Mask 57
Determining the Network IDs to Use. 59
Determining the Range of Host IDs for Each Subnet. 61

4 Dynamic Host Configuration Protocol. 69
How DHCP Works. 73
Microsoft DHCP Components. 75
DHCP Clients. 75
DHCP Scopes 76
DHCP Options Supported by Microsoft Clients. 78
DHCP Initialization Phases. 79
IP Lease Renewal Phases 81
Planning a DHCP Installation 82
Multiple DHCP Servers. 83
DHCP Relay Agent. 84
DHCP Traffic Considerations. 85
Reducing DHCP Traffic. 86
Installing and Configuring DHCP 86
Configuring DHCP Scopes and Options 87
Global, Scope, Default, and Client Options. 89
Creating a Client Reservation 90
Using the Ipconfig Utility 91

5 IP Routing 99
IP Routing Defined 102
How Routing Works. 103
The Routing Table 105
Dead Gateway Detection. 108
IP Routing Protocols 109
Static IP Routing 109

Dynamic IP Routing 110
Configuring Windows NT as an IP Router 114
    Enabling Static IP Routing 114
    Enabling Dynamic IP Routing 116
    Using the Tracert Utility 117

6 Windows Internet Naming Service 123
What Is WINS? 126
    WINS Clients and Servers 126
    Benefits of Using WINS 128
How WINS Works 128
    Name Registration 128
    Name Renewal 130
WINS Installation 132
    Server and Client Requirements 133
    WINS Proxy 134
Configuring WINS 135
    WINS Manager 136
    WINS Statistics 137
    Static Entries for Non-WINS Clients 139
Managing the WINS Server Database 141
    WINS Database Replication 142
    Backing up and Restoring the WINS Database 144
    WINS Database Configuration Options 145

7 Domain Name System 153
DNS Overview 157
    Domains 158
    Zones 159
    Name Server Roles 160
    Name Resolution Methods 163
    Caching and TTL 164

CONTENTS

DNS Configuration and Database Files 164
    The BOOT File 165
    Database Files and Resource Records 166
    The Cache File 169
    The Reverse Lookup File 169
Planning a DNS Installation 170
    Single-domain Design 170
    Multiple-domain Design 171
Installing and Configuring Microsoft DNS Server 171
    DNS Manager and Manual DNS Administration 172
    Using the Nslookup Utility 179

8   IP Address Resolution. 187

The Address Resolution Protocol (ARP) 191
    The ARP Cache. 193
    ARP Cache Aging 193
    ArpCacheLife 194
    Static ARP Entries 194
    The arp Utility 195
Hardware Address Resolution Methods. 196
    Local IP Address Resolution 197
    Remote IP Address Resolution 198
Troubleshooting Address Resolution Problems. 200
    Duplicate IP Addresses 201
    Invalid Subnet Masks. 202
    Invalid Static ARP Entries 203
    Troubleshooting Tools 203

9   NetBIOS Name Resolution 209

What Is NetBIOS? 213
    NetBIOS Components 213
    NetBIOS Naming Services 213

xxxv

Windows NetBIOS Name Resolution...................... 216
    Standard NetBT Name Resolution Modes............... 216
    Other Name Resolution Methods...................... 220
    LMHOSTS File....................................... 221

10 Host Name Resolution................... 231
What Is a Host Name?................................... 235
Host Name Resolution Methods........................... 236
    Resolving Names Using a HOSTS File.................. 237
    Resolving Names Using Domain Name System (DNS).... 239
    Resolving Names Using Microsoft Host Name Methods... 240

11 Internetworking and Connectivity......... 247
Microsoft TCP/IP Connectivity........................... 251
    Protocol Differences................................ 251
TCP/IP Connectivity Utilities............................ 253
    Remote Execution Utilities.......................... 253
    Data Transfer Utilities.............................. 255
Microsoft TCP/IP Printing.............................. 259
    TCP/IP Printing.................................... 260
    Methods of Connecting Printers..................... 260
    Microsoft TCP/IP Printing Service................... 261
    Line Printer Port Monitor.......................... 262
    TCP/IP Printing Utilities........................... 262
Internetwork Browsing................................. 264
    Computer Roles.................................... 264
    How Browsing Works............................... 265
    Browsing an Internetwork........................... 267

12 Setting Up the SNMP Service............. 275
How SNMP Works...................................... 279
    SNMP Components.................................. 279

CONTENTS

      Management Information Base (MIB) 281
      SNMP Communities and Traps 285
      The Microsoft SNMP Service 286
          Installing and Configuring the SNMP Service 286
          Managing SNMP 288

13 Installing and Configuring TCP/IP 297
      Planning Your TCP/IP Installation. 301
          Assigning IP Addresses on Your Network 301
      Installing and Configuring TCP/IP
      on a Windows NT Computer. 304
      Installing and Configuring TCP/IP
      on a Windows 95 Computer 306
      Troubleshooting Your TCP/IP Configuration 309
          Using the Ipconfig and Winipcfg Utilities 309
          Testing Your TCP/IP Configuration Using Ping 311

14 TCP/IP Performance Monitoring 321
      Improving Network Performance. 325
          Hardware Performance 325
          Network Traffic. 326
      Monitoring TCP/IP Activity 326
          TCP/IP Connections and Statistics. 326
          Performance Monitor 327
          Network Monitor. 329
      Troubleshooting TCP/IP Problems. 333
          Resources 333
          Diagnosing TCP/IP Problems. 333

xxxvii

Practice Exam 347

Exam Key 367

Exam Analysis 369

Exam Revealed 379

Glossary 387

Index 413

MCSE TCP/IP ACE IT!

Exam Material in This Chapter

Official Word

Based on Microsoft Objectives
- Be familiar with the layers of the OSI model.
- Understand the TCP/IP model and how it relates to the OSI model.
- Understand the TCP/IP protocols and their functions.

Inside Scoop

Based on Author's Experience
- RFCs
- Network interface layer
- Internet layer
- Transport layer
- Application layer
- IP
- ARP
- ICMP
- TCP
- UDP
- NDIS
- Windows Sockets

Introduction to TCP/IP

Although the Microsoft TCP/IP exam does not cover theory in any depth, you will need to understand the background information in this chapter about TCP/IP and protocols in general to pass the exam. This chapter can also serve as a refresher if you already have experience with networking concepts. Be sure that you are comfortable with each of the protocols, its purpose, and where it fits into the OSI Model.

1: INTRODUCTION TO TCP/IP

Are You Prepared?

Test your knowledge with the following questions to assess how familiar you are with the material in this chapter. This will help you identify problem areas where additional review is necessary.

1. **The User Datagram Protocol (UDP) works at which layer of the TCP/IP model?**

    - [ ] A. Network interface
    - [ ] B. Internet
    - [x] C. Transport
    - [ ] D. Application

2. **Which TCP/IP protocol is responsible for resolving IP addresses to physical addresses?**

    - [ ] A. ICMP
    - [ ] B. IGMP
    - [ ] C. TCP
    - [x] D. ARP

Answers:

1. C *The transport layer of the TCP/IP model is responsible for end-to-end communication between hosts. See the "TCP/IP model" section.*

2. D *The Address Resolution Protocol is used to resolve IP addresses to physical addresses. See the "TCP/IP model" section.*

Communications Systems and Protocols

Modern communications systems rely on open standards, such as communications protocols, to provide compatibility between different types of devices. Communications protocols make it possible to interconnect many different physical networks and have them function as a single entity.

Some of the most important functions of any communications protocol suite include:

- Naming and addressing
- Message segmenting
- Flow control and synchronization
- Error control
- Routing

Naming and Addressing

A communications system must provide a method of managing named objects used on the network. Examples of named objects are hosts, processes, ports, mailboxes, and sessions between users. Users normally refer to objects in a symbolic format, such as gregb@quicklearn.com or ftp.quicklearn.com.

Named objects are much easier for users to remember than the addressing notation required by the underlying communication systems protocols. It is important that sites promote consistency by developing standard naming conventions for commonly used objects. Examples of named objects are:

- www.sales.quicklearn.com
- ftp.demos.quicklearn.com
- printer1.sales.quicklearn.com
- printer5.support.quicklearn.com

With few exceptions, in the inner workings of computer protocols, computers are identified by numbers. TCP/IP makes use of two types of numbers:

- *IP addresses*, which provide a universal and uniform name for assigning a numeric identifier to each computer on the network.
- *Physical addresses*, which are used by the underlying network to identify computers and deliver messages. Each network uses its own system to assign numbers to computers. These diverse physical address schemes are usually masked from the user by translating them into IP addresses.

Message Segmenting

Communications between devices on a network consists of messages. Because networking protocols have a fixed packet length, most messages must be split into multiple segments before they can be sent across a network. After segments reach their destination, they are reassembled into the original message.

Segmenting messages into smaller packets improves network transmission efficiency and reduces error rates by reducing delays, enabling you to configure the optimal transmission settings, and enabling the data to be sent simultaneously on multiple paths.

Flow Control and Synchronization

Communications systems support large numbers of network devices that share a common transmission system. Communications traffic can occur when many users demand access to network services simultaneously. *Flow control* mechanisms are designed to optimize network performance by regulating the flow of information between a pair of network devices.

While the protocols specify the structure and organization of the message, there are subtle differences in the implementations of protocols by different vendors. For example, receiving and sending buffer sizes may differ, or one type of device may be able to transmit information faster than another. *Synchronization* is used to manage the flow of messages between two network devices.

Error Control

One of the most important objectives of a communications system is reliable, error-free data transmission. Data would be useless if a spreadsheet were received from across the network with missing rows, or if a word processing document were received with a paragraph missing. Communications protocols must include error detection, correction, and recovery mechanisms. Error detection methods can be performed by:

- Including redundant information in the message that is compared to the original to detect mismatches.
- Using control information algorithms, such as a check sum, to calculate the contents of a message. Errors can be corrected by comparing the calculated results with those received.
- Assigning sequence numbers to messages and packets to detect lost, duplicated, or out-of-sequence messages.

Communications protocols provide various recovery methods, such as retransmission, to correct these types of errors.

Routing

Normally, when the term *routing* is used, it refers to the mechanisms used to deliver a message to a device that exists on a remote network. Communications protocols must include information that enables two devices on different networks to communicate with one another.

Most of the work involved with network-to-network communications is performed by devices called *gateways* or *routers*. However, the protocol suite must include routing mechanisms for each sending device to determine how to address a destination device that resides on a remote network.

> **KNOW THIS** **Function of TCP/IP Protocols**
> TCP/IP is actually a complete suite of protocols. Protocol suites serve many functions in network communications. These include: naming and addressing, message segmenting, flow control and synchronization, error control, and routing.

The OSI Model

Most networks, including the Internet, are comprised of a number of different functional components (or *layers*). The layered model of communications helps developers of both software and hardware components create products that meet a specific need and are still compatible with other components within the environment.

The *Open System Interconnect* (OSI) model, illustrated in Figure 1-1, describes a network architecture that breaks up the functions of moving data from one point to another into seven different tasks.

The idea is to break out each function of communication and assign it a label. This enables protocols to be broken into modular components with interfaces that communicate with the upper and lower layers. Each layer is shielded from the details of how the other layers are implemented.

The network layer corresponds to the physical and datalink layers of the OSI model. The network layer is responsible for moving frames over the wire. The Internet layer corresponds to the network layer of the OSI model. It is at this level that a packet is encapsulated into an Internet datagram. In addition, all routing algorithms are run at the Internet layer. The transport layer is responsible for providing connection-oriented and connectionless communication between two hosts. The application layer addresses applications such as Telnet, FTP, and SNMP.

MCSE TCP/IP ACE IT!

OSI model

| Application |
| Presentation |
| Session |
| Transport |
| Network |
| Datalink |

Figure 1-1 *TCP/IP services and the OSI model*

The OSI Layered Protocols

All protocol suites include a number of different protocols for handling specific tasks. Combining several protocols, each with its own dedicated purpose, is possible through a defined set of rules that describe how the protocols interact with each other (essentially, a protocol for communications between protocols). Protocol control information is contained in the protocol header. The header is used to transfer information between the adjoining layers.

Network protocols are packaged in a similar fashion:

- Headers and trailers that specify the address of the sending host and the address of the remote host are added to data.
- Network layer protocols contain routing information that enables datagrams to be sent between locations.
- Because it often takes more than one datagram to contain all of the information being sent, sequencing and flow control instructions are managed by the transport layer protocols.
- After receiving an agreed-upon number of datagrams, the remote host is usually required to send an acknowledgment to verify the receipt of the sequence of datagrams.

The physical layer

The *physical layer* is the lowest layer of the OSI model. This layer generates the physical pulses, electrical currents, and optical pulses involved in moving data across the network media and to the network interface card.

Information at this layer is represented as bits by identifying the pulse duration and timing of the signals on the media, as shown in Figure 1-2. Data encoding methods are used at the physical layer to represent bit patterns for purposes such as bit and frame synchronization and as a delimiter (a way of determining the separation point between frames).

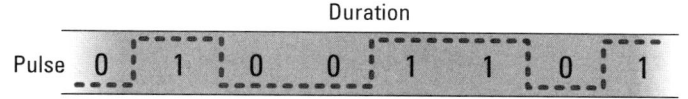

```
                        Duration
Pulse   0   1   0   0   1   1   0   1
```

Figure 1-2 *The physical layer uses signal patterns to represent data.*

The datalink layer

The *datalink layer* assembles the individual bits of data into a useful collection of information called a *packet* or a *frame*. The datalink layer contains error correction and identifying fields used to describe the contents of the frame. For example, as shown in Figure 1-3, an Ethernet frame contains the following:

- A *preamble* that is used to synchronize and separate packets moving across the network
- A *destination address* that specifies the hardware address of the receiver
- A *source address* that specifies the hardware address of the sender
- A *type field* that defines the type of protocol contained in the data field (some implementations of Ethernet use this field to define the length of the data field)
- The *data field,* which contains higher layer protocols that must be interpreted by the protocol software

9

- The *cyclical redundancy check* (CRC) *field* that contains a numeric value used to determine if the frame's contents have been modified during transmission

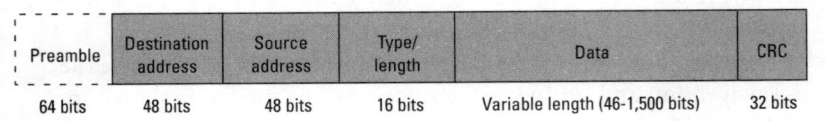

Preamble	Destination address	Source address	Type/ length	Data	CRC
64 bits	48 bits	48 bits	16 bits	Variable length (46-1,500 bits)	32 bits

Figure 1-3 *Ethernet frame format*

The datalink layer is responsible for providing the error-free transfer of these frames from one computer to another through the physical layer. This enables the network layer to assume virtually error-free transmission over the network connection.

The network layer

The *network layer* is responsible for addressing messages and translating logical addresses and names into physical addresses. This layer also controls the operation of the subnet by determining the route to take from the source to the destination computer.

It determines which path the data should take based on network conditions, priority of service, and other factors. It also manages traffic problems such as switching, routing, and controlling the congestion of data packets on the network.

The transport layer

The *transport layer* manages reliable message transfers between hosts using flow control and synchronization fields. This layer repackages messages — dividing long messages into several packets and collecting small messages together in one packet — to provide for their efficient transmission over the network. The transfer of messages must be acknowledged at regular intervals to guarantee the reliability of the data stream.

The session layer

The *session layer* enables two applications on different computers to establish, use, and end a connection, called a *session*. This layer performs name recognition and includes functions that enable two applications to communicate over the network.

Microsoft provides the industry standard NetBIOS interface for managing sessions between Windows-based computers. NetBIOS services provide virtual-circuit session functions that applications can use to manage connections between two computers.

The presentation layer

The *presentation layer*, or the *network's translator*, determines the method used to exchange data between networked computers. At the sending computer, the presentation layer translates data from a format sent down from the application layer into a commonly recognized, intermediary format. The presentation layer also manages network security issues by providing services such as data encryption. This layer also provides rules for data transfers and provides data compression to reduce the number of bits that need to be transmitted.

Microsoft implements a protocol called *Server Messages Blocks* (SMBs) for presentation layer communications. SMB requests are typically commands for file and print transactions sent between a client computer and a server. On the client computer, the Workstation Service (the redirector) uses SMBs when communicating with the Server Service.

The application layer

The top layer of the OSI model is the *application layer*. Applications running on a network can communicate directly with lower layer components, or indirectly as requests that are intercepted by the network components themselves.

The application layer provides an interface to network services to provide the following functions:

- Resource sharing
- Remote file and printer access
- Directory services
- Electronic messaging (e-mail)
- Network management

Layers of the OSI Model

KNOW THIS

The OSI model is used to break network communications into different layers. Each layer is responsible for a different aspect of network communications. The physical layer is responsible for the pulses and currents that are sent across the network media. The datalink layer handles error correction. The network layer handles addressing and routing. The transport layer is responsible for acknowledging packet transfer. The session layer allows applications to communicate across the network. The presentation layer provides data translation, encryption, and compression. Finally, the application layer acts as an interface between the user's application and the network.

The TCP/IP Model

The TCP/IP protocol model differs slightly from the OSI model by dividing protocols into four conceptual layers, which are illustrated in Figure 1-4. Each layer in the figure depicts several of the most significant protocols in the TCP/IP suite.

OSI model	Internet protocol suite
Application	Application
Presentation	
Session	
Transport	Transport
Network	Internet
Datalink	Network interface
Physical	

Figure 1-4 *The four conceptual layers of the TCP/IP protocol suite*

The Network Interface Layer

The bottommost layer of the model is the network interface layer, which contains the protocols that enable TCP/IP to communicate with the physical network. TCP/IP standards do not define specific network interface protocols. Rather, TCP/IP is intended to have the flexibility to adapt to a variety of network types. Some of the techniques that enable TCP/IP to interoperate with specific networks are described in Requests for Comments (RFCs), but the networks themselves, such as Ethernet, are standardized by standards bodies other than the IAB.

The Internet Layer

This is the first layer that is formally defined in Internet standards. Its primary protocol is the *Internet Protocol* (IP), although a variety of other protocols assist IP in its operation. Protocols used at the internet layer include:

- **Internet Protocol (IP):** Responsible for delivering message packets through the network. IP is responsible for host addressing and for routing datagrams between hosts.

- **Internet Control Message Protocol (ICMP):** Carries a variety of messages, including error reports, that relate to packet delivery.

- **Internet Group Management Protocol (IGMP):** Reports host group memberships to support multicast transmissions by routers.

- **Address Resolution Protocol (ARP):** Enables IP to match (resolve) IP addresses of hosts to their physical addresses.

The primary functions performed at the Internet layer are message addressing and translating logical addresses and names into physical addresses. This layer also controls the operation of the subnet by determining the route to take from the source to the destination computer.

It determines which path the data should take based on network conditions, priority of service, and other factors. This layer also manages traffic problems such as switching, routing, and controlling the congestion of data packets on the network.

The Transport Layer

The transport layer is responsible for end-to-end communication between hosts. Two transport layer protocols are available to support two styles of data delivery:

- **Transmission Control Protocol (TCP):** Provides reliable data delivery using connection-oriented communication. Reliable delivery is typically required for transmission of large amounts of data or for extended dialogs between hosts. TCP performs message segmentation and error detection and recovery, relieving applications of those responsibilities.
- **User Datagram Protocol (UDP):** Provides efficient delivery of discrete packets, but does not guarantee delivery will be accomplished. Applications using UDP must perform their own error checking and recovery.

The transport layer manages reliable message transfers between hosts using flow control and synchronization fields. This layer repackages messages — dividing long messages into several packets and collecting small messages together in one packet — to provide for their efficient transmission over the network. The transfer of messages must be acknowledged at regular intervals to guarantee the reliability of the data stream.

The Application Layer

The applications interface is the uppermost layer in the TCP/IP model. A number of TCP/IP applications function at this layer, including *File Transfer Protocol* (FTP), Telnet, *Domain Name Service* (DNS), and *Simple Network Management Protocol* (SNMP).

The application layer includes *application program interfaces* (APIs) that enable non-network applications to communicate with the network. Two network APIs are included with Microsoft TCP/IP protocol suites:

- Windows Sockets is a standard API that enables Microsoft Windows applications to interface with TCP/IP and IPX protocols.

1: INTRODUCTION TO TCP/IP

- NetBIOS is included to support applications that use NetBIOS naming and messaging services. NetBIOS naming has long been used on Microsoft networks using NetBEUI, NWLink (IPX), and TCP/IP protocols.

POP QUIZ — True or False?

1. The Session layer of the OSI model is responsible for choosing the route data should take across the network.
2. The Datalink layer consists of two sublayers.
3. The Physical layer is responsible for encoding and transmitting data.

Answers: 1. False 2. True 3. True

TCP/IP Protocols and Technologies

The core TCP/IP protocols include *Transmission Control Protocol* (TCP), *User Datagram Protocol* (UDP), *Internet Control Message Protocol* (ICMP), *Internet Protocol* (IP), and *Address Resolution Protocol* (ARP). Microsoft supports all of these core protocols. Figure 1-5 shows how these protocols map to the transport and the Internet layers of the Internet protocol suite.

TCP/IP protocol standards concentrate on the upper three layers of the TCP/IP Internet protocol models. At the network interface layer, TCP/IP is intended to take advantage of existing communication technologies such as Ethernet and Token Ring. Consequently, TCP/IP has been adapted to the majority of local and wide area network technologies. Example protocols at the network interface layer are Ethernet II, IEEE 802.3 Ethernet, token ring, and FDDI. By far, the most common network interface technology is Ethernet.

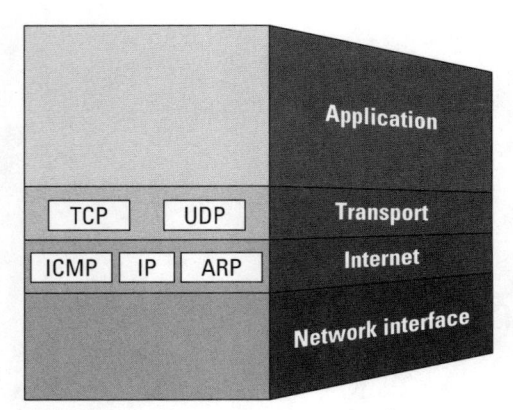

Figure 1-5 *Core TCP/IP protocols correspond to the transport and Internet layers.*

Dial-up Networking Protocols

For dial-up network access, TCP/IP supports two serial-line protocols: *Serial Line Internet Protocol* (SLIP) and *Point-to-Point Protocol* (PPP). Both SLIP and PPP are supported by Microsoft Remote Access service.

SLIP is suited for use only over low-speed serial interfaces. Windows NT RAS supports SLIP client (dial-out) functionality, but does not function as a SLIP server (dial-in).

PPP is a more robust protocol with a richer feature set than SLIP, supported by Windows NT on both the client and server sides of dial-up communication.

Point-to-Point Tunneling Protocol (PPTP) is a new WAN protocol that supports the ability to establish a *Virtual Private Network* (VPN) using the Internet. Using PPTP, remote users who connect to the Internet using a local ISP can connect securely (tunnel) into their corporate network. VPN technology provides secure and encrypted communication across the Internet, enabling organizations to use the public Internet as a secure channel for transmitting confidential data.

1: INTRODUCTION TO TCP/IP

TEST TRAP
It is important to remember that NT supports dialing out to a SLIP server, but cannot function as a SLIP server itself. If you encounter a question on the test concerning the configuration of a dial-in server, remember that NT must be a PPP server.

Internet Layer Protocols

The four protocols that function at the Internet layer are IP, ARP, ICMP, and IGMP.

Internet Protocol (IP)

Internet Protocol (IP) is the mailroom of the TCP/IP stack, where packet sorting and delivery take place. The message unit for IP is the *datagram*. A datagram is a short message that is transmitted discretely — that is, it is not part of a formal sequence of message events. Datagrams are passed to the IP protocol from UDP and TCP above, and from the network adapter below.

IP is responsible for delivering datagrams to hosts. When a destination host resides remotely — on a different physical network from the host that is sending the datagram — then IP is responsible for routing the datagram to the appropriate destination network. IP makes use of routers to transport the datagram to the network on which its final destination resides.

TEST TRAP
The conventional name for a device that moves data between networks is a router. However, in the TCP/IP world, the term *gateway* predated *router* and is still much in evidence. On the test you may see references to gateways and default gateways, but these are simply routers designed to route IP datagrams.

On a given TCP/IP host, more than one single application will usually be running at any given time. Figure 1-6 shows how TCP/IP uses ports and sockets to ensure that messages are delivered to the appropriate upper-layer services, such as an FTP Server or a WWW server.

17

MCSE TCP/IP ACE IT!

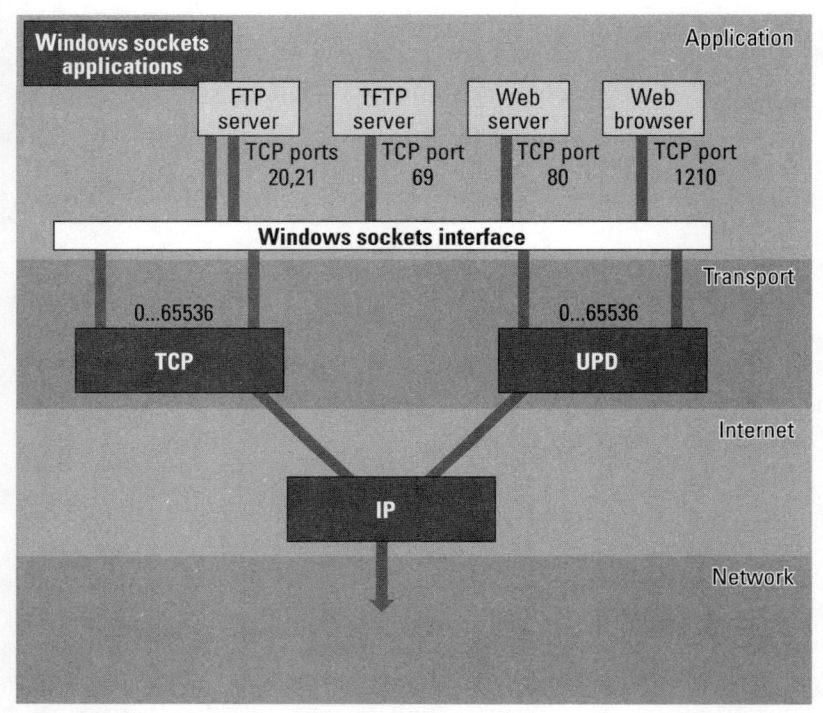

Figure 1-6 *Ports used by the sockets interface*

Each application that is written for the Sockets interface is identified by a port number in the range of 0 – 65536. Each application running on the same host can be associated with a unique port number. To reduce the potential for confusion, many popular applications are assigned *well-known port numbers* by the *Internet Assigned Numbers Authority* (IANA). These well-known port numbers are documented in the RFC titled Assigned numbers, which is currently RFC 1700. Figure 1-6 also illustrates several commonly used port values.

When multiple copies of the same application are executed on a multitasking host, each copy must be assigned a distinct port number.

Each TCP/IP host is configured with a file that documents ports in use on that host. Port numbers on Windows NT are defined in the file `%systemroot%\system32\drivers\etc\services`. This file contains entries for well-known ports as well as for ports that are defined by the administrator.

An application on a host is fully defined by a *socket*, which consists of three pieces of information:

- The IP address of the host
- The type of transport service, where TCP provides connection-oriented service and UDP provides connectionless service
- The port number being used by the application

A communication path is fully defined by the socket numbers associated with the communication endpoints.

Address Resolution Protocol (ARP)

In order for computers to communicate on a network, they must ultimately know each other's physical addresses. As each outgoing IP datagram is encapsulated into a frame, the hardware addresses for both the source and destination hosts must be included. The *Address Resolution Protocol* (ARP) is used to obtain the physical address of a destination TCP/IP host when given the host's IP address.

Address resolution is accomplished when the requesting host sends a broadcast on the local network with the destination host's IP address. The destination host responds to the request by sending a reply containing its physical address.

Internet Control Message Protocol (ICMP)

The *Internet Control Message Protocol* (ICMP) provides a mechanism for reporting errors due to datagram delivery problems. A connectionless system means that datagrams are delivered without any coordination between the originating and destination workstations. Although ICMP does not enable IP to function as a reliable protocol, it does report some errors that occur when IP actions fail. If, for example, the *time-to-live* (TTL) counter expires due to network congestion or the unavailability of the destination workstation, IP fails to deliver the datagram, a failure that will generate an ICMP message. ICMP is a standard component in all TCP/IP implementations.

Another example of an ICMP message is *source quench*. If a host is sending data faster than the receiving host can handle, the receiver may generate an ICMP source quench message to inform the sending host that it should slow down. A Windows NT computer that is configured as a router does not generate source quench messages, but simply discards any datagrams that cannot fit in the router's input buffers. Ping and tracert are examples of utilities that use the ICMP protocol.

The most common ICMP messages are echo request, echo reply, redirect, source quench, and destination unreachable. ICMP messages are contained within IP datagrams. This ensures that the ICMP message will be able to find its way to the appropriate host on a network.

Internet Group Management Protocol (IGMP)

Internet Group Management Protocol (IGMP) provides routers with the identifications of multicast groups that are active on their attached networks. This information is propagated to other routers to enable multicasting support throughout the network. IGMP messages are delivered in IP datagrams and hence delivery of IGMP messages is unreliable.

Transport Layer Protocols

Two protocols, TCP and UDP, are supported at the transport layer, enabling developers to select the appropriate transport service for a given application.

Transmission Control Protocol (TCP)

Transmission Control Protocol (TCP) is a connection-oriented communications protocol that provides reliable transfer of data. TCP views data as a stream of bytes rather than individual frames. Larger messages are broken up and transmitted in segments. TCP mechanisms manage flow control and sequencing of packets to guarantee that no data is lost during transmission. TCP operation is managed by data that is placed in a header that TCP adds to the data to be transmitted.

Session management is one of the functions provided by TCP. TCP is a connection-oriented protocol and requires a session to be opened between hosts that need to communicate. A session establishes a formal dialog between the hosts that enables error recovery to take place. Establishing a session occurs using a three-way handshake process. When the session is finished, a corresponding process closes the session in an orderly manner. The formal procedure for closing the session ensures that all data is transmitted and acknowledged before communication ceases. During the session, for each segment sent, the receiving host must return an *acknowledgment* (ACK) within a specified period for data received. Reliability is achieved by using a checksum on both the header and the data of each segment to reduce the chance of network corruption going undetected. TCP also assigns a sequence number to each segment transmitted so that any lost segments will be detected and retransmitted.

It would be inefficient if the sending host had to wait for individual acknowledgment of each segment that is sent. This would double network traffic by requiring one acknowledgment for each transmitted segment, and would cause the sending host to spend more time waiting than actively transmitting data. Consequently, TCP implements a mechanism called *windowing* that enables the receiving host to acknowledge multiple segments with a single message. When a session is established, the hosts negotiate a window, based on the size of the receive buffers of the host.

User Datagram Protocol (UDP)

User Datagram Protocol (UDP) provides datagram delivery service. In contrast to the reliable, connection-oriented delivery provided by TCP, datagram delivery is unreliable and is performed on a "best effort" basis. UDP does not perform error checking to determine if a datagram is delivered. If error checking is required, it must be performed by the upper-layer application that is sending the data.

POP QUIZ True or False?

1. The TCP port used by Web servers is port 21.
2. TCP/IP is the protocol suite used on the Internet.
3. To view the path across the network between two IP devices, use the tracert utility.

Answers: 1. False 2. True 3. True

> **KNOW THIS**
>
> **The TCP/IP Protocol Stack**
>
> The TCP/IP protocol stack is composed of several components. These components function at various layers of the OSI model. Some of the components of the TCP/IP protocol stack include: TCP, IP, UDP, ARP, ICMP, IGMP, and UDP. Each of these components is responsible for a different function in network communications.

Because a session is established between only two hosts, connection-oriented delivery cannot be used to perform the one-to-many delivery that is required for broadcasting and multicasting. All broadcasts and multicasts must use UDP as a transport protocol.

Because delivery of UDP datagrams is not guaranteed, applications using UDP must supply their own mechanisms for reliability if needed. UDP is used by applications that don't require an acknowledgment of receipt of data. Microsoft networking uses UDP for log-on, browsing, and name resolution.

Like TCP, UDP appends a header to the data it receives from upper-layer protocols.

> **TEST TIP**
>
> Expect a couple of questions on the test about how the TCP/IP suite corresponds to the OSI model. There will be a diagram of the OSI model with the question. Be sure you understand how they relate.

Other Networking Components

The Windows NT operating system provides a number of networking components built into the system itself. The architecture of the operating system provides support for applications and services through well-defined interfaces, as shown in Figure 1-7. The components of the Windows NT network architecture are:

- The *Network Driver Interface Specification* (NDIS)
- The *Transport Driver Interface* (TDI)
- *NetBIOS over TCP/IP* (NetBT)
- Windows Sockets
- The Workstation Service
- The Server Service

Network Driver Interface Specification (NDIS)

Network Driver Interface Specification (NDIS) provides an interface between the transport protocols and the network adapter drivers (the network adapter driver is the software interface between the protocol and the network adapter). For outgoing messages, protocols make calls to NDIS whenever access to the network adapter is necessary. When the network adapter receives incoming messages, the network adapter driver makes a call to NDIS so that the message can be processed by the transport protocols.

				Application
				Presentation
Net BIOS	Redirectors	Servers	Window sockets	Session
TDI interface				Transport
Transport protocols				Network
NDIS interface				Datalink
Network adapter card drivers				
Network interface card				Physical

Figure 1-7 *Windows NT network architecture*

The network driver is provided by the vendor of the network adapter and must conform to the NDIS specification. The NDIS specification provides for multiple protocols and multiple network adapters to exist in a computer.

Transport Driver Interface (TDI)

The *Transport Driver Interface* (TDI) boundary layer provides a common interface between transport protocols and client services. TDI describes a set of functions that transport drivers and clients use to communicate with each other. The redirector and server call TDI functions to communicate with network protocols instead of having to be bound directly to a specific transport protocol.

NetBIOS over TCP/IP (NetBT)

NetBIOS is the standard network API for Windows networks. *NetBIOS over TCP/IP* (NetBT) makes the NetBIOS programming interface available on networks running TCP/IP protocols, enabling the many applications that use the industry standard NetBIOS APIs to work on TCP/IP networks. NetBIOS services include functions for establishing sessions, transferring data, and browsing for network resources.

Microsoft networking services rely heavily on the NetBIOS interface for network communications. The Windows NT Workstation Service, Server Service, Browser, Messenger, and Netlogon services are all examples of NetBIOS clients that require the use of NetBT when using the TCP/IP protocol. NetBIOS over TCP/IP is specified by RFC1001 and RFC1002.

Windows Sockets

The Windows Sockets specification provides an API to which application developers can write TCP/IP programs. *Windows Sockets applications* (also known as *Sockets-based applications*) eliminate the need for NetBIOS to communicate between hosts.

Windows Sockets APIs include functions for sending and receiving data on a network. They include a set of extensions designed to take advantage of the message-driven nature of Microsoft Windows. Applications developed to the Windows Sockets specification form a socket between two ports on different hosts to enable communications.

Sockets-based applications can use a host name or an IP address for communicating with a remote host.

Workstation Service

Windows NT computers include a component called the *Workstation Service*, which also resides just above the TDI. The main function of the Workstation Service is to manage requests for local files and outgoing connections to another computer. The Workstation Service consists of two components:

- The *user-mode interface* passes network commands down to the redirector. These commands are initiated from Windows NT Explorer or from a command line using commands such as "Net Use."

- The *redirector* is a file system driver that interacts with the lower-level network drivers by means of the TDI interface.

The redirector intercepts file *input/output* (I/O) calls and determines whether the request is for a local physical device or a logical remote device. If the request is for a local device, the redirector passes the request to the appropriate device driver for the local device. If the request is for a remote device, the redirector translates the request into a *Server Message Block* (SMB) protocol message. An SMB is a protocol that specifies server I/O requests.

Server Service

The *Server Service* provides the capability for a computer to provide shared resources to other clients. The Server Service is composed of two parts:

- The *server* is the service that is used to manage incoming requests for resources from other computers across the network.
- A *file system driver* handles the interaction with various file system devices to satisfy file and print requests from a client.

> **KNOW THIS**
>
> ### Elements of the NT Network Architecture
>
> Microsoft has included some helpful elements in the NT network architecture. One of these elements is NDIS. NDIS provides support for multiple protocols and adapters in each computer. TDI allows network services to communicate directly with protocols. NetBT enables NetBIOS APIs to function on TCP/IP networks. Windows Sockets eliminate the need for NetBIOS in network communications. The Workstation Service allows a computer to make requests on the network. The Server Service allows a computer to provide resources on the network.

Have You Mastered?

Now it's time to review the concepts in this chapter and apply your knowledge. These questions will test your mastery of material covered in this chapter.

1. **FTP functions at which layer of the OSI model?**

    ☐ A. Application layer
    ☐ B. Presentation layer
    ☐ C. Session layer
    ☐ D. Transport layer

    A. FTP functions at the Application layer of the OSI model. This is explained in the "OSI Model" section.

2. **Which layer of the OSI model is responsible for data encryption on the network?**

    ☐ A. Application layer
    ☐ B. Presentation layer
    ☐ C. Session layer
    ☐ D. Transport layer

    B. The Presentation layer is responsible for handling encryption of data on the network. The responsibilities of the Presentation model are covered in the "OSI Model" section.

MCSE TCP/IP ACE IT!

3. Which of the following is not supported on an NT dial-in RAS server?

☐ A. SLIP
☐ B. PPP

A. NT RAS servers cannot function as SLIP dial-in servers. NT supports PPP for dial-in; SLIP and PPP are supported for dial-out connections. Dial-up connections are covered in the "TCP/IP Protocols and Technologies" section.

4. Which of the following allows multiple adapters and protocols in a single computer?

☐ A. TDI
☐ B. NetBT
☐ C. Windows sockets
☐ D. NDIS

D. NDIS allows multiple protocols and adapters to coexist in a computer. NDIS is explained in the "Other Networking Components" section.

5. Which of the following enables an NT computer to provide network resources?

☐ A. Windows sockets
☐ B. NetBT
☐ C. Server service
☐ D. Workstation service

C. The Server service enables an NT computer to share resources on the network. The Workstation service enables computers to request resources on the network. These services are covered in the "Other Networking Components" section.

2

IP Addressing

THERE ARE A FEW IMPORTANT rules that network administrators must be follow when defining network IDs and host IDs on an internetwork. If a network will be connected to the worldwide Internet, an organization must acquire a network ID from the InterNIC. The InterNIC will assign an organization either a Class A, Class B, or Class C network ID. Each of these classes of network IDs is covered in this chapter.

MCSE TCP/IP ACE IT!

Exam Material in This Chapter

Official Word

Based on Microsoft Objectives
- Diagnose and resolve IP addressing problems.
- Understand binary conversion.

Inside Scoop

Based on Author's Experience
- Dotted decimal notation
- Class A
- Class B
- Class C

2: IP ADDRESSING

Are You Prepared?

Test your knowledge on this subject with the following questions, which will help you pinpoint problem areas requiring further review.

1. **Class A addresses begin with which binary form?**
   - ☐ A. 0
   - ☐ B. 01
   - ☐ C. 11
   - ☐ D. 111

2. **Which of the following is the broadcast address?**
   - ☐ A. 127.0.0.1
   - ☐ B. 0.0.0.0
   - ☐ C. 255.255.255.255
   - ☐ D. 255.0.0.0

3. **Which of the following is responsible for assigning an IP address to a device?**
   - ☐ A. The hardware manufacturer
   - ☐ B. IEEE
   - ☐ C. Class addressing
   - ☐ D. Network designer

Answers:

1. A   See the "Class A addresses" section.
2. C   See the "Host Addressing Guidelines" section.
3. D   See the "IP Addressing Overview" section.

IP Addressing Overview

IP addressing is a general term that encompasses the conventions and tools used to identify devices on TCP/IP networks and enable them to communicate. Any person responsible for managing a TCP/IP network must have a complete understanding of how IP addresses work and the methods used to assign IP addresses to network devices.

Physical Addresses

At the lowest level of network communications, all networking devices must communicate by using a *physical address*. Any device on a network needing to communicate with another networking device must eventually determine the destination device's physical address or the physical address of a router that will be used to communicate with the remote device if it exists on a different subnet.

> **TEST TRAP**
> For the test, be aware that terminology may be different. For example, *a physical address is often referred to as a hardware address* or *media access control* (MAC) *address*.

The manufacturer of the network interface adapter normally encodes this address into the hardware. Manufacturers of Ethernet devices are allocated a fixed value for a portion of the physical address by the IEEE (Institute of Electrical and Electronics Engineers). Every piece of equipment supporting Ethernet made by that vendor is programmed with a physical address that begins with a 24-bit *vendor code*.

The manufacturer is responsible for making sure every Ethernet device it makes has the same first three bytes, which make up the manufacturer's unique code. The vendor allocates the remaining three bytes to each device so that every device in the world has a unique 48-bit physical address. This guarantees that no two manufacturers will ever create the same address on two different devices. Otherwise, there would be no way of uniquely identifying and communicating with a specific device.

Assigned IP Addresses

Assigned IP addresses are necessary because:

- Not all hosts have a hardware network adapter. IP addresses enable hosts such as dial-up clients to connect to an IP network without having a physical address.
- Physical addresses are long, cryptic, and not very user-friendly. Using TCP/IP, an organization can assign IP addresses by creating a numbering system that meets the needs of its network. This enables the network designers to use a more logically ordered addressing scheme.
- Physical addresses are only used when both devices reside on the same physical network. IP addresses provide a method of addressing devices that reside on remote networks. The physical address often does not reference the same machine as the IP address.

Another advantage of IP addressing is if a network adapter fails or is upgraded, it can be replaced without getting a new IP address. Also, if a host is moved from one network to another, it can be given a new IP address without requiring a new adapter card.

The formats of physical addresses versus IP addresses are shown in Table 2-1. Notice how physical addresses appear as random numbers whereas IP addresses can be assigned using a selected numbering system.

TABLE 2-1 Physical addresses versus assigned IP addresses

Physical addresses	Assigned IP addresses
2c-40-95-e0-5d-c7	172.25.16.21
00-c0-1b-00-5a-f6	172.25.16.22
00-3d-87-14-3a-d9	172.25.16.32

Finally, higher-level addressing schemes, such as IP, are necessary so protocols can determine whether packets should remain on the local network or be transmitted to other networks. Hosts on a network must be assigned an IP address from a defined range of numbers. When a host attempts to communicate with another host that has an IP address outside of this range, TCP/IP automatically forwards the datagram to the default gateway. This happens because the destination host is assumed to reside outside of the local network since it is out of range.

IP Address Contents

The addressing conventions for IP start with a broad identification that refers to a unique network and then narrows down the focus to identify individual hosts on that network. Once this granular identification has been determined, any host can communicate with any other host on that network or on a network that is connected through the Internet.

The IP address is the set of numbers many people see on their workstations or terminals, such as `172.25.16.51`. This is the number that uniquely identifies the device on a TCP/IP network. However, like most computer programs, the TCP/IP software running on a host computer performs computations and routing decisions based on the binary value of this number.

Dotted decimal notation

Because it would be too difficult to remember the binary representations of IP addresses, they are presented in a format called *dotted decimal notation*. Each octet is separated with a period. An *octet* of an IP address is an eight-bit binary number (also referred to as a *byte*) that represents a decimal number in the range 0–255. For example:

    Binary format: `10101100   00011001   00010000   00110011`

When converted to decimal becomes:

    Dotted decimal notation: `172.25.16.51`

While the TCP/IP software always works with the binary format of an IP address, all TCP/IP configuration screens and diagnostic utilities allow you to refer to the addresses in dotted decimal notation.

2: IP ADDRESSING

TEST TIP Be sure to know how to convert a dotted decimal address to its corresponding binary address. You will need to convert addresses on the test.

POP QUIZ **True or False?**

1. The conversion for the decimal value 176 to binary is 1011 0000.
2. ANDING is the process of comparing the IP address to the subnet mask to determine the network address.
3. LMHOSTS files are used to map hostnames to IP addresses.

Answers: 1. True 2. True 3. False

IP Network Address Classes

Internet standards define five classes of IP addresses. The three classes that you need to be aware of are Class A, Class B, and Class C. The class of network determines what portion of the Internet address is to be used to designate the network and what portion is to be used to identify individual hosts on the network. The class that will be used for a given network depends on the number of host IDs that need to be defined on the local network and on the internetwork.

TEST TIP The TCP/IP exam extensively tests your knowledge on the differences between different IP network address classes. You need to have a thorough understanding of the capabilities and limitations of the different address classes. You should also make sure that you know how to tell the difference between address classes from the value of the first octet in a given IP address.

35

If a network is not connected to the Internet, it can be assigned a network ID from any address class to meet the needs of the organization. However, if the network is connected to the Internet, the network address must be assigned by the InterNIC. The InterNIC manages the allocation of network addresses to guarantee that each network ID is unique on the Internet.

Determining the class of an IP address

The class of an address defines which bits are used for the network ID and which bits are used for the host ID. It also determines the number of subnets and the number of hosts that can be assigned on an internetwork.

Table 2-2 shows how network and host ID octets are segmented according to the address class. A Class A network address allocates 24 bits for use as host IDs, providing more available host IDs for network devices. A Class B network address provides an equal number of network IDs and host IDs per network ID, enabling administrators to configure a larger number of networks but permitting fewer hosts per network. A Class C network address provides for many network IDs but permits a small number of host IDs per network ID.

TABLE 2-2 Network and host ID octets

Class	IP address	Network ID	Host ID
A	w.x.y.z	w	x.y.z
B	w.x.y.z	w.x	y.z
C	w.x.y.z	w.x.y	z

Class A addresses Class A addresses are assigned to very large networks with many host computers. A Class A address will always have the high-order bit (first bit of the first octet) set to 0. This indicates that all IP addresses on the internetwork will be divided so that the first octet will specify the network ID and the last three octets (24 bits) will specify the host ID.

2: IP ADDRESSING

Because there are only seven bits available for creating unique network IDs using a Class A address, only 126 networks can be allocated by the InterNIC. A Class A address provides 24 bits for the host address. Each of the 126 Class A networks can accommodate more than 16 million (16,777,214 to be exact) unique host IDs per network.

> **KNOW THIS — Subnetting**
>
> Sixteen million is a lot of hosts to put on a single network. Too many, in fact. Most of the time, an organization that has been assigned a Class A address will divide the host ID further to create many different internal subnetworks (usually referred to as *subnets*). This practice, called subnetting, is valuable with other address classes as well, enabling an organization to spread its valuable IP address assignments across a larger network.

The range of IP addresses that can be assigned with a Class A address is:
`1.x.y.z to 126.x.y.z`.

> **TEST TRAP**
>
> While the binary value `0111 1111` (127 decimal) is technically a Class A address, this address (called the *loopback* address) is reserved for connectivity testing purposes.

Class B addresses Class B addresses, more commonly assigned (even to large organizations) than Class A addresses, always have the high-order bits set to 10. This indicates that all IP addresses on the internetwork will be divided so that the first two octets will specify the network ID and the second two octets (16 bits) will specify the host ID.

Class B addresses have 14 bits available (after discounting the first two bits, which must always be 10) for assigning network IDs and 16 bits for assigning host IDs. This provides for:

- 16,384 networks
- 65,534 hosts per network

37

The range of IP addresses that can be assigned with a Class B address is:
128.0.0.1 to 191.255.255.254.

Class C addresses Class C addresses are normally reserved for smaller LANs, although the scarcity of Class A and B addresses has forced the use of Class C addresses on large WANs, as well. Class C addresses always have the high-order bits set to 110. This indicates that the IP address will be partitioned so that the first three octets will specify the network ID and the last octet (16 bits) will specify the host ID.

Class C addresses have 21 bits available for assigning network numbers (after discounting the first three bits, which must always be 110). This provides for:

- 2,097,152 networks
- 254 hosts per network

The range of IP addresses that can be assigned with a Class B address is:
192.0.0.1 to 223.255.255.254

Obtaining an Internet IP Address

To connect to the Internet or create an internetwork for your organization, you will need to determine an addressing scheme for your network. If an organization plans to build a TCP/IP network that will never be connected to another TCP/IP network outside of the organization, then any Class A, Class B, or Class C network number can be selected that provides for an appropriate number of hosts.

This, however, is a shortsighted approach, because the organization would have to completely reconfigure the network if ever there was a need to connect outside of the organization or to the Internet. A better strategy is to contact the InterNIC's registration services and acquire an officially assigned network number.

Assigning Host IP Addresses

Table 2-3 summarizes Class A, B, and C network addressing. The class of an IP address can be determined from the three high-order bits, with two bits being sufficient to distinguish among the three primary classes (Class A, Class B, or Class C). Microsoft only supports the use of Class A, B, and C addresses for assigning host IP addresses.

TABLE 2-3 Internet address classes

Class	Bits for network IDs	Range (first octet)	Number of networks	Bits for host IDs	Number of host IDs
A	7	1–126	126	24	16,777,214
B	14	128–191	16,384	16	65,534
C	21	192–223	2,097,152	8	254

Table 2-4 lists the valid ranges of host IDs for a network in a given network class.

TABLE 2-4 Valid ranges of host IDs

Class	Beginning range	Ending range
A	1.0.0.1	126.255.255.254
B	128.0.0.1	191.255.255.254
C	192.0.0.1	223.255.255.254

Assigning Host IDs

Because a host ID is used to identify a specific host interface on a network, each host interface, including the interface to a router, must have a unique host ID. Hosts that have multiple network adapters (called multihomed hosts) must also have a unique host ID for each interface.

A unique host ID is required for each computer and printer that is connected to the network. Additionally, every interface that a router has to a network requires its own host ID.

Grouping host computers by host ID

There are only a couple of rules for how to assign valid host IDs on a network. Hosts must not be assigned an IP address that contains all 0s or all 1s. Also, the host must be assigned an IP address that is within range of the other hosts on the same subnet.

Hosts can be numbered sequentially or grouped by the type of device for easy identification. For example:

Routers	172.25.16.1 to 172.25.16.11
Servers	172.25.16.21 to 172.25.16.50
UNIX hosts	172.25.16.51 to 172.25.16.99
Workstations	172.25.16.100 to 172.25.16.254

Consider growth planning in your addressing scheme to accommodate the addition of different types of host computers.

Host addressing guidelines

The Internet community has defined a number of special addressing conventions that need to be followed when assigning host IDs. Failure to follow these guidelines can create compatibility problems between devices from different manufacturers.

- A host ID must be unique within a network.
- A host ID cannot be all 1s (the sum, 255, indicates a broadcast address).
- A host ID cannot be all 0s (0 indicates a local network).

Assigning Network IDs

An IP address is logically divided into two components. Some bits function as a network ID, and the remaining bits comprise a host ID. A network ID identifies those TCP/IP hosts that are located on the same network, similar to the way your street name is specified when a letter or parcel is addressed to you. Because the IP address specifies not only the device's host ID but also identifies the machine's connection to the network, the IP address must be changed when the device is moved to a different network.

> **KNOW THIS**
>
> ### Understanding Network Interfaces
>
> Although it is commonly stated that each device must have a unique IP address, it is more accurate to say that each network *interface* must have a unique IP address. Some TCP/IP devices have more than one interface. A router, for example, must have two or more interfaces. Each physical interface must be assigned a distinct IP address. If you think of IP addresses as being assigned to network interfaces rather than to devices, you will find several TCP/IP processes easier to understand.

An IP addressing scheme must ensure that no two interfaces on a network will ever have the same ID. Correct addressing of hosts on a network requires the following:

- Each network in an internetwork must have a unique network ID.

- A connection between two routers is a network even though the routers are the only devices attached to the connecting network. The network between the routers also requires a unique network ID.

- Each device connected to the same network must be configured with the same network ID or they will be unable to communicate.

- Each host on the same network must be assigned a unique host ID; otherwise, hosts will receive each other's messages.

MCSE TCP/IP ACE IT!

TEST TIP: There are several exam questions that will test your knowledge on the difference between valid and invalid IP addresses. You will need to know which addresses can be used and the kinds of problems that will result when an invalid address is specified.

Internet addressing guidelines

Internet standards define a number of special addressing conventions that must be followed when assigning network IDs.

- A network ID must be unique on an internetwork.
- A network ID cannot be all 1s (the sum, 255, indicates a broadcast address).
- A network ID cannot be all 0s (0 indicates a local network and cannot be routed).
- A network ID cannot begin with 127 (127 is reserved for loopback testing).

POP QUIZ True or False?

1. The address `192.64.114.68` is a Class B address.
2. The address `127.0.0.1` is a Class A address.
3. The address `200.200.200.200` is a Class C address.

Answers: 1. False 2. True 3. True.

2: IP ADDRESSING

Have You Mastered?

Now it's time to review the concepts in this chapter and apply your knowledge. These questions will test your mastery of material covered in this chapter.

1. **A device receives network transmissions when sent to which type of address?**

    ☐ A. Physical
    ☐ B. IP
    ☐ C. Computer name
    ☐ D. Network

    A. The physical address of the network adapter is the address used to receive data. See the "Physical Addresses" section.

2. **Which of the following is an example of dotted decimal notation?**

    ☐ A. http://www.microsoft.com
    ☐ B. 9.43.98.126
    ☐ C. 1110 0010
    ☐ D. 00-C0-6D-10-47-8D

    B. Dotted decimal notation consists of four octets separated by periods. See the "Dotted decimal notation" section.

43

MCSE TCP/IP ACE IT!

3. Which class of address offers the most host IDs?

- A. Class A
- B. Class B
- C. Class C
- D. Class D

A. Class A addresses allow the largest possible number of host IDs. See the "Class A addresses" section.

4. What is the largest possible number of hosts on a Class C network?

- A. 16 million
- B. 65 thousand
- C. 256
- D. 254

D. Class C addresses are capable of supporting 254 hosts. See the "Class C addresses" section.

5. Which of the following is acceptable for a host ID?

- A. 0
- B. 255
- C. 127.0.0.1
- D. 45

D. A host ID cannot be all 0s or 255s. 127.0.0.1 is known as the loopback address and is not available for use on the network. See the "Assigning Host IDs" section.

3

Subnet Addressing

SUBNET ADDRESSING IS AN important part of managing a large TCP/IP network, and a knowledge of subnet addressing indicates a good knowledge of TCP/IP. For this reason, the TCP/IP exam covers this subject extensively. Therefore, you should study this chapter a couple of times until you are comfortable doing the subnetting math calculations in your head. Your knowledge of subnet addressing may mean the difference in passing or failing the TCP/IP exam.

MCSE TCP/IP ACE IT!

Exam Material in this Chapter

Based on Microsoft Objectives
- Given a scenario, identify valid network configurations.

Based on Author's Experience
- Subnet Addressing
- Subnet Masks
- Host IDs
- Network IDs
- Supernetting
- Address Classes

3: SUBNET ADDRESSING

Are You Prepared?

Start out by testing your knowledge on this topic with the following questions. After checking your answers, you'll be able to identify any areas you need to study further.

1. **What method is used to combine Class C addresses to create larger networks?**

    ☐ A. Subnetting
    ☐ B. Supernetting
    ☐ C. Masking
    ☐ D. Routing

2. **What is not a consideration when determining the subnet mask?**

    ☐ A. Number of host computers
    ☐ B. Number of networks
    ☐ C. Expected network growth
    ☐ D. Router location

Answers:

1. B   See the "Supernetting" section.
2. D   See the "Subnet Masks" section.

Subnets

For administrative, performance, and security purposes, many organizations divide a single network into multiple physical networks and connect them with routers. *Subnetting* is a technique that enables a single network address to span multiple physical networks. Each physical network on an internetwork is referred to as a subnet.

> **TEST TRAP**
> The word *internetwork*—frequently shortened to *internet*—means one or more networks connected by routers. This is typically used to refer to an organization's internal network. The word *Internet* (uppercase I) refers to a specific network that connects millions of computers worldwide.

A common reason for subnetting is because a Class A or Class B address space is simply too large to be implemented in a single, unrouted network. To use the address space efficiently, it is necessary to allocate the available addresses to multiple smaller networks. In other cases, routing is required by the network design.

With subnets, an organization can divide a large network into smaller portions that are more manageable. Some of the administrative reasons for dividing a large network into subnets are:

- Subdividing administrative responsibility
- Increasing performance
- Providing additional security

Subnet Addressing

Subnet addressing is the most complex problem you will face in configuring a TCP/IP network, and can best be understood by imagining a site with a single IP network address assigned to it, but with two or more physical networks, each of which uses a portion of the available host IDs. When a network is properly subnetted, only the routers know that there are multiple physical networks and how to route traffic among them.

TEST TIP — Subnet addressing is the most complex topic in configuring a TCP/IP network. It's also a very important topic for managing a large network containing many subnets. Use your binary math skills to determine how to select a subnet mask and create a range of IP addresses for each subnet. Study the examples given and try creating some of your own scenarios.

Partitioning the IP Address

An organization is assigned a network portion of an IP address by the InterNIC. Figure 3-1 shows how the host portion can be further partitioned by the network administrator to identify a specific subnet that a host resides on.

This results in a form of hierarchical addressing scheme that supports routing between subnets on an internetwork and, at a higher level, between an internetwork and the worldwide Internet. On an internetwork, the three-part division consists of the *network ID*, the *subnet ID*, and the *host ID*.

Network ID	Host ID	
Network ID	Subnet ID	Host ID

Figure 3-1 *IP addresses can be further partitioned to support subnetting.*

Partitioning the host portion of IP addresses into two parts enables the creation of additional subnet addresses. One part of an IP address is then used to identify the subnet as a unique network within the internetwork.

The network administrator must decide how this partitioning should occur by specifying a custom subnet mask on each host within the subnet. All hosts on that subnet must be configured with the same subnet mask. Subnet addressing involves careful management of IP addresses and properly defined subnet masks.

How you partition the host address (the number of bits you reserve for the subnet portion) depends on your needs. The more bits you reserve for the subnet portion, the fewer bits you have available for assigning to host computers, which means fewer host computers can reside on any one subnet.

Sites that need fewer subnets and have a large number of hosts will define a subnet mask that uses fewer bits for subnetting. Sites that need to create many subnets but have fewer hosts will define a subnet mask that uses more bits for subnetting.

Subnet Masks

A subnet mask is a 32-bit number used to inform TCP/IP hosts which bits of the IP address correspond to the network address and which bits correspond to the host address. The TCP/IP protocols use the subnet mask to determine if a destination host address is located on the local subnet or on a remote subnet.

Determining this is accomplished by *masking* the network address. Masking is simply designating where the division between the network ID and host ID occurs. All bits in the subnet mask that correspond to the network address are set to 1. All bits in the subnet mask that correspond to the host address are set to 0.

The computation TCP/IP performs when comparing the subnet mask against the IP address is a `logical bitwise AND`. Performing a bitwise `AND` on any two bits results in 1 (or TRUE) if the two values are both 1. If either of the values is 0, then the result is 0 (or FALSE).

Subnet rules

RFC 950, which defines subnet addressing specifications, applies two rules to the subnet portion of a network ID:

- Because a network ID of all 0s conventionally is equivalent to "this network," the subnet portion of the network ID cannot be all 0s because that designates "this subnet."
- Because a network ID of all 1s is a broadcast address, the subnet portion of the network ID cannot be all 1s, because the all-1s address is used to address broadcasts to the subnet.

These rules limit the kinds of subnets you can create. A single bit can have values of only 0 and 1, and neither is a valid subnet number according to the RFC.

Subnet shortcuts

Subnet masks do not always end on even byte boundaries, and you are likely to encounter subnet masks such as `255.255.240.0`. To understand how a particular subnet mask functions, you need to convert the decimal representation into binary.

> **KNOW THIS**
>
> ### Decimal-Binary Conversions
>
> Memorizing the following decimal-binary conversations will be extremely helpful in answering questions on the exam related to subnetting.
>
> Although others are possible, there are only a few common subnet masks. If you remember just nine decimal-binary conversions, you can easily understand the bits in nearly every subnet mask you will encounter. Here are the conversions:
>
> | 255 | 11111111 |
> | 254 | 11111110 |
> | 252 | 11111100 |
> | 248 | 11111000 |
> | 240 | 11110000 |
> | 224 | 11100000 |
> | 192 | 11000000 |
> | 128 | 10000000 |
> | 0 | 00000000 |

How IP determines the destination of a packet

Whenever a host attempts to communicate with another host, IP checks the source and destination IP addresses and compares them against the subnet mask that has been assigned on the sending host. IP can then determine if the remote host is on the local subnet or a remote subnet. IP does this by performing a binary calculation on each of the addresses:

- If the result of the bitwise AND computations on the network IDs for both the source and destination hosts are the same, then IP assumes both hosts reside on the same subnet. The source host then uses ARP to determine the hardware address of the destination host.
- If the result of the bitwise AND computations on the network IDs for both the source and destination hosts are different, then IP assumes each of the hosts resides on a different subnet. The source host then uses ARP to determine the hardware address of the default gateway and forwards all datagrams to the default gateway for delivery.

KNOW THIS

Configuring Subnet Masks

Misconfiguration of subnet masks is a frequent source of network problems. All hosts on a subnet must be configured with the same subnet mask, even if all their IP addresses are correct. A host assumes its subnet mask applies to the entire local subnet, and uses its subnet mask to perform the bitwise AND comparison with the destination host's IP address. If the destination host is configured with a different subnet mask, it may or may not receive packets from the source. But the destination host will certainly be unable to reply, because its incorrect subnet mask forces it to assume that the source host is on a remote subnet. Therefore, the destination host will send its reply to a router rather than sending it to the source host.

Default subnet masks

A default subnet mask is used on TCP/IP networks that are not divided into subnets. Remember that all hosts require a subnet mask even if the site consists of a single-segment network. The default subnet mask used depends on the address class. Table 3-1 shows the default subnet masks for each address class.

TABLE 3-1 Default subnet masks for address classes

Address class	Dotted decimal notation	Bits used for the subnet mask
A	255.0.0.0	1111 1111 0000 0000 0000 0000 0000 0000
B	255.255.0.0	1111 1111 1111 1111 0000 0000 0000 0000
C	255.255.255.0	1111 1111 1111 1111 1111 1111 0000 0000

Private Internetworks

A network address from the InterNIC is only required if you plan on accessing resources on the Internet. If your internetwork is private, you can assign any valid network address to a network as long as it's unique within your internetwork. If this is the case, subnetting is not required, so you can designate any Class A, Class B, or Class C network address to each of your subnets. This eliminates the need to define custom subnet masks on your internetwork.

> **KNOW THIS** **Reserved IP Addresses**
>
> Specific Class A, B, and C addresses have been assigned for use on private internetworks by the IETF, so as not to conflict with registered IP addresses. These addresses are as follows:
>
> Class A   10.0.0.0 through 10.255.255.255

Class B   172.16.0.0 through 172.31.255.255
Class C   192.168.0.0 through 192.168.255.255

Supernetting

Because of the limited availability of Class B network addresses, the Internet authorities have provided the ability to consolidate multiple Class C network addresses into one logical network.

To use supernetting, the InterNIC allocates eight Class C network addresses. The addresses that are to be combined must share the same high-order bits, and the subnet mask is "shortened" to take bits away from the network portion of the address and add them to the host portion.

When routing decisions are made, only the bits covered by the subnet mask are used. This makes addresses in Class C networks appear as if they are on the same subnet. IP will use ARP to resolve these addresses locally instead of using ARP to forward messages to a router.

Subdividing a Network

To divide your network into different subnets, you must assign each subnet its own network ID. Before you can do this, you need to determine how many subnets you require and the maximum number of host IDs that you need to assign on each subnet. With this information, you can define a subnet mask, a range of network IDs, and a range of host IDs for each subnet. The factors involved in subdividing a network are:

1. Determining how many network IDs will be required to uniquely identify every subnet on your internetwork
2. Determining how many host IDs will be required to identify each host on each physical network (subnet)
3. Defining a custom subnet mask that meets the requirements of your internetwork
4. Determining the network IDs that will be used to identify each subnet
5. Determining the range of host IDs that will be used on each subnet

Determining How Many Network IDs Will Be Required

The first step in subnetting your network is to determine how many network IDs will be required to assign a unique network ID to each subnet. A unique network ID is required for:

- Each subnet
- Each *wide area network* (WAN) connection

Determining How Many Host IDs Will Be Required

The next step is to determine the maximum number of host IDs that you will need on each subnet. A unique host ID is required for:

- Each TCP/IP host
- Each router interface

Keep in mind a TCP/IP host includes any device that uses a network adapter to connect it to the network. This includes routers and printers that are directly attached to the network. There are also cases in which a computer has been installed with two network adapters. In this case, each adapter requires a unique host ID.

Don't forget to factor in future growth in the number of subnets and hosts as part of your plan. Once you have determined the total number of subnets that will be required on your network and the maximum number of host IDs that will be required per subnet, you can define the following:

- A subnet mask that you will use on your entire internetwork
- A unique network address for each subnet based on the subnet mask
- A range of valid IP addresses for each subnet

MCSE TCP/IP ACE IT!

Defining a Custom Subnet Mask

Once you decide to subnet your network and you determine your requirements for the number of network IDs and host IDs, you can define a subnet mask that supports the needs of your internetwork.

Tables 3-2, 3-3, and 3-4 show the differences between a default subnet mask and a custom subnet mask. As you can see, with the custom subnet mask, additional bits have been masked from the host ID for the purpose of defining subnets.

TABLE 3-2 Class A Example

	Dotted decimal notation	Bits used for the subnet mask
Default	255.0.0.0	1111 1111 0000 0000 0000 0000 0000 0000
Custom	255.255.0.0	1111 1111 1111 1111 0000 0000 0000 0000

TABLE 3-3 Class B Example

	Dotted decimal notation	Bits used for the subnet mask
Default	255.255.0.0	1111 1111 1111 1111 0000 0000 0000 0000
Custom	255.255.240.0	1111 1111 1111 1111 1111 0000 0000 0000

TABLE 3-4 Class C Example

	Dotted decimal notation	Bits used for the subnet mask
Default	255.255.255.0	1111 1111 1111 1111 1111 1111 0000 0000
Custom	255.255.255.192	1111 1111 1111 1111 1111 1111 1100 0000

The number of additional bits that the subnet mask defines beyond the number specified by the default subnet mask determines the possible number of subnets that can be defined and the number of hosts that can be assigned IDs on each subnet. Before you define a subnet mask, you should plan ahead and consider the possibility that you may need to add additional subnets and hosts at some future time.

Selecting the Appropriate Subnet Mask

The following process is used to choose the correct subnet mask for a network:

1. Determine the number of subnets required.
2. Convert the number of subnets to the binary numbering format. For example, if six subnets are required, use the third and the second bits.
3. Convert the number of required bits to high order and pad all leading bit values of 0 to 1s (make sure there are no 0s to the left).
4. Convert all of the subnet bits to decimal format to determine the value for the subnet mask.

TEST TIP: There's one time you won't be able to have this book with you to refer to the conversion tables: when you are taking the exam. Better read the previous section one more time!

Use Tables 3-5, 3-6, and 3-7 to determine the appropriate subnet mask to use based on your requirements.

TABLE 3-5 Subnet masks for Class A networks

Number of subnets	Number of hosts per subnet	Required number of bits	Subnet mask
0	Invalid	1	Invalid
2	4,194,302	2	255.192.0.0

Continued

TABLE 3-5 *Continued*

6	2,097,150	3	255.224.0.0
14	1,048,574	4	255.240.0.0
30	524,286	5	255.248.0.0
62	262,142	6	255.252.0.0
126	131,070	7	255.254.0.0
254	65,534	8	255.255.0.0

TABLE 3-6 Subnet masks for Class B networks

Number of subnets	Number of hosts per subnet	Required number of bits	Subnet mask
0	Invalid	1	Invalid
2	16,382	2	255.255.192.0
6	8,190	3	255.255.224.0
14	4,094	4	255.255.240.0
30	2,046	5	255.255.248.0
62	1,022	6	255.255.252.0
126	510	7	255.255.254.0
254	254	8	255.255.255.0

TEST TIP

Try to memorize these tables (especially for Class B and Class C network addresses). Before you start the exam, you might want to write these down on the scratch paper that will be provided to you prior to starting the exam. This will enable you to use your time more efficiently.

TABLE 3-7 Subnet masks for Class C networks

Number of subnets	Number of hosts per subnet	Required number of bits	Subnet mask
0	Invalid	1	Invalid
2	62	2	255.255.255.192
6	30	3	255.255.255.224
14	14	4	255.255.255.240
30	6	5	255.255.255.248
62	2	6	255.255.255.252

TEST TRAP You can use more than eight bits for the subnet mask. Remember: The more bits used for the subnet mask means fewer hosts per subnet.

Determining the Network IDs to Use

The next step is to determine the subnet network IDs that will be created for each of the subnets. A range of valid network addresses is defined by applying the custom subnet mask — which you have selected from the previous tables — to the network ID that has been assigned to you by the InterNIC (or the network ID you have selected). The possible bit combinations supported by the chosen subnet are evaluated, and then each is converted to a decimal format. The resulting subnet network IDs can then be assigned to each subnet. Each host can then be assigned an IP address that conforms to the network ID on which the host resides.

Once you have defined a subnet mask that meets your requirements, you can determine the available network IDs that can be used as follows:

1. Using the same bits that were used to define the subnet mask — not including those bits used in the default subnet mask — list all possible bit combinations.

2. Cross out any values that would result in all 1s or 0s, as these values should not be used for network IDs.
3. Convert the remaining bits to decimal format.

Using a shortcut to define network IDs

The more bits that are used for the subnet network ID, the more bit combinations there are. Listing and converting so many bit combinations becomes tedious and impractical when more than four bits are used for the subnet mask. There is another method of defining a range of network IDs:

1. List the additional octet added to the default subnet mask in binary format.
2. Convert the right-most bit with a value of 1 (the lowest bit value) to decimal. This becomes the incrementing value for each subnet.
3. Convert the bits to low order and determine the decimal value. Subtract 1 to determine the possible number of subnets.
4. Starting with 0, increment the value from Step 2 by the number of bit combinations from Step 3.

When you append this decimal value to the original network ID of 172.25.0.0, you will have defined your subnet network IDs as follows:

    172.25.32
    172.25.64
    172.25.96
    172.25.128
    172.25.160
    172.25.192

3: SUBNET ADDRESSING

POP QUIZ — True or False?

1. The default subnet mask for a Class C address is 255.255.255.255.

Answer: 1. False.

Determining the Range of Host IDs for Each Subnet

Once you have defined the subnet network IDs that will be used on your internetwork, you must determine the range of host IDs that can be used on each subnet.

The first host ID in a range starts with the incrementing value followed by .1 in the last octet. The last host ID in a range starts with one less than the next incrementing value. Remember, though, that the last octet cannot be 0 or 255.

Table 3-8 shows the range of addresses that can be used on each subnet for a Class B network 172.25.0.0 and a subnet mask of 255.255.224.0. The incrementing value for the given subnet mask is 32. Therefore, the first valid IP address for the first subnet network ID (subnet 32) is 172.25.32.1, and the last valid address for that subnet is 172.25.63.254 (one less than the next subnet network ID, discounting the broadcast value 255).

Table 3-8 Determining the ranges of host IP addresses

Bit value	Subnet	First IP address	Last IP address
00100000	32	172.25.32.1	172.25.63.254
01000000	64	172.25.64.1	172.25.95.254
01100000	96	172.25.96.1	172.25.127.254
10000000	128	172.25.128.1	172.25.159.254
10100000	160	172.25.160.1	172.25.191.254
11000000	192	172.25.192.1	172.25.223.254

Given the subnet mask 255.255.224.0, any IP address less than 172.25.32.1 and any IP address greater than 172.25.223.224 would be invalid. One of the common mistakes that beginners make when they first learn these concepts is assuming that the only valid addresses within a given subnet have to start with the same value as the subnet (for example, 172.25.32.1 – 172.25.32.254). This would only provide 254 host IDs. The full range of host IDs actually available with Subnet 32 is 172.25.32.1 through 172.25.63.254. This means that there are 8,190 possible host ID addresses available on each of the six subnets in the example above.

3: SUBNET ADDRESSING

Have You Mastered?

Now it's time to review the concepts in this chapter and apply your knowledge. These questions will test your mastery of material covered in this chapter.

1. **How many subnets can be created on a Class C network with a subnet mask of** `255.255.255.224`**?**

    ☐ A. 12
    ☐ B. 6
    ☐ C. 20
    ☐ D. 9

    B. See the "Defining a Custom Subnet Mask" section.

2. **How many subnets can be created on a Class B network with a subnet mask of** `255.255.252.0`**?**

    ☐ A. 50
    ☐ B. 16
    ☐ C. 84
    ☐ D. 62

    D. See the "Defining a Custom Subnet Mask" section.

MCSE TCP/IP ACE IT!

3. **How many hosts can be created on a Class C network with a subnet mask of** 255.255.255.192**?**

    ☐ A. 50
    ☒ B. 62
    ☐ C. 20
    ☐ D. 12

B. See the "Selecting the Appropriate Subnet Mask" section.

4. **How many hosts can be created on a Class B network with a subnet mask of** 255.255.248.0**?**

    ☐ A. 256
    ☐ B. 1,012
    ☐ C. 2,046
    ☐ D. 592

C. See the "Selecting the Appropriate Subnet Mask" section.

Practice Your Skills

The following exercises provide you with a practical opportunity to apply the knowledge you've gained in this chapter.

1. Implementing subnets

EXERCISE You are the administrator of a single segment network that contains 100 host computers. Users report that network performance is very slow. Using network monitoring tools, you determine there is excessive traffic on the network. You are asked to implement a solution that will improve the performance of the network. How should you modify your network design to improve performance? What additional hardware will be required?

ANALYSIS Subdivide the network into two or more subnets to improve performance. One or more gateways (routers) will be required. Each subnet will require a connection to a router.

2. Configuring host computers for subnetting

EXERCISE You are the administrator for a single-segment network that contains 150 Windows-based computers. Your company is assigned a Class B network address. You plan to divide your network into multiple subnets. Other than a unique IP address, each host computer has been configured with default IP address settings. Which TCP/IP address settings will you need to configure for each computer in order to implement subnetting?

ANALYSIS Each computer will need to be configured with the following: (1) a custom subnet mask, (2) an IP address that is within the range of addresses allowed for the subnet on which the computer resides, and (3) an IP address for the default gateway (the router on the computer's subnet).

3. Determining the class of an IP address

EXERCISE You are the administrator for a network containing 150 Windows-based computers. Currently, all computers are assigned an IP address in the range `135.109.7.1` to `135.109.7.254`. All computers use a subnet mask of `255.255.0.0`. What is the current class of the IP addresses used? How can you determine this?

ANALYSIS Class B is the current class. The first octet of a TCP/IP address determines the class of the address. In this case, the first octet is 135, which is in the range of a Class B address (128–191).

4. Selecting a subnet mask for use on a network

EXERCISE Your company is assigned a Class B network address. You are asked to divide the network into 12 different subnets to increase performance and provide some isolation between different departments. Each subnet will never have more than 250 hosts. For future expansion, you want to design a subnet addressing scheme that provides for the greatest number of subnets. Which subnet mask should you use? How many subnets will you be able to create using this subnet mask?

ANALYSIS Use subnet mask 255.255.255.0. You will be able to create 254 subnets with this mask.

5. Subnetting a Class B network address

EXERCISE You are the administrator of a single-segment network containing 150 host computers. Your organization has been assigned a Class B network address. What is the default subnet mask for a Class B network address? You want to divide your network into 25 subnets. You want to allow for the largest possible number of hosts on each of the subnets. Which subnet mask should you use? What is the maximum number of host IDs that can exist on the network using this subnet mask?

ANALYSIS The default subnet mask is 255.255.0.0. To allow for the largest possible number of hosts on each subnet, use subnet mask 255.255.248.0. This will enable you to create 2,046 host IDs.

6. Subnetting a Class C network address

EXERCISE You have been assigned a Class C network address. You want to divide your network into three different subnets. Each subnet will have as many as 25 hosts. Which subnet mask should you use? Using this subnet mask, what is the maximum number of host IDs that can be defined on any one subnet? What is the maximum number of subnets that can defined using the subnet mask?

ANALYSIS You should use subnet mask 255.255.255.224. This will enable you to have 30 host IDs on each subnet, and 6 subnets.

4

Dynamic Host Configuration Protocol

DYNAMIC HOST CONFIGURATION PROTOCOL (DHCP) can solve many administration problems by providing a special protocol and database service for managing IP configuration settings. DHCP planning and traffic considerations are emphasized so you can understand how DHCP can be implemented on a large network with multiple subnets.

Exam Material in This Chapter

Official Word

Based on Microsoft Objectives
- Given a scenario, identify valid network configurations.
- Configure scopes by using DHCP Manager.
- Configure a RAS server and dial-up networking for use on a TCP/IP network.

Inside Scoop

Based on Author's Experience
- Dynamic Host Configuration Protocol
- DHCP Scopes
- DHCP Initialization Phases
- DHCP Lease Renewal
- DHCP Relay Agents
- DHCP Options
- Client Reservations

4: DYNAMIC HOST CONFIGURATION PROTOCOL

Are You Prepared?

Test your knowledge with the following questions. Then you'll know if you're prepared for the material in this chapter or if you should review problem areas.

1. **Which of the following is not required when creating a DHCP scope on a DHCP server?**

    - [ ] A. IP addresses
    - [ ] B. Subnet mask
    - [ ] C. Default gateway
    - [ ] D. Lease duration

2. **Which of the following options is used for all scopes on a DHCP server?**

    - [ ] A. Global
    - [ ] B. Scope
    - [ ] C. Client
    - [ ] D. Server

3. **Which command is used to view the IP configuration on a Windows 95 computer?**

    - [ ] A. `ipconfig`
    - [ ] B. `winipcfg`
    - [ ] C. `renew`
    - [ ] D. `release`

Answers:

1. C   See the "DCHP Scopes" section.
2. A   See the "DCHP Scopes" section.
3. B   See the "IP Lease Renewal Phases" section.

How DHCP Works

One of the biggest complaints about managing and maintaining a TCP/IP network is the difficulty of keeping track of all of the addresses and names. *Dynamic Host Configuration Protocol* (DHCP) helps with addressing problems by using centralized databases to manage IP address configuration. The databases are stored on DHCP servers, which are configured to hand out unique IP addresses and other TCP/IP configuration information on an as-needed basis. DHCP reduces the administrative burden of adding, moving, and configuring computers on TCP/IP networks by using a dynamic method of IP address assignment. DHCP was designed as an open, industry-standard specification intended to reduce the complexity of TCP/IP network administration.

The two major components of DHCP are:

- A protocol for communicating TCP/IP configuration parameters between a DHCP server and a client (the DHCP protocol is encapsulated within the *User Datagram Protocol* [UDP] datagram.)

- A service that manages requests from DHCP clients and maintains the database of TCP/IP configuration parameters

> **TEST TIP** DHCP is covered heavily in the TCP/IP exam. You should have a good understanding of all aspects of how to install, configure, and manage DHCP servers and clients on a network.

Using DHCP to automatically configure IP addressing information provides several benefits:

- IP addressing information is accurately provided by a DHCP server, which reduces the chance of clerical and typing errors.

- IP addressing information is changed automatically when a computer is moved to a different subnet. The changes may include a new default gateway or a new DNS or

WINS server. When the DHCP client computer starts up on the new subnet, the client will be automatically reconfigured with appropriate TCP/IP configuration information for that subnet.

- Changes to IP addressing information that need to occur on all computers can be centrally configured on a DHCP server.
- The available and used IP addresses can be more accurately monitored and controlled. This is especially important when there are a large number of computers and a limited number of IP addresses available for a network or subnet.
- You can manage many aspects of your TCP/IP client configurations from a central location. Bulk management is possible, enabling you to change settings for groups of computers with one simple operation.
- Manual configuration of this information requires good record keeping and can be time-consuming. Automatically assigning an IP address to a computer can eliminate many of the typical IP addressing problems, such as a user entering incorrect IP address values, or duplicate addresses.

You can use Microsoft DHCP Server to automatically assign TCP/IP configuration parameters to DHCP clients that start on the network. The configuration parameters that can be dynamically assigned by a Microsoft DHCP Server include:

- An IP address for each network adapter installed in a computer
- A subnet mask
- Optional parameters, such as the IP addresses of a default gateway, DNS servers, WINS servers, node type, and a NetBIOS Scope ID

Microsoft DHCP Components

Microsoft DHCP consists of DHCP Server, a Windows NT service that manages all DHCP activity, and a graphical administration tool called DHCP Manager. Clients must be configured to use DHCP to automatically receive their IP configuration settings using DHCP.

> **POP QUIZ — True or False?**
> 1. Class A addresses have a default subnet mask of 255.0.0.0.
> 2. Class B addresses have a default subnet mask of 255.0.0.0.
> 3. Class C addresses have a default subnet mask of 255.255.255.255.
>
> *Answers: 1. True 2. False 3. False*

DHCP Server manages the requests from DHCP clients and maintains the database of TCP/IP configuration parameters. A DHCP Server database is automatically created when Microsoft DHCP Server is installed on a computer running Windows NT Server and the TCP/IP protocol.

DHCP Manager is used to configure basic IP address settings and all optional parameters. You add data to the DHCP Server database by defining DHCP scopes and DHCP options using DHCP Manager. DHCP Manager can be used to configure other DHCP servers on the network by adding them to the list of DHCP servers that can be managed, as shown in Figure 4-1.

DHCP Clients

The easiest method for installing and configuring network clients to use TCP/IP on a network is to enable automatic DHCP configuration on each client computer. During system startup, DHCP-enabled clients will contact a DHCP server to receive configuration information, such

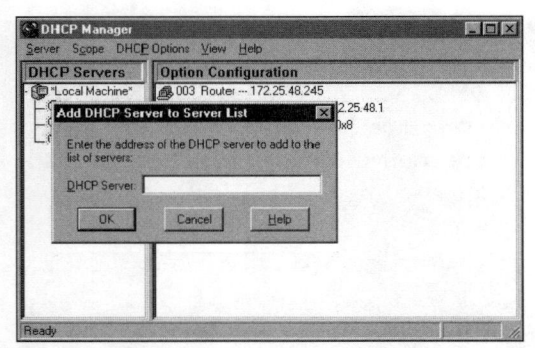

Figure 4-1 *DHCP Manager is used to configure a DHCP server.*

as an IP address, a subnet mask, or the IP address of the default gateway. Computers running the following operating systems can be configured as DHCP clients:

- Windows NT Server (except DHCP servers)
- Windows NT Workstation
- Windows 95
- Windows for Workgroups 3.11 with the Microsoft 32-bit TCP/IP installed
- Microsoft Network Client version 3.0
- LAN Manager version 2.2c

After DHCP has been properly configured on both the server and the client, DHCP will be used to set all IP configuration parameters on the client during startup. The DHCP server will provide a lease for an IP address to the client for a specified period of time. The DHCP client must renew its lease within the lease period interval to retain use of the IP configuration settings.

DHCP Scopes

A *DHCP scope* is an administrative grouping that identifies the configuration parameters for all DHCP clients grouped together on one physical segment. The scope must be defined before DHCP clients can use the DHCP server for dynamic TCP/IP configuration. At a minimum, a DHCP scope must be configured to provide the DHCP client with the following information:

4: DYNAMIC HOST CONFIGURATION PROTOCOL

- A range of valid IP addresses that are available to be leased
- A subnet mask that will be assigned to all hosts on a subnet
- A time interval (known as *lease duration*) that specifies how long a DHCP client can use an assigned IP address before it expires

> **KNOW THIS — DHCP Scopes**
> On a given DHCP server, only one scope can be created per subnet, and a scope cannot span multiple subnets.

In addition to the required DHCP scope information, you can define individual scope options using DHCP Manager. Additional scope options enable you to automatically assign advanced TCP/IP configuration options, such as the IP addresses of a WINS server and a DNS server.

> **TEST TRAP —** Don't confuse DHCP scopes with the NetBIOS scopes encountered elsewhere in this book; NetBIOS scopes are extensions to NetBIOS names, and have nothing to do with TCP/IP configuration management.

The three types of scope options available are:

- **Global options:** Used to set options for all scopes (all subnets). For example, global options are often used to set options like the DNS Server addresses when there are only two DNS Servers on your internetwork.
- **Scope options:** Used to set options individually for a scope. For example, each subnet requires a different default gateway address.
- **Client options:** Used to set options for a specific DHCP client. A client reservation must be created in order to do this. This is discussed later.

77

> **KNOW THIS** **DHCP Option Priorities**
>
> When using DHCP options, keep in mind that options are assigned in the following order:
> Client options override scope or global options. Scope options override global options (scope options are assigned to all hosts that obtain their IP address assignments from a given DHCP scope). Global options apply to all hosts unless there are overriding client or scope settings for a particular configuration parameter.

DHCP Options Supported by Microsoft Clients

Although there are many options defined in the DHCP specification, Microsoft clients support only a subset of the available options. You can configure the following DHCP options for Microsoft DHCP clients:

- Routers (default gateways)
- DNS servers
- Domain name
- WINS/NBNS servers
- WINS/NBT node type
- NetBIOS scope ID

> **KNOW THIS** **DHCP Client Options**
>
> All Microsoft and non-Microsoft DHCP clients receive standard options to specify the IP address lease time, renewal time, and rebinding time.

4: DYNAMIC HOST CONFIGURATION PROTOCOL

Because Microsoft DHCP Server can provide DHCP services to non-Microsoft clients, all the options in the DHCP specification can be supplied by Microsoft DHCP Server to those clients that support the use of these options.

POP QUIZ True or False?

1. DHCP scopes are capable of spanning multiple subnets.
2. Each server can have multiple scopes.
3. The same scope can be used on multiple servers.

Answers: 1. False   2. True   3. False

DHCP Initialization Phases

The DHCP client obtains its configuration in the form of a lease that is granted by the DHCP server, usually for a limited period of time. While the lease is in force, the client has the right to use the assigned IP address on the network. As the lease approaches expiration, the client must attempt to renew the lease. If lease renewal is unsuccessful, the client must obtain a new lease.

DHCP uses a four-phase process to configure DHCP-enabled clients. The basic TCP/IP configuration parameters that must be provided to a DHCP client include an IP address, a subnet mask, and optionally the IP address of a default gateway. When a DHCP client is started on a TCP/IP network, it attempts to locate a DHCP server to get its TCP/IP configuration information in four phases:

- Phase 1: IP Lease Request
- Phase 2: IP Lease Offer
- Phase 3: IP Lease Select
- Phase 4: IP Lease Acknowledgment

During Phase 1, when the client first starts TCP/IP, it sends a broadcast request (destination IP address `255.255.255.255`), called a `DHCPDISCOVER` packet. Because this is a broadcast packet, it is received

79

MCSE TCP/IP ACE IT!

by all DHCP servers on the local network. If the DHCP relay agent is installed on routers, the broadcast is also forwarded (using a mechanism called *BOOTP forwarding*) to other DHCP servers that reside on remote networks. The client's source address is 0.0.0.0 because the client does not yet have an IP address. However, the client sends its hardware address and computer name in the packet so the DHCP server can respond directly back to the client computer.

> **KNOW THIS**
>
> **DCHPDISCOVER Intervals**
>
> If the client does not receive a response to a DHCPDIS-COVER message within 1 second (perhaps no DHCP servers are active), it makes three more attempts to obtain a lease at 9-, 13-, and 16-second intervals, along with a random attempt at between 0 and 1,000 milliseconds. If none of these attempts results in a lease offer, the client continues to try at 5-minute intervals.

The IP lease request phase occurs only under one of the following circumstances:

- This is the first time this computer has started as a DHCP client.
- The client is denied when attempting to request a specific IP address. (This can happen when the lease expires or when the original DHCP server that supplied the address is unavailable.)
- The client has released its lease and requires a new one.
- An existing DHCP client has been moved to a new subnet.

During Phase 2, all DHCP servers that receive the DHCPDISCOVER packet determine if they can offer an address lease for the subnet on which the client resides. When a DHCP server receives the request and can offer a lease, it selects an available (not currently leased) IP address from the DHCP database. The DHCP server offers the following configuration settings to the DHCP client using a DHCPOFFER packet:

- IP address
- Subnet mask
- A lease duration that specifies how long the IP address can be used by the client computer

The DHCP server temporarily reserves the IP address so that it will not be offered to any other DHCP clients.

During Phase 3, the client selects the IP address information from the first offer that it receives (in case there are multiple DHCP servers). The client then responds to the DHCP server by broadcasting a DHCPREQUEST packet that confirms the selection of the offered IP address. If there were offers from other DHCP servers, those servers also receive the broadcast message, informing them that they can retract their offers and make their offered IP addresses available again.

During Phase 4, the DHCP server with an offer that has been accepted by the client acknowledges the client's request by sending back a DHCPACK packet. The DHCP server also returns any options that have been configured in a global or scope option. For example, the lease may include the IP addresses of the DNS server and the WINS server that are to be used by the client.

> **KNOW THIS** **Saving the DHCP Configuration**
> The IP addresses and other configuration settings are saved on the DHCP client computer (in the registry on Windows 95 and Windows NT computers and in a file on MS-DOS based computers). The settings are saved so the client can attempt to renew its previous settings instead of having to request a new IP address each time the computer starts.

IP Lease Renewal Phases

A DHCP client automatically attempts to renew its IP address lease when 50 percent of its lease time has expired. The client can be forced to renew its DHCP lease by typing the **ipconfig /renew** command at a command prompt (use `winipcfg /renew` on a Windows 95 client). Lease renewal for a DHCP client occurs in two phases:

- Phase 1: IP Lease Renewal
- Phase 2: IP Lease Renewal Acknowledgment

To renew its lease, a DHCP client sends a `DHCPREQUEST` message directly to the DHCP server from which it originally received the lease. A `DHCPREQUEST` message is generated in each of the following cases:

- The client is running and 50 percent of the lease time has expired.
- The client has been restarted after the DHCP server had previously configured it with an IP address. The client attempts to lease the same IP address that it had originally received from the DHCP server.

The DHCP client always attempts to renew with the DHCP server that provided its current lease. If that DHCP server is unavailable at the 50 percent interval, the client continues to attempt to renew the license while continuing to use the IP address until 87.5 percent of the lease time has expired. If the DHCP server is still unavailable, the client will broadcast a `DHCPREQUEST` message to which any DHCP server (not only the original DHCP server) will respond. The new DHCP server may be able to renew the lease or send a message indicating that the lease should be terminated, which causes the client to return to the process of leasing a new IP address.

When a client receives the acknowledgment, it updates its configuration, including the IP address lease expiration date and time.

Planning a DHCP Installation

Once you have decided that you will use DHCP on your network, you need to consider how it will be implemented. Some of the considerations include:

- How many DHCP servers will you need?

- Where should you locate your DHCP servers?
- How should you configure your DHCP scopes?

> **TEST TIP**
> The TCP/IP exam will include questions that test your knowledge of how to plan and manage a network that has multiple DHCP servers. You will need to know how to implement a DHCP relay agent and how to configure scopes when multiple DHCP servers are used. You should also be familiar with how to define different options for the scope and how to create a client reservation.

Multiple DHCP Servers

It is recommended that there always be two or more available DHCP servers on the network that can provide all DHCP clients with IP address configuration settings. When there are multiple DHCP servers, regardless of whether the DHCP server is located on the local subnet or not, the client accepts the first offer it receives. DHCP servers cannot communicate with one another to exchange information about currently leased IP addresses, so it is vital to carefully allocate ranges of IP addresses so that the same IP addresses cannot be assigned by any two DHCP servers.

One strategy is to define one DHCP scope per server for each of the subnets. In each scope, define the range of IP addresses to be used on that subnet. Allocate only half of all IP addresses available for a subnet to each scope. On the second DHCP server, define one DHCP scope for each of the subnets. In each scope, define the range of IP addresses to be used on that subnet. Be sure to allocate a range of IP addresses that does not overlap with the range of IP addresses defined on the first DHCP server.

To determine where to install the DHCP Servers, use the physical characteristics of your network and not the domain groupings defined in the Windows NT Server directory services.

> **KNOW THIS** **Configuring Multiple Scopes**
> For configuring multiple scopes for two or more DHCP servers, the typical configuration method is to assign a larger number of IP addresses (75 percent for example) to the local scope (the scope for the subnet that the DHCP Server resides on). On the DHCP server on the remote subnet, the remaining 25 percent of the available addresses would be available as a backup in case the local DHCP Server was down or all of the IP addresses had been assigned. The same configuration would be reversed for the remote subnet.

DHCP Relay Agent

A DHCP *relay agent* is a program that is used to pass specific types of IP packets between subnets. A DHCP/BOOTP relay agent enables a router to pass messages between subnets according to the RFC 1542 specification. If the router cannot function as a relay agent, each subnet that has DHCP clients must have its own DHCP server.

In addition to passing DHCP/BOOTP messages from one subnet to another, the relay agent also adds additional information to the DHCP request packet. The relay agent includes information in the packet that indicates from which subnet the request originated. This is done so that the DHCP server can determine which scope to use when providing addressing information to the DHCP client.

A DHCP-enabled client broadcasts a DHCPDISCOVER message on the local subnet to request IP address configuration settings. A DHCP relay agent that has been installed on the same subnet as the host receives the request. The DHCP relay agent consults a list of DHCP servers that has been established by the network administrator and forwards the DHCPDISCOVER message to each remote DHCP server. The forwarded DHCPDISCOVER messages are not broadcast, and are sent directly to each known DHCP server. The DHCP Server then responds directly back to the DHCP client with a DHCPOFFER message.

A DHCP relay agent must be configured with the TCP/IP addresses of the DHCP servers. This enables the DHCP relay agent to forward

DHCP requests directly to the DHCP servers. This eliminates the need to use a broadcast to locate the DHCP server, which may reside on a remote subnet. The DHCP relay agent is installed by adding a service to the Network section under Control Panel.

DHCP Traffic Considerations

DHCP traffic should not have a significant effect on network traffic, even if multiple DHCP clients are acquiring or renewing addresses simultaneously. Traffic generated by DHCP activity occurs during two phases of configuration: IP address lease acquisition and IP address lease renewal.

When a new client initializes TCP/IP for the first time (has never received an IP address from DHCP) or has been moved to a new subnet, the first step is to acquire an IP address using DHCP. This process, called *IP address lease acquisition*, results in an exchange of four packets between the DHCP client and the DHCP server. Each packet transferred during this phase is 342 bytes in size and normally occurs in less than 1 second (Windows NT 3.5 and Windows for Workgroups clients use 590-byte frames).

When an existing DHCP client starts, it attempts to renew its IP address with its DHCP server. This process, called *IP address lease renewal*, results in an exchange of two packets (the second two packets that are used during the IP address lease phase). The other difference between the IP lease acquisition phase and the IP renewal phase is that the conversation is directed, and not a broadcast, because the client already knows the IP address of the DHCP Server. The IP address renewal phase also occurs automatically when the lease time of the DHCP client falls to half of the configured lease duration. The length of the lease duration, by default, is 72 hours, which causes the IP address renewal phase to take place once every 36 hours. Finally, an IP address renewal occurs whenever a client manually refreshes or releases its address by using the `ipconfig /release` (or `winipcfg /release`) command.

The general guideline for determining how many DHCP servers are needed on a network is that one DHCP server can support 10,000 clients. However, it is recommended to have a backup DHCP Server in case the first one fails. When deciding how many DHCP servers you will need, you should consider the locations of routers on the network and whether you will want a DHCP Server in each subnet.

Reducing DHCP Traffic

If you wish to reduce the amount of traffic generated by DHCP, it is possible to adjust the lease duration for IP address leases. Increasing the lease duration reduces the frequency with which the DHCP clients need to query the DHCP server to renew their leases. If there are a large number of IP addresses available in the DHCP scope and relatively few DHCP clients, the lease duration should likely be increased in length.

Reducing the lease duration causes DHCP clients to renew their leases more frequently but ensures that any unused IP addresses in the pool are made available to other DHCP clients as soon as possible. If there are a limited number of IP addresses available in a DHCP scope for a subnet, it may be beneficial to reduce the lease duration. This causes unused IP addresses to be returned to the address pool more quickly.

Reducing the lease duration is also desirable if DHCP clients on a network frequently change subnets, therefore requiring a different IP address, as is often the case with laptop users. The lease duration is specified as part of the DHCP scope. DHCP manager is used to set this and other DHCP configuration settings as described in the next sections.

Installing and Configuring DHCP

To start using DHCP, you must:

- Install the DHCP Server service on a Windows NT Server computer.
- Configure the DHCP server by creating a scope containing a range of valid IP addresses and other IP configuration settings into the DHCP Server database.

- Configure all host computers to use DHCP. This is done by selecting the option Enable Automatic DHCP Configuration checkbox from the Network applet in Control Panel.

DHCP can be installed during setup of a Windows NT server, or, if DHCP is not installed as part of the setup, it can be installed (by using an Administrator account) in the Network section of Control Panel by adding the DHCP server service.

> **TEST TRAP** Remember, a Windows NT server that is a DHCP server cannot be a DHCP client as well. Its IP address configuration settings must be set manually. This is important to remember for the test because the IP address of the DHCP server must be excluded from the range of available IP addresses in the scope.

The DHCP Manager contains a list of the servers that it can administer. Before you can begin to manage any DHCP servers, you must add the servers to the list. This includes the first DHCP server installed on the network.

Configuring DHCP Scopes and Options

Before you can use DHCP to provide IP addressing information to computers, you must configure the DHCP Server database. The DHCP Server database is configured by defining DHCP scopes and DHCP options using DHCP Manager. One DHCP scope must be defined for each subnet.

Some of the things that you will need to configure are:

- The range of IP addresses (the *address pool*) that the DHCP server can lease to DHCP clients on a subnet, for example 172.25.16.1 to 172.25.16.254.
- The subnet masks that are used to identify which subnets the IP addresses in the pool belong to. DHCP Manager checks to make sure that you are entering a valid range of

IP addresses for a selected subnet mask. Or, you can choose a range of IP addresses that are to be excluded from the scope. This is for computers that must be configured with TCP/IP configuration settings manually. By creating an exclusion range, you prevent DHCP from allocating any duplicate IP addresses within that range.
- The IP address lease duration (*time interval*) used to specify how long a DHCP client can use an address before it must renew its configuration with the DHCP server. The default time is 72 hours.
- IP address reservations for specific clients that require specific IP addresses. This way you can still use DHCP Server to manage and allocate the address, but the same address will be used each time the client computer starts.

> **KNOW THIS** **Excluding IP Addresses**
>
> An exclusion range can be a single IP address or a range of addresses. You can create any number of exclusion ranges. This is important, because each subnet can be associated with only one scope on a given server. Addresses in the scope must consist of a single continuous range of IP addresses.
>
> If you want to create several ranges within a scope, create a scope with a continuous range that encompasses all of the addresses you want to allocate to the DHCP server pool. Then manually exclude the addresses that fall between these specific ranges for those addresses that you want to prevent DHCP from using.

In addition to the standard DHCP configuration settings (IP address, subnet mask, and lease duration), there are about 60 other predefined configuration parameters, called *options*, that can be configured by an administrator for DHCP clients. Although Microsoft DHCP

Server can offer all of the 60 different options, Microsoft DHCP clients utilize only these options:

- 003 Router: Specifies the IP addresses for one or more routers (default gateways) on the client's subnet. If the client has been configured manually with a gateway address, the manually configured gateway address overrides the DHCP option.
- 006 DNS Servers: Specifies the IP addresses for DNS name servers that are available to the client.
- 044 WINS/NBNS Servers: Specifies the IP addresses of WINS servers. If the client has been configured manually with WINS server addresses, the manually configured addresses override the DHCP option.
- 046 WINS/NBT node type: Specifies the type of NetBIOS-over-TCP/IP (NetBT) name resolution that will be used by the client. The values include: b-node (broadcast), p-node (peer), m-node (mixed), and h-node (hybrid).
- 047 NetBIOS Scope ID: Specifies a text string that is the NetBIOS-over-TCP/IP scope ID for the client, as specified in RFC 1001/1002. When scope IDs are used, NetBIOS computers can communicate only with other computers that are configured with the same scope ID. On multihomed computers, the node type is assigned to the entire computer, not to individual adapter cards

Global, Scope, Default, and Client Options

A *global option* takes effect for all DHCP scopes defined on a selected DHCP server. Global options are used when all DHCP clients on all subnets require the same configuration parameters, for example, if your company uses one or two WINS servers or DNS servers. Global options appear with a globe icon preceding them in DHCP Manager.

Setting a scope DHCP option will set the option only for the selected scope. Use a scope option to set configuration parameters that are to be set only on DHCP clients that reside on the same subnet. For example, you would use a scope option to set the default gateway address for all clients on one subnet. DHCP options configured for a scope are displayed with a series of computer icons preceding them in DHCP Manager.

Setting a default DHCP option modifies the default value for one of the DHCP options. When a default value is set, the selected option and associated value are used on each new scope that is created. Default options are used to simplify administration when creating multiple scopes that need the same configuration parameters. The default options you establish take effect only when the option is entered in a global, scope, or client option configuration.

A client option can be used to configure one or more of the DHCP options for a specific DHCP client. DHCP options can be set for a client only if a client reservation has been created for the DHCP client.

Configuring a DHCP option for a specific DHCP client is performed in a different location from the global, scope, and default options.

POP QUIZ True or False?

1. Client options can only be used when a client reservation has been created.
2. WINS servers are used to resolve host names.
3. DNS servers are used to resolve host names.

Answers: 1. True 2. False 3. True

Creating a Client Reservation

The DHCP Manager enables the reservation of a specific IP address for a computer. This *client reservation* enables you to assign a fixed address for a computer while still providing the benefits of central management for IP addressing and client configuration.

A client reservation is created by specifying the following information:

- **IP address:** This is the IP address that will be assigned to the client when the client sends a DHCP request to the DHCP server.
- **Unique identifier:** This is the hardware address for the network interface that is installed in the client's computer. This information must be specified correctly or it will not match the information sent by the DHCP client. Keep in mind that you will have to change the hardware address if a new network interface is installed in the client computer.
- **Client name:** This name is used for identification purposes only. You can view the client name when scrolling through client reservations using DHCP Manager.
- **Client comment:** The comment field is optional for any other client description.

Using the Ipconfig Utility

`Ipconfig` is a valuable tool for solving DHCP configuration problems. `Ipconfig` is a command line utility used to display current TCP/IP network configuration settings and update or release TCP/IP network configuration settings on a DHCP client.

TEST TRAP
Pay careful attention to test questions that ask you to use this utility. Windows 95 computers use `winipcfg` in place of `ipconfig`.

When `ipconfig` is used with the `/renew` switch, it causes the client to issue a DHCP request (`DHCPREQUEST`) message to the DHCP server to get any updated options and a new lease time. The request message is sent to the original DHCP server that provided the configuration settings.

To renew a DHCP lease, from a command line, type:

ipconfig /renew

When `ipconfig` is used with the `/release` switch, it causes the client to issue a DHCP release message (`DHCPRELEASE`) to notify the DHCP server that the DHCP client will be giving up its lease. The DHCP server can then use the IP address for other DHCP clients. This command is useful when the client computer is moving to a different subnet.

Microsoft DHCP clients do not release a lease when they shut down, which provides an opportunity for the client to retain the same IP address over a period of time. This is because the DHCP lease information is stored locally on the client computer so that each time the DHCP client starts, the DHCP settings, including IP address, are reused. This reuse occurs only when the DHCP client has been restarted during the lease period.

If the computer has not been started within the lease period, the DHCP server will release the IP address and make it available for other clients. When the DHCP client whose lease has expired restarts later, that computer will receive a new IP address from the DHCP server.

To release a DHCP lease, from a command line, type:

ipconfig /release

> **TEST TIP**
>
> The troubleshooting portion of the TCP/IP exam includes a number of questions regarding the use of `ipconfig` to solve IP address configuration problems. You should be familiar with how to use `ipconfig` to solve problems when using DHCP and when configuring IP settings manually.

4: DYNAMIC HOST CONFIGURATION PROTOCOL

Have You Mastered?

These exercises provide you with an opportunity to apply the knowledge you've gained in this chapter about TCP/IP performance monitoring and troubleshooting.

1. **Which of the following is required on a DHCP relay agent?**

    - [ ] A. The BOOTP protocol
    - [ ] B. The IP address of the DHCP servers
    - [ ] C. DHCP manager
    - [ ] D. ARP

    A. The physical address of the network adapter is the address used to receive data. See the "DHCP Relay Agent" section.

2. **When using a DHCP relay agent, where is the DHCPOFFER message delivered?**

    - [ ] A. DHCP relay agent
    - [ ] B. Router
    - [ ] C. DHCP client
    - [ ] D. Broadcast across the network

    C. The DHCP server delivers the message directly to the DHCP client. See the "DHCP Initialization Phases" section

MCSE TCP/IP ACE IT!

3. **After what percentage of lease duration does the DHCP client attempt to renew its IP lease?**

   ☐ A. 25%
   ☐ B. 50%
   ☐ C. 75%
   ☐ D. 90%

   B. DHCP clients attempt to renew the lease at the halfway point of the lease duration. See the "IP Lease Renewal Phases" section

4. **When using multiple DHCP servers on a network, what should be done to ensure that IP addresses are distributed in the event that one of the servers goes down?**

   ☐ A. Configure identical scopes on all servers.
   ☐ B. Configure 95% of addresses on the remote scope and 5% of addresses on the local scope.
   ☐ C. Configure 5% of addresses on the remote scope and 95% of addresses on the local scope.
   ☐ D. Configure 25% of addresses on the remote scope and 75% of addresses on the local scope.

   D. The majority of the addresses should be assigned to the local scope with a portion used on the remote scope. See the "DHCP Initialization Phases" section.

5. **When a DHCP client initializes, how does it request an IP address?**

   ☐ A. Broadcasts a request to the network
   ☐ B. Sends a request to the router
   ☐ C. Sends a request directly to the DHCP server
   ☐ D. Sends a request to the DHCP relay agent

   A. DHCP clients are not configured with the IP addresses of the DHCP server or relay agent. To obtain an IP address, they must

4: DYNAMIC HOST CONFIGURATION PROTOCOL

broadcast a request to the network. See the "DHCP Initialization Phases" section.

6. **What happens when DHCP client options, scope options, and global options have different values?**

    ☐ A. Global options overwrite all others.
    ☐ B. The user can choose which options to use.
    ☐ C. The administrator can choose which options to use.
    ☐ D. Global options are overwritten by scope options which are overwritten by client options.

D. Global options are overwritten by either scope or client options; scope options can be overwritten by client options. See the "Global, Scope, Default, and Client options" section.

Practice Your Skills

The following exercises provide you with a practical opportunity to apply the knowledge you've gained in this chapter.

1. Configuring Dynamic Host Configuration Protocol

EXERCISE You want to use DHCP to assign IP address settings to all Windows NT Workstation computers on your network. You install the DHCP Server on a Windows NT Server computer. How must you configure the workstations so they can use the DHCP Server to receive IP address settings? What must be defined on the DHCP Server before clients can use DHCP? The network contains a number of UNIX computers that do not support DHCP. How can you prevent DHCP from assigning IP addresses that have already been assigned to the UNIX computers?

ANALYSIS On each workstation, modify the Network option in Control Panel to modify TCP/IP properties. Choose the option to obtain an IP address from a DHCP Server. A DHCP scope must be created containing a range of addresses, a subnet mask, and other optional settings such as the default gateway. In the DHCP scope, create an exclusion range to block out a range of addresses so that DHCP will not assign them to any computer.

2. Configuring DHCP for the Windows Internet Naming Service

EXERCISE Your network contains five different subnets. You have installed one DHCP Server and one WINS Server to support all Windows NT Workstation and Windows 95 computers on the network. How should you configure the DHCP Server to assign the address of the WINS Server to all of the workstations regardless of what subnet they reside on? How can you specify the order and method of name resolution used by the workstations that use WINS? How should you configure the DHCP Server to assign the address of the default gateway to each workstation?

ANALYSIS Use DHCP Manager to create a global option to set the IP address of the WINS Server on all workstations that use DHCP. Use DHCP Manager to create a global option to set the WINS/NBT node type for all workstations. Use DHCP Manager to create a scope option for each subnet to set the IP address of the default gateway on each workstation.

3. Configuring DHCP scopes and a DHCP relay agent

EXERCISE Your network consists of two subnets. You want to install a single DHCP Server to manage all IP addresses on your network. You want to guarantee that all client computers receive the same IP address each time the computer is turned on. If a computer has not been turned on within 30 days, you want the IP address to be made available to other computers. You want all Windows NT Server computers to always receive the same IP address. How should you configure DHCP to support client computers and servers on both subnets? How should you configure DHCP for the client computers? How should you configure DHCP for the Windows NT Server computers?

MCSE TCP/IP ACE IT!

ANALYSIS On the subnet that does not contain the DHCP Server, install a DHCP relay agent to pass all DCHP messages to the subnet that contains the DHCP Server. Create a DHCP scope for each subnet with a lease period of 30 days. Create a client reservation for each Windows NT Server computer.

4. Configuring multiple DHCP Servers

EXERCISE Your network consists of two subnets. You want to install one DHCP Server on each of the subnets. You want to configure the DHCP Server on Subnet A so it can respond to DHCP requests from clients on Subnet B in case the DHCP Server on Subnet B fails. You also want to configure the DHCP Server on Subnet B so it can respond to DHCP requests from clients on Subnet A in case the DHCP Server on Subnet A fails. How should you configure the DHCP Servers to support this? What must you install on each subnet so that DHCP requests can be passed to the other subnet?

ANALYSIS Create a scope on each DHCP Server for the other subnet. In the scope, specify a range of addresses that does not overlap with the range of addresses created for that subnet on the other DHCP Server. A DHCP relay agent must be installed so the requests can be passed.

5

IP Routing

INTERNET PROTOCOL MAKES ROUTING DECISIONS BASED on the contents of the routing table that must reside on each host computer and router. A number of different routing protocols are available to dynamically maintain routing table entries on routers. You must know the differences between these protocols so you can understand the issues involved in using each routing protocol on a network. You will see several questions on the exam that test your knowledge of the routing protocols.

Exam Material in This Chapter

Official Word

Based on Microsoft Objectives
- On a Windows NT Server computer, configure Microsoft TCP/IP to support multiple network adapters.

Inside Scoop

Based on Author's Experience
- Routing
- Router
- Routing table
- Static routing
- Dynamic routing
- Distance-vector routing
- Link-state routing
- RIP
- OSPF

5: IP ROUTING

Are You Prepared?

Test your understanding of this subject with the following questions, which will help you pinpoint problem areas that require further review.

1. **Which type of routing is used to transmit data between two machines located on the same subnet?**

    - [ ] A. Link-state routing
    - [ ] B. Distance-vector routing
    - [ ] C. Direct routing
    - [ ] D. Indirect routing

2. **Which method of building a routing table requires the least amount of work from the administrator?**

    - [ ] A. Direct routing
    - [ ] B. Indirect routing
    - [ ] C. Static routing
    - [ ] D. Dynamic routing

3. **Which routing protocol is Windows NT capable of using?**

    - [ ] A. RIP
    - [ ] B. OSPF
    - [ ] C. IGRP7
    - [ ] D. Link-state routing

Answers:

1. C   See the "Direct and indirect routing" section.
2. C   See the "Direct and indirect routing" section.
3. A   See the "Common routing protocols" section.

IP Routing Defined

When two hosts communicate on a network, the hosts are said to be *local* (on the same subnet) or *remote* (on different subnets). If the hosts are located on different subnets, IP routing is used so that the hosts can communicate. *IP routing* is the process of choosing a path through the routers of an internetwork that enables IP datagrams to be delivered to a destination host. A *router* (also called a *gateway* in IP terminology) is the computer that makes the choices of where the packets will be sent. Routing is a critical function of IP.

Routers behave much like the post office does. If you want to deliver a message to someone very close (for example, on the same street), you would most likely deliver it yourself. But if the destination address were far away, you would deliver the message to the nearest mail drop or post office. The post office then uses the addressing information to determine how to deliver the message. The message may pass through a number of post offices before finally being delivered.

A router is a computer that forwards messages between hosts on different networks based on the network IDs of the networks on which the hosts reside. Because they make use of network identifiers, routers operate at the internet layer of the TCP/IP protocol stack. Each packet sent over a network has a packet header that contains source and destination address fields. Routers match each packet header to a network segment and choose the best path for the packet, optimizing network performance.

A router is usually a special computer dedicated to performing routing functions. However, it is possible to configure a Windows NT computer to be a router by installing multiple network adapter cards, each attached to a different subnet. A computer configured in this way is called a *multihomed host*. A multihomed host is then configured to forward data between the attached subnets, enabling it to function as a router.

How Routing Works

Ordinarily, hosts are not configured with routing protocols, which would use up the host's limited memory and processing resources. The host is instead provided with just enough information to enable it to send packets to a router, which is identified as its *default router* (or *default gateway*). When the host needs to deliver a datagram to a host that is not attached to the local network (as determined from the network and subnet addresses of the destination), the host directs the datagram to its default router. The default router is then responsible for forwarding the datagram to a different network or to another router until the datagram reaches its ultimate destination. Message delivery is the responsibility of the router. From the host's perspective, the network is viewed simply as an entity that delivers packets.

Thus, both hosts and routers participate in IP routing decisions. When a network application attempts a connection to another host, one or more datagrams are generated. The host makes a routing decision when it chooses where to send the datagrams.

Direct and indirect routing

In Figure 5-1, assume that all hosts use a default subnet mask for the Class B address (`255.255.0.0`). Because the destination host address (`172.25.16.54`) for the datagram is located on the same subnet as the sending host, the host can use *direct routing* (without the need for a router) to deliver the datagram. Direct routing is accomplished when IP uses ARP to get the hardware address of the host computer on the local subnet.

In the second example, the TCP/IP software on the sending host has determined that the destination address is located on a different network. This is because the destination host address (`172.31.24.101`) is not within the range of IP addresses for the subnet on which the sending host is located. The datagram is then sent to the IP address of the default gateway (a router) for processing, as shown in Figure 5-2. Delivery of the datagram to the remote host is left up to the router, which makes routing decisions on how best to deliver the datagram to the destination network. This is called *indirect routing* because the two hosts do not communicate directly but instead pass all network requests through one or more routers.

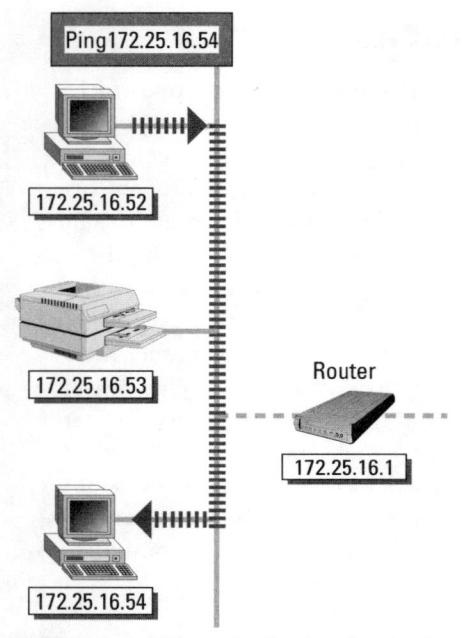

Figure 5-1 *When the destination and source hosts both reside on the same subnet, the hosts can communicate directly with each other without needing a router.*

POP QUIZ — True or False?

1. DHCP scopes must have a range of IP addresses, subnet mask, lease duration, and router settings.
2. In TCP/IP, the terms *router* and *gateway* refer to the same device.
3. ARP is used to resolve IP addresses to MAC addresses.

Answers: 1. False 2. True 3. True

5: IP ROUTING

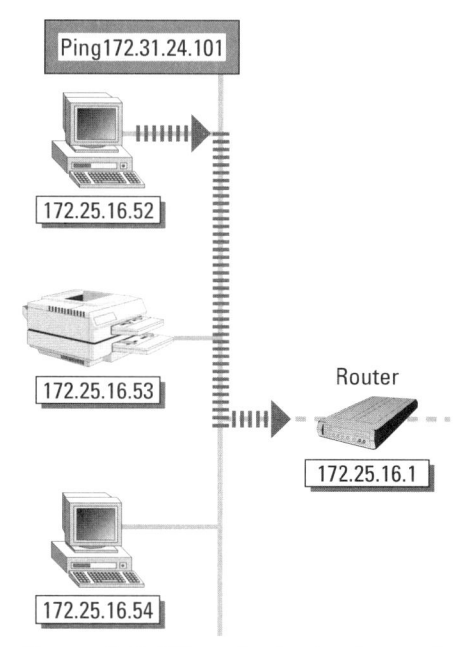

Figure 5-2 *When the destination and source hosts each reside on different subnets, the hosts require the use of a router to communicate.*

The Routing Table

For routers to fulfill their roles as the "post offices" of the network, they need to know which networks are reachable and how to get to them. To accomplish this, the router uses algorithms based on the contents of a table that stores information about the topology of the network. This *routing table* contains a list of entries that specifies the IP addresses of the router interfaces to other networks with which the router can communicate. Whenever the IP routing software in a host or gateway needs to transmit a packet, it consults the routing table to decide where the packet should be sent.

> **TEST TIP**
> The exam includes several questions on working with the routing tables on a TCP/IP host. You should understand how to read and maintain entries in the routing table.

105

Every host that runs TCP/IP makes routing decisions based on entries found in the routing table. A default routing table is initially created by using the IP settings that have been entered in the host's TCP/IP configuration settings. The contents of the routing table are managed using the route utility. You can display the routing table by opening a command prompt on a Windows NT TCP/IP host and entering the command **route print**.

Reading the routing table

The following items describe each of the columns found in a route print listing:

- **Network address:** The *network address* is the IP address or network name of the destination network. An IP address is used, for example, to determine if the destination address is the same as the sending host's IP address. If a network name is used as a destination, the name is looked up in a local file called NETWORKS. The search order of entries in the routing table is from unique routes (specific IP addresses) to general routes (multicast and broadcast addresses). The network address and netmask work together to determine the search order.

> **KNOW THIS** **Default Route**
> The entry with the network address 0.0.0.0 is the default route, corresponding to the default gateway that was defined for the host's TCP/IP configuration.

- **Netmask:** A *netmask* is the subnet mask for the route entry. The netmask defines what portion of the network address must match for the route to be used. For example, a 255.255.255.255 mask is used for a host entry (the network card address). This means the destination address of the packet to be routed must match this IP address exactly for this route to be used (for example, the loopback address 127.0.0.1). In another example, the network address 172.25.16.0 has a netmask of 255.255.255.0. This netmask indicates that the first three octets must match exactly, and that the last octet does not matter. Thus, any address with the first three octets that start with 172.25.16 will use this route. Because this is a netmask for a subnet route, it is also called the *subnet mask*.

- **Gateway address:** The *gateway address* specifies where the packet needs to be sent if a match is found in the routing table. This address must be associated with a router interface on the local subnet.

- **Interface:** The *interface* specifies the IP address of the network card on which the packet should be sent. On a single-homed host, most entries (except the loopback entries) will have the same entry in the Interface column. On a multihomed host, some entries will exist for each interface in the host.

- **Metric:** A *metric* specifies the preference level for the route. The metric has no effect unless the routing table contains more than one route to a given destination, in which case the router will prefer the routing table entry that has the lowest metric. Typically, the metric is a hop count that reflects the number of routers that must be crossed to reach the destination. The administrator, however, can raise or lower the metric, if desired. The administrator might assign a lower metric to a high-bandwidth path than to a low-bandwidth path, even though the high-bandwidth path incorporates the higher number of routers.

Standard routing table entries

The route table maintains four different types of routing entries. When a host prepares to send a packet, it scans the table in the following order:

1. *Host route* (a route to a single, specific destination IP address)

2. *Subnet route* (a route to a subnet)

3. *Network route* (a route to an entire network)
4. *Default route* (uses the default gateway when there is no other match)

If a match is found, the host stops scanning the routing entries and uses the IP address of the interface specified in the routing entry. When TCP/IP protocols are installed on a host computer, a standard routing table is created. A description of the entries that are created in a standard routing table for a host computer is shown in the list below:

- 0.0.0.0 (default route): This is the default route entry that is used when there are no other matches found in the routing table. It normally specifies the default gateway address.
- 127.0.0.1 (loopback address): The IP address used to test IP configurations.
- 172.25.16.0 (local subnet address): Used to send packets addressed to hosts on the local subnet.
- 172.25.16.51 (network card address): The address of the local host. It uses the local loopback address.
- 172.25.255.255 (subnet broadcast address): The address used to send subnet broadcasts.
- 224.0.0.0 (multicast address): Used to address multicast messages sent to predefined groups of hosts.
- 255.255.255.255 (limited broadcast address): An address used to broadcast to the local network. (IP broadcasts do not propagate across routers.)

Dead Gateway Detection

Windows-based clients can detect whether a default gateway for a host is still functioning. If the default gateway fails to respond to TCP requests after several tries, IP will direct packets to the address specified for a backup gateway by making an adjustment to the IP routing table to use another default gateway. This is called *dead gateway detection*.

For the dead gateway detection to work correctly, you must specify more than one default gateway address for the TCP/IP configuration on each computer. Additional default gateways can be entered on the

Advanced IP Addressing dialog box by clicking the Advanced button on the Microsoft TCP/IP Properties dialog box. Or, if a computer is a DHCP client, the default gateway may be automatically configured for that computer. A DHCP scope option can be created to configure all DHCP clients with the IP addresses of multiple gateways.

> **POP QUIZ** **True or False?**
>
> 1. Data going to any address not located on the subnet is sent to the default gateway address.
> 2. The route command is used to change the routing table.
> 3. SNMP must be installed for the TCP/IP counters to appear in Performance Monitor.
>
> *Answers: 1. True 2. True 3. True*

IP Routing Protocols

Routers rely on local routing tables to determine how to deliver packets to other networks based on the destination network address. There are two common methods of building a routing table on an IP router.

A *static routing table* uses a local file configured with entries containing routes to all known networks on each router. Static routing requires that fixed routing tables be manually configured. A *dynamic routing table* uses specialized protocols to evaluate traffic load and messages from other routers to define an internal table. The main advantage of dynamic routing is the routing table is automatically updated, so there is no need for manual configuration of routing information. A disadvantage is that network traffic increases on larger networks.

Static IP Routing

Static table routing requires manual adjustment by an administrator to adapt to changes in network topology. With static routing, the person installing the router is responsible for typing in various fields to configure the routing table. This means telling the router which networks are reachable, how far away they are, and which routers will be used to reach them.

A static router can only communicate with networks with which it has a configured interface. To route packets to other networks, each static router must be configured with one of the following:

- An entry in the routing table for each network
- A default gateway address of another router's locally connected interface

For simple networks, or networks whose configurations change infrequently, creating a static routing table using the TCP/IP route command is often efficient, but when networks grow larger, the need for more sophisticated routing decisions becomes important.

Dynamic IP Routing

The dynamic table routing approach is achieved by means of one or more routing protocols. The dynamic table is best for adapting to changes in network topology but requires more control and more complex software and creates additional network traffic. However, with the increasing complexity of large networks, the advantages of the dynamic approach far outweigh the disadvantages.

Dynamic IP routing protocols allow a router to exchange routing information with neighboring routers. As a router becomes aware of any change in the network layout (for instance, a downed router), it broadcasts (or uses multicasts) to send the information to neighboring routers. Routers also send periodic broadcast packets containing all routing information known to the router. These broadcasts between routers keep all network routers synchronized.

Classification of routing protocols

When dealing with network routing, routing protocols are divided into two different classes: *interior routing protocols* and *exterior routing protocols*.

An interior routing protocol, sometimes known as an *interior gateway protocol* (IGP), is used by a group of routers that is part of an *autonomous system* (AS), a group of networks that manages routing with a common protocol. An autonomous system uses routers that are connected into one large network, as might be found in a large corporation.

Large networks, such as the Internet, contain gateways that change constantly. *Exterior routing protocols*, sometimes known as *interdomain routing protocols*, are used to exchange routing information between different autonomous systems.

Depending on the algorithm used to determine routes, routing protocols are further classified as either *distance-vector routing protocols* or *link-state routing protocols*.

Distance-vector routing protocols With distance-vector-based protocols, each router keeps a routing table with its own perspective of the network. Distance-vector routing protocols select the best route based on a metric (an agreed-upon unit of measurement that may be arbitrary or may be tied to a physical measurement of the network). The metric used is different based on the protocol. One drawback of distance-vector protocols is that when routers send updates, they send their entire routing tables. To keep the information up to date, the updates are broadcast at regular, fixed intervals. Because routers broadcast their entire routing tables at frequent intervals, distance-vector routing can generate high amounts of network traffic.

Link-state routing protocols Link-state routing protocols calculate a "tree" of the entire network, with each router acting as the root of its own routing tree. Under link-state, each router distributes information only about its directly connected networks and their associated metrics. Link-state routers transmit routing messages only when changes are detected, greatly reducing the amount of network traffic they generate. When a router detects a change in the state of its direct link, the router broadcasts the change to all other routers through a process called flooding. Flooding updates every router's database with only the changes. Normally these packets are small and sent infrequently.

Common routing protocols

Several routing protocols are used in the TCP/IP world. However, they are generally not compatible with each other. The most common routing protocols include:

- Routing Information Protocol (RIP)
- Interior Gateway Routing Protocol (IGRP)
- Open Shortest Path First (OSPF)

Routing Information Protocol (RIP) *Routing Information Protocol* (RIP) is a simple protocol that enables routers to tell each other what networks they know about and how far away they are. A RIP router is a computer or other piece of hardware that broadcasts routing information, such as network addresses, and directs data packets on IP networks. RIP is a distance-vector routing protocol that uses broadcasts every 30 seconds to update routing tables with neighboring routers. These broadcasts keep all routers on the internetwork synchronized, but do so at a high cost, generating large amounts of network traffic.

The distance-vector algorithm implemented by RIP is subject to numerous limitations. One is that it can take considerable time for routers on the network to become aware of changes to the network; another is that RIP routers can establish routing loops that prevent data from being delivered. To prevent datagrams from endlessly circulating a routing loop, each router decrements the time-to-live (TTL) field in the datagram header. When the TTL value is zero, the datagram is removed from the network. To reduce the effects of loops, RIP specifications establish a maximum size for the network. At most, a datagram can cross 15 routers to reach its destination. Datagrams that cross more than 15 routers are assumed to be in a routing loop and are removed from the network.

Windows NT Server supports RIP for dynamic management of IP routing tables. RIP eliminates the need to establish static IP routing tables. This version of RIP routing does not support RIP over dial-up connections.

5: IP ROUTING

> **KNOW THIS** **RIP**
> Windows NT supports RIP version 1 (RIP v1), which does not include subnet addresses in route broadcasts. Although RIP v1 routers can learn subnet masks on directly attached networks by examining their own configurations, they cannot learn the subnet masks of remote networks. When designing a network that uses RIP v1, it is important to locate all subnets of a given network ID contiguously. RIP version 2 (RIP v2) comprehends subnet masks but is not as widely implemented as RIP v1.

Open Shortest Path First (OSPF) *Open Shortest Path First* (OSPF) is a link-state protocol that uses a "cost" as the metric. This enables routes to be selected based on the cost of the connection when there are multiple paths between networks. More and more sites are converting to OSPF from RIP because of its much lower traffic overhead. OSPF can support a much larger internetwork than RIP.

OSPF also supports variable-length subnetting, which enables the network administrator to use a different subnet mask on each segment of an internetwork. Among other things, this enables companies to select any Class A or Class B address for most of their internal network and designate one subnet as the InterNIC registered network.

OSPF is not supported by the multiprotocol router included with Windows NT Server 4.0.

With the release of NT 4.0, Microsoft has introduced the Routing and Remote Access Service, which offers greatly enhanced routing capabilities, including support for OSPF.

Interior Gateway Routing Protocol (IGRP) *Interior Gateway Routing Protocol* (IGRP) was developed by Cisco Systems, Inc., and is commonly used for routers connected to the Internet. IGRP is a distance-vector routing protocol that uses a number of variables to determine the metric, including:

113

- Bandwidth of the link
- Delay due to the link
- Load on the link
- Reliability of the link

By considering the variables, IGRP has a much better capability to optimize the routing of packets between networks.

Configuring Windows NT as an IP Router

A Windows NT Server computer can be configured as an IP router using both static and dynamic routing methods. LAN-to-LAN routing is supported by installing multiple network adapter cards in a server and configuring routing between them.

Multiprotocol routing support can be installed on a Windows NT Server, which enables routing over IP using RIP. The server can be connected between local subnets or between wide area networks (WANs) without needing to purchase a dedicated router.

> **TEST TIP**
> Most of the exam questions related to routing test your knowledge on using a Windows NT computer as a static or dynamic IP router. You should be familiar with how to install and configure both types of routing on a Windows NT computer.

Enabling Static IP Routing

To enable static routing on a multihomed Windows NT computer, you must:

- Have at least two network adapters and appropriate drivers installed in the Windows NT computer
- Configure each adapter with a valid IP address and subnet mask
- Enable IP forwarding

5: IP ROUTING

> **KNOW THIS: Enabling Static Routing**
> If you have installed RIP for IP, you must remove it first, before you can enable static routing. You can do this from the Services tab in the Network folder in the Control Panel.

Static routing may require the configuration of static routing tables. You can use the route utility to configure static routing tables. At the command prompt, type **route** with the appropriate options.

The route command

The `route` command, shown below, is used to print and manage entries in the routing table.

route [-f] [-p] [command [destination] [**MASK** netmask] [gateway] [**METRIC** metric]]

The syntax of the route command is as follows:

- `-f`: Clears all gateway entries from the routing tables. If used with a command, it clears the tables before the command is run.

- `-p`: Enables persistent, or permanent, routes. Routing table changes are reloaded automatically when you restart the computer. Persistent routes are stored in the Registry and are reloaded when you restart the router. If you enter a route without the -p parameter, it will be lost when the router is restarted.

- command `Print`: Prints a route.

- command `Add`: Adds a route.

- command `Delete`: Deletes a route.

- command `Change`: Modifies an existing route.

- *Destination*: The network or host to which you want to route.

115

- **MASK**: Indicates the next parameter to be interpreted as *netmask*.
- *netmask*: The subnet mask value with which this route entry is to be associated. Defaults to 255.255.255.255.
- *Gateway*: The gateway to the destination.
- **METRIC**: Indicates the next parameter to be interpreted as *metric*.
- *metric:* Designates a cost/hop count for the destination the route entry specifies. The distance is normally specified in number of hops from the destination. Set to 1 by default.

Enabling Dynamic IP Routing

Installing RIP for Internet Protocol provides dynamic routing support for a Windows NT Server computer. When you install RIP for Internet Protocol, the RIP routing service is automatically enabled, and the Enable IP Forwarding checkbox in the Routing tab of the Microsoft TCP/IP Properties is automatically selected. RIP for Internet Protocol runs as a service and can be stopped and started through the Services icon in the Control Panel. Because dynamic routers exchange routing information automatically, no manual configuration of the routing tables is necessary.

To enable a multihomed Windows NT computer with dynamic routing, you must:

- Have at least two network adapters and appropriate drivers installed in a Windows NT Server computer
- Configure each adapter with a valid IP address and subnet mask

Install the RIP for Internet Protocol service.

POP QUIZ — True or False?

1. RIP uses the distance-vector routing method for building its routing tables.
2. FTP allows users to run programs remotely.
3. A WINS server must be installed on each subnet of the network.

Answers: 1. True 2. False 3. False

Using the Tracert Utility

The `tracert` diagnostic command traces the connection between a local host and a destination host. Tracert works by determining the route taken to a destination host by sending Internet Control Message Protocol (ICMP) echo packets with varying TTL values to the destination. The `tracert` command determines the route by sending the first echo packet with a TTL of 1 and incrementing the TTL by 1 on each subsequent transmission until the target responds or the maximum TTL is reached (usually 30 hops). The route is determined by examining the ICMP Time Exceeded messages sent back by the intermediate routers. While `tracert` won't solve routing problems, it can show you why an IP address might work one day, but not the next, by showing you where the problem is in the route.

MCSE TCP/IP ACE IT!

Have You Mastered?

Now it's time to review the concepts in this chapter and apply your knowledge. These questions will test your mastery of material covered in this chapter.

1. **Which command is used to add an entry to the routing table?**

    ☐ A. route
    ☑ B. route add
    ☐ C. route new
    ☐ D. route entry

    B. `Route add` is the command used to add an entry to the routing table. See the "Standard routing table entries" section.

2. **Which of the following is not a requirement of a Windows NT computer functioning as a static router?**

    ☑ A. Enable IP forwarding
    ☐ B. At least two network adapters
    ☐ C. IP address and subnet mask for all installed adapters
    ☑ D. RIP

    D. Windows NT cannot function as a static router with RIP installed. See the "Enabling Static IP Routing" section.

5: IP ROUTING

3. Which of the following is not a requirement of a Windows NT computer functioning as a dynamic router?

- ☑ A. Enable IP forwarding
- ☐ B. At least two network adapters
- ☐ C. IP address and subnet mask for all installed adapters
- ☐ D. RIP

A. Windows NT cannot function as a static router with IP forwarding enabled. See the "Enabling Dynamic IP Routing" section.

4. Which utility can be used to follow the path of data across routers on the network?

- ☐ A. route
- ☑ B. tracert
- ☐ C. RIP
- ☐ D. OSPF

B. The `tracert` utility is used to view the path of data across the network. See the "Using the Tracert Utility" section.

5. Which of the following is not a standard routing table entry?

- ☐ A. Default route
- ☐ B. Network route
- ☐ C. Subnet route
- ☑ D. Device route

D. The four standard routing table entries are: default route, network route, subnet route, and host route. See the "Standard routing table entries" section.

MCSE TCP/IP ACE IT!

Practice Your Skills

The following exercises provide you with a practical opportunity to apply the knowledge you've gained in this chapter.

1. Implementing IP routing

EXERCISE Your network is divided into five different subnets. You have assigned a valid TCP/IP address and a subnet mask to each computer on the network. One of the subnets contains only four Windows NT Server computers; the other four subnets contain 25 Windows NT Workstation computers on each subnet. What additional TCP/IP configuration setting must be specified on each workstation? How does the TCP/IP software running on a workstation determine that a server resides on a remote subnet? How can you find out what decisions a workstation makes when determining whether a datagram should be sent to a remote subnet?

ANALYSIS The address of the default gateway (router) must be specified. It is determined when the destination host (server) has an IP address that is not within the range of addresses allowed for the subnet on which the client resides. You can find out what decisions are made by displaying the contents of the route table by typing **route print** from a command line.

2. Configuring a Windows NT Server computer as a static router

EXERCISE Your network contains three subnets. You want to configure a Windows NT Server computer as a static router between Subnet A and Subnet B. What additional hardware is required on the server? How many TCP/IP addresses must be assigned on the server? In addition to TCP/IP address configuration settings, what must be configured on the server?

ANALYSIS Two network adapters — one attached to each subnet — are required. You must assign two addresses, one for each network adapter. TCP/IP protocol settings must be configured to Enable IP Forwarding.

3. Configuring a static router

EXERCISE Your network contains three subnets. You have installed a Windows NT Server computer to be a static router between Subnet A and Subnet B. You have installed another server to be a static router between Subnet B and Subnet C. How should you configure the server connected between Subnet A and Subnet B so that hosts on Subnet A can communicate with hosts on Subnet C? Which command should you use to configure this?

ANALYSIS Create an entry (static route) in the routing table on each server that specifies where datagrams should be forwarded if the router does not have a direct connection to the destination subnet. Use the command: `route add ip_address mask netmask` (where the *ip_address* is the address of the router port to Subnet B and *netmask* is a valid subnet mask for Subnet B).

MCSE TCP/IP ACE IT!

4. Configuring multiple default gateways

EXERCISE Your network contains six subnets, and you have installed two routers on each. You want to configure Windows NT Workstation computers on all subnets so that they can continue to communicate outside of their local subnet even when the router specified as the default gateway has failed. How should you do this? How does a workstation determine which router to use when it needs to communicate with a host on a different subnet? In which case will the other default gateway be used? How can you determine which default gateway is being used by the computer?

ANALYSIS Configure the default gateway setting on each workstation with the TCP/IP addresses for both of the routers on the local subnet. When the workstation needs to communicate with a host on a different subnet, the IP address of the first default gateway is used. The workstation determines which router to use when there is no response from the first listed default gateway. Determine by the default gateway with the `ipconfig` utility by typing **ipconfig /all**.

6

Windows Internet Naming Service

THIS CHAPTER EXPLAINS HOW the *Windows Internet Name Service* (WINS) works to address NetBIOS naming and resolution problems on a large internetwork, as well as how to plan, install, and configure one or more WINS servers on a network. Also presented here is how to use the WINS administration tool, called *WINS Manager*, to view and configure WINS database settings.

Exam Material in This Chapter

Official Word

Based on Microsoft Objectives
- Given a scenario, identify valid network configurations.
- Install and configure a WINS server.

Inside Scoop

Based on Author's Experience
- WINS
- Name Registration
- Name Renewal
- Name Release
- WINS Proxy
- Static Entries
- WINS Replication
- Backing up WINS

Are You Prepared?

Review your knowledge of this subject by answering the following questions. Checking the answers will tell you what areas of study you need to concentrate on.

1. **When a device attempts to register a name that is already in use, what does the WINS server do?**

    - [ ] A. Registers the name to the new device
    - [ ] B. Refuses to register the name to the new device
    - [ ] C. Attempts to contact the device that has registered the name
    - [ ] D. Assigns an alternate name to the new device

2. **Which of the following should not be configured on a WINS server?**

    - [ ] A. Static IP address
    - [ ] B. Subnet mask
    - [ ] C. Default gateway
    - [ ] D. Multiple network adapters

Answers:

1. C   See the "Duplicate Names" section.
2. D   See the "Server and Client Requirements" section.

What Is WINS?

When two Windows-based computers reside on different subnets, they are unable to communicate because they cannot use NetBIOS broadcasts to exchange name registrations or to resolve each other's addresses. Microsoft's first technique for extending NetBIOS naming to an internetwork was the use of a mapping file called LMHOSTS, which contains a list of IP addresses with matching NetBIOS names for all of the computers on remote subnets that a Windows-based computer needs to communicate with. A copy of LMHOSTS must reside on each computer on the network. The disadvantage of this method is that each entry in the LMHOSTS file must be entered manually. WINS solves these problems by providing a central NetBIOS name database that all computers on an internetwork can access.

The use of WINS on an internetwork eliminates many of the broadcasts that occur for NetBIOS name resolution. It also enables computers located on different subnets to communicate with each other. WINS consists of two main components, the *WINS client* and the *WINS server*.

> **KNOW THIS** **Computer Names**
> A NetBIOS name is also called a computer name on Microsoft-based clients.

WINS Clients and Servers

WINS clients are configured with the IP address of at least one WINS server. A WINS client registers its computer name and IP address with a WINS server when the client initializes TCP/IP during startup. After a WINS client has registered its computer name with a WINS server, other WINS clients can communicate with the registered WINS client. WINS clients also use the WINS server to resolve computer names to IP addresses when connecting to other computers.

KNOW THIS: Configuring NT Server for WINS

All Windows NT Server computers, including the WINS server itself, should be configured as WINS clients.

WINS must be installed on a Windows NT Server computer. The WINS server manages name registration requests from WINS clients and responds to queries for computer names from WINS clients. The WINS server responds to queries by returning the IP address of the requested name if the name has been registered with the WINS server. It also maintains a database that maps the IP addresses of registered WINS clients to their computer names. When a WINS client requests the IP address for a computer name, a WINS server retrieves the IP address from its database and returns it to the WINS client.

Most networks should be configured with more than one WINS server in order to provide load balancing and backup in case the primary WINS server fails. When multiple WINS servers are installed, they can be configured to exchange their databases with each other, so the information on all WINS servers is kept synchronized.

POP QUIZ: True or False?

1. A DHCP server can only receive broadcast requests from clients on the same subnet.
2. WINS proxy agents provide name resolution for non-WINS clients.
3. Windows NT supports printing to IP printers.

Answers: 1. True 2. True 3. True

Benefits of Using WINS

The use of WINS on a network provides the following benefits:

- **A dynamic database:** WINS provides a dynamic database with which WINS clients register upon startup. The use of WINS for name resolution eliminates the need for network administrators to maintain static entries in the `LMHOSTS` file.
- **Reduced broadcast traffic:** The use of WINS reduces the amount of broadcast traffic on a network. Instead of using broadcasts to resolve a computer name to an IP address, the WINS client sends a message directly to a WINS server to find out the IP address for a given computer name.
- **Prevention of duplicate computer names:** Because all WINS clients must register their computer names with a central database, the WINS server can detect when a WINS client is attempting to register a duplicate computer name.
- **Ability of Windows-based clients to locate computers on remote subnets:** In addition to using the WINS server to resolve computer names located on remote subnets, WINS supports the capability to pass browse lists (lists of computer names) between computers configured as browsers on different subnets. This is possible because browser servers register a special group name with the WINS servers that enables them to locate each other.

How WINS Works

WINS supports standard NetBIOS services such as *name registration, name resolution,* and *name release,* as follows.

Name Registration

Each WINS client is configured with the IP address of a primary WINS server and, optionally, the IP address of a secondary WINS server. On startup, the WINS client sends a *name registration request* to the WINS server. The name registration request contains the WINS client's IP address and the name the client wants to register. The name registration request is sent directly to the WINS server, even if the WINS server is located on a different subnet.

When the WINS server receives a name registration request, it checks the WINS database to ensure that the name being registered is unique. If the name is unique in the WINS database, the WINS server responds with a positive name registration response. The response includes a *time-to-live* (TTL) value that indicates when the WINS client will need to renew its registration.

Computers always register multiple NetBIOS names for different services or applications, such as the Workstation service, the Server service, and the Messenger service. Typing **nbtstat -n** on a Microsoft TCP/IP client displays the names that are registered.

Duplicate names

The following describes what happens when a name registration request is received for a name that already exists in the WINS database:

1. A WINS client starts and sends a name registration request for the name `Wkstal`.

2. The WINS server finds an existing name registered as `Wkstal` and sends a challenge to the currently registered owner of the name `Wkstal`. This is to verify that the current owner is actually running with the registered name. The WINS server sends the challenge three times in 500-millisecond intervals. If the computer is multihomed, the WINS server tries each of the registered IP addresses for the name.

3. If the current registered owner of the name is running, it responds to the WINS server to indicate that the name is still in use.

4. The WINS server sends a negative name registration response back to the WINS client that was attempting to register the name.

129

Name Renewal

A WINS client must renew its lease to continue using the same NetBIOS name. If the client does not renew its lease before it expires, the WINS server releases the name and makes it available in the WINS database for other WINS clients. A WINS client initiates attempts to refresh its NetBIOS name when 1/8 of the TTL has expired. The default configuration for the WINS server sets a renewal interval of 144 hours, or six days. The WINS TTL value can be set on the WINS server.

When a WINS client renews its name registration, it sends a *name refresh request* to the WINS server asking its primary WINS server to refresh its registration. The WINS server responds to the WINS client with a *name refresh response* containing a new TTL. If the WINS client does not receive a response to a name refresh request, it continues attempts to contact the WINS server at two-minute intervals. These attempts continue until half of the TTL has expired. If the primary WINS server has not responded by that time, the WINS client attempts to renew its name with its secondary WINS server. If it is unable to refresh its registration by half of the TTL expiration, it reverts to the primary WINS server and again attempts to refresh its registration.

After the WINS client has successfully refreshed its registration one time, it makes subsequent refresh attempts when half of the TTL has expired.

> **KNOW THIS** **Altering the Renewal Interval**
> Changing the renewal interval to less than 96 hours can unacceptably increase the amount of network traffic. Increasing the renewal interval can cause NetBIOS names to remain in the database longer than desired. You should configure the primary and backup WINS servers with the same renewal interval.

Name release

When a WINS client is shutting down normally, it notifies the WINS server by using a name release request. After receiving a name release request, the WINS server checks the WINS database for the specified name. When the name and corresponding IP address are found in the WINS database, a positive name release response is returned to the WINS client containing the released NetBIOS name and indicating a TTL of 0.

A negative name release response is sent back to the WINS client if the WINS server encounters a database error or if the IP address of the WINS client does not match the IP address stored in the WINS database.

In either case, the WINS client ignores the name release response, so if the WINS server sends a negative name release response, the client will shut down anyway. However, when the WINS client does not receive any response from the WINS server, it will send three b-node broadcasts to notify all computers on the local subnet to remove the NetBIOS name from their local NetBIOS name cache, if it exists.

Name query and resolution

WINS clients resolve computer names to IP addresses by using *NetBIOS over TCP/IP* (NetBT). NetBT supports four different name resolution modes. By default, WINS clients use the h-node method of name resolution. This means WINS clients will always attempt to use the WINS server before trying another method of name resolution.

TEST TIP
On the test you may be asked to view the IP configuration and determine whether the computer is a WINS client and if it has been configured correctly. You can verify the name resolution mode by typing `ipconfig /all` command from a command line. Remember that if a computer is configured as a WINS client, the node type should be set to *hybrid*.

NetBIOS name resolution occurs whenever a user attempts to access a resource using a computer name such as `net use h: \\Computer3\apps`. NetBIOS name resolution also occurs when a user is browsing and connecting to a computer using the Windows NT Explorer.

The process used to resolve NetBIOS computer names works as follows:

1. The user initiates a command that uses a computer name.
2. The local NetBIOS name cache is checked for a matching name. If the name exists, the name can be resolved from the cache.
3. If the name does not exist in the cache, a name query request is sent to the primary WINS server. If no response is received, the WINS client will attempt two more requests before switching to the secondary WINS server. If a WINS server can resolve the name, a name query response is sent back to the WINS client containing the IP address for the requested name.
4. If no WINS server can resolve the name, a name query response is sent back to the WINS client indicating that the requested name does not exist.
5. The WINS client then attempts to use a broadcast (b-node) to resolve the name.

If the name cannot be resolved using WINS or b-node, it may still be possible to resolve the name using an `LMHOSTS` file, a `HOSTS` file, or DNS.

WINS Installation

Although you really need only one WINS server on a network, there should always be two or more WINS servers installed. This provides for a backup WINS server in case the first one is not available. In addition, multiple WINS servers can be used to balance the load of name registration and resolution requests.

WINS clients can be configured with the IP addresses of a primary and a secondary WINS server. If the primary server is unavailable, the WINS client will automatically switch to the secondary WINS server. For load-balancing purposes, you should allocate half the WINS clients to one of the WINS servers as the primary and allocate the other half of the WINS clients to the other WINS server as the primary.

Tests have shown that a single WINS server can manage approximately 1,500 name registrations per minute and 4,500 name resolution requests per minute.

> **KNOW THIS**
>
> **Running WINS with Multiple Processors**
>
> One way to increase WINS server performance is to install WINS on a computer with multiple processors. When multiple processors have been installed, WINS starts a separate thread for each processor, resulting in roughly a 25 percent performance gain per extra processor. Also, using the WINS Manager, logging can be turned off to enable names to be registered faster. Turning off logging, however, can result in the loss of the last few updates if the WINS server should fail.

Server and Client Requirements

Implementing WINS on your network requires the installation and configuration of a WINS server and the configuration of each WINS client. Requirements for a WINS server include:

- A Windows NT Server computer with TCP/IP installed. The Windows NT Server computer can be configured as a domain controller or a stand-alone server.
- The Windows NT Server computer should be configured with a static IP address, subnet mask, and default gateway.
- The WINS server cannot be a multihomed computer. A WINS server can be registered on only a single network.

> **KNOW THIS**
>
> **Configuring WINS Servers for DHCP**
>
> You can use DHCP to set the TCP/IP parameters on a WINS server, but you should create a client reservation for the WINS server. Because all clients are configured with the IP address for the WINS server, the WINS server IP address must not change.

133

The following operating systems can be configured as WINS clients:

- Windows NT Server version 4.0
- Windows NT Workstation version 4.0
- Windows 95
- Windows for Workgroups (WFWG) 3.11, with Microsoft 32-bit TCP/IP installed
- Microsoft Network Client for MS-DOS with real-mode TCP/IP driver
- LAN Manager for MS-DOS 2.2c

Each client must be configured with the IP address of the primary WINS server. Or, it may be configured with the IP address of the secondary WINS server.

WINS Proxy

A WINS proxy is a WINS-enabled computer that helps resolve name queries for non-WINS-enabled computers on an internetwork. A WINS proxy extends the capability of WINS to computers that are not capable of becoming WINS clients. A WINS proxy acts as an agent on a subnet that does not contain a WINS server. It listens for NetBIOS name registrations and resolution broadcasts from non-WINS clients on that subnet and forwards those requests to a WINS server on a different subnet. The WINS proxy can be a Windows 95 or Windows NT computer and must be configured as a WINS client.

> **TEST TIP**
> For the test, remember that a WINS server cannot be configured as a WINS proxy.

When a non-WINS client broadcasts a name registration request, the WINS proxy accepts the broadcast and passes it to the WINS server to verify that no other WINS client has registered that name. The WINS server responds to the WINS proxy with a message indicating whether the non-WINS client can use the name. In either case, the non-WINS client is not registered on the WINS server. The process used to resolve NetBIOS computer names using a WINS proxy works as follows:

6: WINDOWS INTERNET NAMING SERVICE

1. A non-WINS client uses a broadcast when attempting to resolve a NetBIOS name.
2. The WINS proxy receives the broadcast and first checks its cache to see if it has the NetBIOS computer-name-to-IP address mapping. If the requested name does not reside in the cache, the WINS proxy contacts the WINS server to resolve the name.
3. The WINS proxy receives the response from the WINS server and stores the mapping in its cache before returning the information to the non-WINS client. By default, the mapping remains in the cache on the WINS proxy for six minutes. This enables the WINS proxy to respond to any subsequent name query broadcasts from other non-WINS clients for the same mapping.
4. The WINS proxy directs a message to the non-WINS client, providing the required name resolution.
5. The non-WINS client can now communicate with the desired computer.

If a proxy agent cannot resolve a name through the internal cache or by using the WINS server, the proxy agent will not return any response to the non-WINS client, causing the client to fail in its request for the NetBIOS name.

> **KNOW THIS** **Planning WINS Proxies**
> You should have no more than two WINS proxies on any one subnet. This is because all proxies will respond to broadcasts and will cause multiple requests and responses to be sent. This can cause the WINS server to become overloaded.

Configuring WINS

A WINS server can be installed as part of the process of installing or configuring Microsoft TCP/IP on a Windows NT Server computer, or it can be installed later. To install WINS, you must be logged on as a

135

member of the Administrators group. When the computer restarts, WINS can start processing NetBIOS name registration and resolution requests from WINS clients immediately. However, you may need to configure some of the WINS server parameters for your network.

> **POP QUIZ** **True or False?**
>
> 1. The WINS server can receive requests only from clients on the same subnet.
> 2. `IPCONFIG` is a utility that displays the IP configuration of a Windows 95 computer.
> 3. NT server supports static routing.
>
> Answers: 1. False   2. False   3. True

Client computers must be configured to use WINS before they can use a WINS server for name resolution (except when a WINS proxy is being used). A WINS client must be configured with the IP address of a primary WINS server and, optionally, the IP address of a secondary WINS server if one exists. This is done by modifying the TCP/IP properties.

One of the easiest ways to configure all client computers to use WINS is by using DHCP. A DHCP server can be configured to supply WINS configuration settings in addition to other TCP/IP parameters.

When using a DHCP server to supply WINS configuration settings to a client computer, you must also specify the WINS node type. The WINS node type is used to specify the method and order of name resolution that WINS clients will use to resolve NetBIOS names.

WINS Manager

When WINS has been installed on a Windows NT Server, a new menu item on the Administrative Tools (Common) menu will be created for WINS Manager. WINS Manager is used to configure parameters for WINS. Some of the parameters you may want to configure include:

- Creating static entries for non-WINS clients
- Database replication between WINS servers
- Importing an `LMHOSTS` file

In order to manage multiple WINS servers on a network, you must add the remote WINS servers to the Server List using WINS Manager. Once a WINS server has been added to the list, remote configuration of the WINS server can take place.

WINS Statistics

When you start WINS Manager, the basic statistics about the selected WINS server are displayed. The following is a WINS server statistics summary:

- `Database Initialized`: The last time that the static mappings have been imported into the WINS database.
- `Statistics Cleared`: The last time when statistics for the WINS server were cleared using the Clear Statistics command from the View menu.
- `Last Replication Times`: The last times that the WINS database was replicated.
- `Periodic`: The last time that the WINS database was replicated according to the replication interval specified in the Preferences dialog box.
- `Admin Trigger`: The last time that the WINS database was replicated as a result of the administrator clicking the Replicate Now button in the Replication Partners dialog box.
- `Net Update`: The last time that the WINS database was replicated as a result of a push notification message to request propagation.
- `Total Queries Received`: The number of name query request messages that have been received by this WINS server. Successful indicates the number of names that were successfully matched in the database, and Failed indicates the number of names this WINS server was not able to resolve.

- **Total Releases:** The number of messages that have been received indicating that a NetBIOS program has stopped. Successful indicates the number of names that were successfully released, and Failed indicates the number of names this WINS server could not release.
- **Total Registrations:** The number of messages received for client name registrations.

WINS server statistic details are:

- **Last Address Change:** Indicates the last time that the WINS database change was replicated.
- **Last Scavenging Times:** Indicates the last times that the WINS database was cleaned for specific types of entries. (For information about database scavenging, see "Managing the WINS Server Database" later in this chapter.)
- **Periodic:** Indicates when the WINS database was cleaned based on the renewal interval specified in the WINS Server Configuration — (Local) dialog box.
- **Admin Trigger:** Indicates when the database was last cleaned because the administrator chose Initiate Scavenging.
- **Extinction:** Indicates when the database was last cleaned based on the Extinction interval specified in the WINS Server Configuration dialog box.
- **Verification:** Indicates when the database was last cleaned based on the verify interval specified in the WINS Server Configuration dialog box.
- **Unique Registrations:** Indicates the number of name registration requests that have been accepted by this WINS server.
- **Unique Conflicts:** The number of conflicts encountered during registration of unique names owned by this WINS server.
- **Unique Renewals:** The number of renewals received for unique names.

- `Group Registrations`: The number of registration requests for groups that have been accepted by this WINS server.
- `Group Conflicts`: The number of conflicts encountered during registration of group names.
- `Group Renewals`: The number of renewals received for group names.

Static Entries for Non-WINS Clients

If your network will consist of non-WINS clients, you can add static computer name-to-IP-address mappings for those computers on the WINS server. A static mapping creates a permanent entry in the WINS server database that cannot be challenged or removed by a WINS client. A WINS static mapping can be removed only by the administrator using the WINS Manager utility. WINS static mappings are useful in situations where a specific computer must always be able to register its computer name.

There are two methods of adding static mappings to a WINS database using WINS Manager:

- Enter individual static mappings for each computer in a dialog box.
- Import one or more files that contain static mappings.

The types of static mappings you can enter in WINS include:

- **Unique:** This is a unique name in the WINS database. It permits only one address per name. The unique name is the WINS client's computer name.
- **Group:** This indicates a normal group for which the IP addresses of the individual clients are not stored. A normal group is the name to which broadcasts are sent and is the domain name used for browsing purposes. When a WINS server receives a request for the group name, the WINS server returns the limited broadcast

address (255.255.255.255), which the WINS client will then use to broadcast to the subnet.

- **Domain Name:** A domain name defines a group that can consist of the addresses of up to 25 members. If additional names are registered, WINS overwrites a replica address if one exists or overwrites the oldest address registration if a replica does not exist.
- **Internet Group:** Internet groups are user-defined groups used to define lists of group resources. Printers are examples of resources that might be registered in an internet group. Up to 25 entries can be made to an internet group. Static entries made using WINS Manager or imported from LMHOSTS are not overwritten by dynamic entries.
- **Multihomed:** This is similar to a unique name in that it is the WINS client's computer name; however, it can have up to 25 addresses and is for use by multihomed systems.

TEST TRAP
If both WINS and DHCP are used on a network, any IP addresses that have been reserved on the DHCP server will cause WINS static mappings to be overwritten. Remembering this can help reduce confusion when taking the test.

If you would like to use the static mappings that are currently listed in the LMHOSTS file, you can import (load) the contents of the LMHOSTS file into the WINS database as static mappings for all unique names and all group names. The import file does not actually have to be the LMHOSTS file, but it must be the same format as the LMHOSTS file. When the LMHOSTS file is read, a static mapping is created for each computer name and address. When the #DOM keyword is included for any entry in the LMHOSTS file, an Internet group is created and the address is added to that group.

Managing the WINS Server Database

WINS Manager enables you to view the contents of the database that can be sorted in a number of different ways. If you will be using WINS on an internetwork, you will most likely want to replicate (copy the WINS database) between different WINS servers so that all WINS clients can locate any computer on the network.

The information for the mappings that are maintained in the WINS database include:

- **Mappings:** Under the Mappings column unique names (computer names) have a single computer icon in front of the name. The group, internet group, and multihomed names show an icon with multiple computers.

- **'A' and 'S':** A check in the 'A' column indicates that the WINS Client is active and a check in the 'S' column indicates that this is a static mapping.

- **Expiration Date:** Shows when the entry will expire. If the database includes replicated mappings, the expiration date is set to the time on the current server plus the renewal interval.

- **Version ID:** The Version ID is assigned by the WINS server when the name is registered with the WINS server. It is used by the WINS server's pull partners to request the entries in the WINS database that are newer than the last entry the pull partner received during the last replication.

The following options are available when viewing the mappings from the Show Database window:

- **Display Options — Owner:** You can choose to view the mappings from a specific WINS server, or all mappings, including those replicated from other WINS servers. To view the mappings in the database for a specific WINS server, select Show Only Mappings From Specific Owner; then from the Select Owner list, select the WINS server

141

whose database you want to view. By default, the Show Database dialog box shows all mappings for the WINS database on the currently selected WINS server.

- **Display Options — Sort Order:** You can change the order that mappings are displayed by selecting one of the following for Sort Order:
  - IP address
  - Computer name
  - Expiration date
  - Version ID (a time stamp used for replication)
  - Type (unique, group, multihomed, or Internet group)
- **Set Filter:** You can limit the range of IP addresses or computer names displayed in the Static Mappings or Show Database dialog boxes. You can specify a portion of the computer name or IP address or both when filtering the list of mappings.
- **Delete Owner:** You can remove all mappings from the database for a specific WINS server by selecting the WINS server in the Select Owner list and then clicking Delete Owner.

WINS Database Replication

WINS servers on an internetwork can be configured to replicate database entries with other WINS servers. This allows all WINS servers on an internetwork to remain synchronized when new mappings are registered or released from any WINS server. This is especially important for two WINS clients who need to communicate with each other but have registered their names with different WINS servers.

Push partners and pull partners

A *push partner* is a WINS server that sends a message to its pull partners to notify them when changes have been made to the WINS database. After receiving the message, a pull partner responds to the push partner with a replication request. The push partner sends a copy of the new database entries. A push partner notifies the pull partner of the need to perform replication when:

- A specified number of updates have occurred on the push partner (called the *update count*). The update count is configurable.
- The administrator initiates an immediate replication using WINS Manager.
- The WINS server has been started.

A *pull partner* is a WINS server that pulls (requests) WINS database mappings from its push partners. After being notified by the push partner, the pull partner requests all entries from the push partner's database that have a higher version number than the last update. A pull partner can request updates from the push partner when:

- A specified, configurable amount of time (called the time interval) has passed.
- The administrator initiates an immediate replication using WINS Manager.

Deciding on whether to configure a WINS server as a pull partner or a push partner depends mostly on the configuration of the internetwork. Some guidelines include the following:

- When two WINS servers are separated by slow-link connections, configure a pull partner between the locations because the replication can be configured to occur at a specified interval. In addition, a pull partner can be configured to replicate at a specific time such as after business hours.
- When two WINS servers are separated by fast-link connections, configure a push partner between locations because the replication interval can be configured to occur after a specific number of updates have occurred. Typically, WINS servers that are located near each other will replicate more frequently than WINS servers across WAN links. Always configure both WINS servers to be either both push partners or both pull partners to each other to keep the databases in synch.

Replication trigger

You can force replication partners to immediately replicate their databases by selecting the WINS server to which you want to send a replication trigger. Under Send Replication Trigger Now, click Push or Pull, depending on which partners you want to trigger.

If Push With Propagation is not selected, the selected WINS server does not send the trigger to its other partners. If Push With Propagation is selected, the selected WINS server sends a push trigger to its pull partners after it has received the latest information from the source WINS server. If it does not need to pull in any replicas because it has the same or more up-to-date replicas than the source WINS server, it does not propagate the trigger to its pull partners.

Backing up and Restoring the WINS Database

There is no limit to the number of mappings that can be contained in the WINS database. The database will grow to accommodate entries as they are added. Over time, as WINS client entries are released from the database, the file can become fragmented. The compacting of the database occurs in the background even while the WINS server is being used. The WINS server database consists of the following files:

- `J50.log` and `J50#####.log`: A log of all transactions done with the database. This file is used by WINS to recover data if necessary.
- `J50.chk`: A checkpoint file. During a recovery, it indicates where the recovery should start.
- `Wins.mdb`: The WINS server database file, which contains two tables, the IP Address-Owner ID mapping table, and the Name-to-IP-Address mapping table.
- `Winstmp.mdb`: A temporary file that is created by the WINS server service. This file is used by the database as a swap file during index maintenance operations and may remain in the `%systemroot%\System32\Wins` directory after a crash.

POP QUIZ — True or False?

1. WINS proxies are used to resolve name queries for non-WINS enabled devices.
2. `HOSTS` files are case sensitive.
3. `LMHOSTS.txt` provides name-to-IP resolution.

Answers: 1. True 2. False 3. False

WINS Database Configuration Options

You can change the default setting for how WINS manages database maintenance. The configuration options listed below enable you to specify time intervals for various settings:

- **Renewal Interval:** Specifies how often a client reregisters its name. The default is 144 hours (six days).
- **Extinction Interval:** Specifies the interval between when an entry is marked as *released* (no longer registered by a computer) and when it is marked as *extinct*. The default is the same as the renewal interval.
- **Extinction Timeout:** Specifies the interval between when an entry is marked *extinct* and when the entry is finally scavenged (removed) from the database. The default is the same as the renewal interval.
- **Verify Interval:** Specifies the interval after which the WINS server must verify that old names it does not own are still active. The default is 576 hours (24 days).

The advanced configuration options for the WINS server are:

- **Logging Enabled:** Specifies whether logging of database changes to `J50.log` files should be turned on.

- **Log Detailed Events:** Specifies whether logging events is verbose mode. (This requires considerable computer resources and should be turned off if you are tuning for performance.)
- **Replicate Only With Partners:** Specifies that replication occurs only with configured WINS pull or push partners. If this option is not checked, an administrator can ask a WINS server to pull or push from or to a non-listed WINS server partner. By default, this option is checked.
- **Backup On Termination:** Specifies that the database is backed up automatically when WINS Manager is closed.
- **Migrate On/Off:** Specifies that static unique and multihomed records in the database are treated as dynamic when they conflict with a new registration or replica. This means that if they are no longer valid, they are overwritten by the new registration or replica. Check this option if you are upgrading non-Windows NT-based computers to Windows NT. By default, this option is not checked.
- **Starting Version Count:** Specifies the highest version ID number for the database. Usually, you do not need to change this value unless the database becomes corrupted and needs to start fresh. In such a case, set this value to a number higher than appears as the version number counter for this WINS server on all the remote partners that earlier replicated the local WINS server's records.
- **Database Backup Path:** Specifies the directory where the WINS database backup is stored. If you specify a backup path, WINS automatically performs a full backup of its database to this directory every 24 hours. WINS uses this directory to perform an automatic restoration of the database in the event that the database is found to be corrupted when WINS is started. Do not specify a network directory.

Have You Mastered?

Now it's time to review the concepts in this chapter and apply your knowledge. These questions will test your mastery of material covered in this chapter.

1. **Which of the following is not a reason to install multiple WINS servers?**

    - ☐ A. Fault tolerance
    - ☐ B. A WINS server should be installed on each side of a WAN link.
    - ☐ C. A WINS server must be installed on each subnet.
    - ☐ D. Load balancing

    C. WINS servers do not need to be installed on each subnet because the clients know the IP address of the WINS server and traffic can be routed to them. See the "WINS Installation" section.

2. **Which of the following is not a valid static mapping type on a WINS server?**

    - ☐ A. Unique
    - ☐ B. Host
    - ☐ C. Group
    - ☐ D. Domain name

    B. There is no host mapping in WINS. To create a mapping for a single device, you should create a Unique mapping. See the "Configuring WINS" section.

MCSE TCP/IP ACE IT!

3. A WINS client with multiple network adapters must be configured with which type of static mapping?

☐ A. Multiple
☐ B. Multihomed
☐ C. Unique
☐ D. Group

B. To create a mapping for a device with more than one network adapter, you should create a Multihomed mapping. See the "Configuring WINS" section.

4. How can LMHOSTS files be used on a WINS network?

☐ A. Import the file into the WINS database as static mappings.
☐ B. Copy the LMHOSTS file to the root directory of all clients.
☐ C. Create an LMHOSTS file with a single mapping that points to the WINS server.
☐ D. Extract the WINS database to an LMHOSTS file.

A. LMHOSTS files can be imported into the WINS database as static mappings. See the "How WINS Works" section.

5. Which type of WINS replication is beneficial for WINS servers separated by a WAN link?

☐ A. Push
☐ B. Pull
☐ C. Backup
☐ D. Trigger

B. WINS servers separated by a WAN link should be configured as pull partners. This allows replication to be configured for a specific time of the day after normal business hours. See the "Push partners and pull partners" section.

6: WINDOWS INTERNET NAMING SERVICE

Practice Your Skills

The following exercises provide you with a practical opportunity to apply the knowledge you've gained in this chapter.

1. Configuring Windows-based computers to use WINS

EXERCISE Your network consists of four different subnets. You install a single WINS Server on one of the subnets, which will be used to support Windows NT Workstation computers that reside on all subnets. How must you configure the workstations so that they can use the WINS Server? What must you do to configure the WINS Server so it can be used by all workstations? What is the easiest way to assign the IP address of the WINS Server to all workstations?

ANALYSIS To configure workstations using WINS, you need to specify the IP address of the WINS Server on each of the workstations. When the WINS Server is installed, it is automatically available to all WINS clients that can connect to it, so you don't need to take any special steps during configuration. To assign the IP address of the WINS Server to all workstations, use DHCP Manager (assuming that DHCP is used on your network) to create a global option.

2. Configuring the WINS Server to prevent duplicate computer names

EXERCISE You have installed a WINS Server on your network. All Windows NT Workstation computers and Windows NT Server computers have been configured to use WINS. How can you prevent a workstation from registering a computer name that is used by one of the servers? What happens when a workstation attempts to register, with the WINS Server, a computer name that has already been registered? How long will computer names remain registered with the WINS Server by default?

ANALYSIS To prevent a workstation from registering a computer name used by one of the servers, create a static entry for each of the servers in the WINS database using WINS Manager. When a workstation attempts to register a computer name that is already registered, the WINS Server will send a challenge to the currently registered owner of the computer name. If the current owner responds (or if the name has been registered as a static entry), a negative name registration response is returned. Otherwise, the name is released from the current owner and registered to the new owner. By default, computer names will be registered for 96 hours (four days). If a computer does not renew its name within that time, the computer name will be released from WINS.

3. Configuring multiple WINS servers

EXERCISE Your network consists of four subnets. Subnet A and Subnet B are located in San Diego, and Subnet C and Subnet D are located in Dallas. You install a WINS Server on Subnet A for all WINS clients in San Diego, and a WINS Server on Subnet C for all WINS clients in Dallas. Subnet B contains 25 Windows for Workgroups computers that are not

6: WINDOWS INTERNET NAMING SERVICE

WINS-enabled. How can you configure the network so that the Windows for Workgroups computers can use WINS for NetBIOS name resolution? You want to enable any WINS client in Dallas to be able to connect to servers in San Diego. You also want to allow any WINS client in San Diego to be able to connect to servers in Dallas. How do you do this? You want to enable WINS clients in San Diego to be able to use the WINS Server in Dallas as a backup in case the WINS Server in San Diego fails. How should you do this?

ANALYSIS In order for Windows for Workgroups computers to use WINS for NetBIOS name resolution, configure one Windows NT computer or a Windows 95 computer on Subnet B as a WINS proxy. To enable WINS clients in Dallas and San Diego to connect to the server in the other city, you need to configure the WINS Servers as replication partners so that they exchange their lists of registered computer names with one another. To enable WINS clients in San Diego to use the WINS server in Dallas as a backup server, you need to specify the IP address of the Dallas WINS Server as the secondary WINS Server on each WINS client in San Diego. (The easiest way to do this is to use DHCP.)

4. Configuring WINS replication

EXERCISE Your network consists of three subnets. Subnet A is in Miami, Subnet B is in Toronto, and Subnet C is in Denver. You install a WINS Server on each subnet. There are 500 WINS clients in Miami, 250 WINS clients in Toronto, and 100 WINS clients in Denver. There is a fast communications link between Miami and Toronto. The communications link between Denver and Miami is slow. You want to replicate WINS database changes between Miami and Toronto whenever there are ten or more changes to the WINS database. How should you do this? You want to replicate WINS database changes between Denver and Miami only after business hours. How should you do this?

ANALYSIS To replicate WINS database changes between Miami and Toronto whenever there are ten or more changes to the WINS database, configure the WINS replication between Miami and Toronto as push partners. To replicate WINS database changes after business hours only, configure the WINS replication between Miami and Denver as pull partners.

7

Domain Name System

MICROSOFT INCLUDED A FULL version of a *Domain Name System* (DNS) server for the first time with the release of Windows NT 4.0. DNS provides a naming system for computers and other resources on an internetwork or on the Internet. Read this chapter to review how to plan the implementation of a DNS on an internetwork, and how to install and configure a Microsoft DNS server for various roles.

MCSE TCP/IP ACE IT!

Exam Material in This Chapter

Official Word

Based on Microsoft Objectives
- Given a scenario, identify valid network configurations.
- Install and configure the Microsoft DNS Server service on a Windows NT Server computer.

Inside Scoop

Based on Author's Experience
- DNS
- Resolvers
- Name servers
- Domains
- Zones
- Recursive and iterative queries
- Inverse queries
- BOOT file
- `Nslookup`

7: DOMAIN NAME SYSTEM

Are You Prepared?

Test your knowledge with the following questions, which will help you determine if you're prepared for the material covered in this chapter, or if you need additional study in problem areas.

1. **The file copy procedure used to replicate the contents of the DNS database from the primary name server to a secondary name server is known as a:**

    - ☐ A. Forwarder
    - ☐ B. Replicator
    - ☐ C. Zone transfer
    - ☐ D. Inverse queries

2. **Which record is used to establish aliases for hosts?**

    - ☐ A. Name server record
    - ☐ B. Address record
    - ☐ C. CNAME record
    - ☐ D. Mail exchanger record

3. **Where are the zone files stored?**

    - ☐ A. \SYSTEMROOT\SYSTEM32\DNS
    - ☐ B. \SYSTEMROOT\SYSTEM32\DRIVERS\ETC
    - ☐ C. \SYSTEMROOT\SYSTEM32\
    - ☐ D. \SYSTEMROOT\CONFIG

Answers:

1. C   See the *"Name Server Roles"* section.
2. C   See the *"Database Files and Resource Records"* section.
3. A   See the *"DNS Manager and Manual DNS Administration"* section.

7: DOMAIN NAME SYSTEM

DNS Overview

The *Domain Name System* (DNS) was created because of the enormous growth of the Internet. It provides a centralized database that registers and translates host names to IP addresses, and prevents duplication. Using DNS, the name space can be partitioned into different domains and allow multiple servers to be used for manageability, performance, and redundancy.

> **TEST TIP**
> The exam will test your knowledge of basic DNS concepts and your ability to configure a Microsoft DNS server. You should understand the different roles a DNS server can perform on a network and how to use Microsoft DNS Manager to perform common DNS administrative tasks.

A host computer on a network provides a domain name to a DNS and the IP address of the domain name is returned, working much like a telephone directory by providing cross references.

Specifications for DNS are defined in RFCs 974, 1034, and 1035. RFC 1034 identifies the three main components of DNS as: name resolvers, domain name space, and name servers.

The main purpose of DNS is to resolve resource names to IP addresses. In DNS terminology, DNS clients are called *resolvers*. The resolver queries the DNS server to obtain the IP address of the requested host.

The resolver software is usually built into the application or is provided as a library routine on the host computer. The resolver software for Windows-based computers is contained in the Windows sockets libraries that are installed on each computer.

The DNS database is a tree structure called the *domain name space*. Each domain is named and can contain subtrees (or subdomains). The domain name identifies the domain's position in the database in relation to its parent domain. A period (.) separates each part of the name for the network nodes of the DNS domain.

DNS name servers store information about portions of the domain name space. The *name server* is the computer running the programs that manage the DNS database. Name servers can either respond directly to a request for information by performing a lookup in local

157

resource records or pass the request to other name servers. If a name server contains the resource record for a portion of the name space, it is said to have *authority* for that part of the name space.

Domains

DNS domains define different levels of authority in a hierarchy. These levels are the *root domain*, *top-level domains*, and *second-level domains*.

Root domain

The highest level of the hierarchy is the *root domain*. All other domains fall below the root domain. Because every host name falls below the root domain, it is clear that it is an essential part of the DNS database. In fact, because the root domain is so important, it is serviced by seven root domain servers on the Internet.

Top-level domains

The next level in the hierarchy is divided into a series of nodes called *top-level* (or *first-level*) *domains*. The top-level domains are assigned by the type of organization and by country. The top level of the domain space is divided into three primary areas: *organizational domains*, *geographical domains*, and *reverse domains*, as described below.

Top-level domains are located directly below the root domain in the DNS hierarchy. Each top-level domain is identified by a three-character code to indicate the primary function or activity of the organization that has obtained a domain name. The familiar .com domain is an example of a top-level domain.

Organizational domains, the primary top-level domain names used in the U.S., are defined as follows:

.com	Commercial: The InterNIC assigns portions of the domain name space under this level to commercial organizations, such as quicklearn.com.
.edu	Educational: The InterNIC assigns portions of this domain name space to educational organizations, such as the Massachusetts Institute of Technology (mit.edu).

.gov   Government: The InterNIC assigns portions of this domain name space to governmental organizations, such as the White House in Washington, D.C. (whitehouse.gov).

.mil   Military: U.S. government military organizations.

.org   Nonprofit organizations, such as iana.org.

.net   Networking organizations: The InterNIC assigns portions of this domain name space to networking organizations, such as the National Science Foundation (nsf.net).

As the Internet grew internationally, it became necessary to introduce *geographical domains* to identify countries. The Internet community has adopted the two-character country codes established by ISO 3166. For example, www.bplus.au denotes a Web site in Australia; ftp.quicklearn.ca is the name of an FTP server in Canada, and www.medus.tra.gr identifies a Web site in Greece.

In most instances, DNS is used to determine the IP address associated with a given host name. But there are times when it is necessary to work from the IP address to the host name. To support address-to-name lookups, a special domain name called in-addr.arpa exists. Records in the reverse lookup file are named by their IP addresses instead of domain name. Address-to-name lookups are also called *reverse name lookups*.

Second-level domains

Below the top-level domains are the *second-level domains*. In most cases, second-level domains are associated with specific organizations. If an organization decides it wants its domain name to be available on the Internet, it must register a second-level name under the appropriate top-level domain. In the majority of cases, second-level domains are registered with the InterNIC.

Zones

The administrative unit for DNS is the *zone*. A zone is a portion of a DNS domain that can be administered as a separate entity. A zone can consist of a single domain or a domain that has been divided into subdomains. A single DNS server can be configured to manage one or more zone files. Each zone is anchored at a specific domain node, referred to as the zone's *root domain*.

A domain may be partitioned into a hierarchical organization of subdomains and zones that are controlled by different DNS name servers. Breaking up domains may be necessary to provide distributed management and performance load balancing.

> **KNOW THIS** **Authoritative Servers**
> A name server that maintains records for a domain or a zone is said to be *authoritative* for that domain or zone.

Name Server Roles

Information on DNS servers is stored differently based on the role of the server. The role of the server describes how zone information will be maintained on that server. The various types of name servers are:

- Primary
- Secondary
- Master

Primary name server

A *primary name server* is a name server that obtains configuration data for its zones from files that are stored and maintained locally on that name server. All changes to a zone, such as adding a domain or host, are performed at the primary name server. A given zone can be associated with only one primary name server.

Secondary name server

A *secondary name server* gets the data for its zones from another name server across the network in a process called a *zone transfer*. The other server can be a primary name server or another secondary name server. Secondary name servers provide the following benefits:

7: DOMAIN NAME SYSTEM

- **Redundancy:** Each zone requires a primary name server and at least one secondary name server for redundancy. Like any good fault tolerant system, having multiple systems guarantees that if one of the name servers fails, the other one can still be used for host name resolution.
- **Distribution:** Secondary name servers should be placed at remote locations that have a large number of clients. This eliminates the need for clients to generate additional traffic on a wide area network for host name resolution.
- **Load Balancing:** The use of secondary name servers can help reduce the load on the primary name server. Distributing the load for host name resolution requests to a secondary name server can increase response time.

Because the zone information is maintained in specific files on a name server, it is possible to configure one name server to be a primary name server for one zone and to configure a secondary name server for another zone.

Master name server

A *master name server* is the name server that is the source of zone information for a secondary name server. The master name server can either be a primary or a secondary name server for the zone.

When a secondary name server starts up, it contacts the master name server and initiates a zone transfer for each zone for which it is acting as a secondary name server. Zone transfers also occur periodically when information has been updated on the master.

Forwarders and slaves

When a DNS name server receives a DNS query, it attempts to locate the information in its local zone files. If the name server is not authoritative for the domain that has been requested, it will attempt to communicate with other DNS name servers to resolve the request.

Typically, these requests are for resources outside of an organization's internetwork. DNS enables specific name servers to be designated as *forwarders* for this purpose. Only forwarders are enabled to communicate across the Internet. All other DNS servers are configured to use forwarders to resolve requests for Internet resources.

161

The forwarder carries out the request and passes the results back to the requesting DNS name server. If a forwarder is unable to resolve the query, the original DNS server will attempt to resolve the query on its own. The capability of a DNS server to resolve its own query when the forwarder is unavailable is referred to as *nonexclusive mode*.

In *exclusive mode*, a DNS server is configured to return an error message when the forwarder is unable to resolve a query. A DNS server configured this way is also called a *slave*. A slave will not attempt to contact other name servers when the forwarder is unavailable.

Caching-only server

All DNS servers cache queries they have resolved for a certain amount of time. A *caching-only server* is a name server whose only job is to cache queries it has received. A caching-only server does not contain any zone information files and therefore does not perform any zone transfers.

Initially, when a caching-only server starts up, it must forward all queries to a different DNS name server until the cache has been built up and can service queries on its own. For this reason, caching-only servers will generally create traffic when they start up, but because they do not perform any zone transfers, they will generate less traffic over time.

A *zone transfer* is a file copy procedure that replicates the contents of the DNS database from the primary (or master) name server to a secondary name server. A zone transfer occurs automatically when a secondary name server starts up. The refresh parameter on the primary name server is used to configure the frequency of zone transfers after the initial zone transfer that occurs at startup. A name server can act as a secondary name server for more than one zone, in which case the zone transfer occurs for each zone that the secondary is configured for.

Zone transfers can also be configured to occur when there has been a change to the zone information on the primary name server. You can also configure a primary name server to send a DNS change notification message to all servers listed in the notify list. Once notified, the secondary name servers will request an immediate zone transfer without waiting for the refresh interval.

How often you should configure a zone transfer to occur is a balance between the amount of network traffic and server load versus how long it may take for changes on the primary server to be copied to the secondary server.

Name Resolution Methods

DNS clients use one of three methods when making queries to a DNS name server: *recursive*, *iterative*, and *inverse*. Remember: A DNS name server can also be a client to another DNS name server.

Recursive and iterative queries

A *recursive query* typically occurs between a DNS client and a DNS name server. With a recursive query, a request is made to the DNS name server to respond with the requested data or to return an error message indicating that the specified domain or host does not exist. The server receiving the recursive query is responsible for resolving it and cannot forward the request to another server. It can, however, make iterative queries of other servers in an effort to locate the server that is authoritative for the target domain.

An *iterative query* typically occurs between name servers attempting to resolve a recursive query from a resolver. With an iterative query, a DNS name server will respond with the best answer it can provide. Typically, this is a referral to another name server that may be able to fulfill the client's original request.

Inverse queries

With an *inverse query*, a resolver sends a request to a DNS server to resolve the host name for a known IP address. (Remember: Most DNS requests are used to resolve a TCP/IP address for a known host name.) This process is known as *reverse lookup*. Reverse lookup is most often used for special applications, such as security programs, or for troubleshooting. To successfully resolve an IP address to a host name, a special domain, called `in-addr.arpa`, must be created. Entries in the `in-addr.arpa` domain are organized by IP address.

Caching and TTL

Resolving a domain name can require a bit of effort on the part of the DNS server, and it would be wasteful to repeat the task for names that are frequently used. Consequently, the name server stores information it receives in a local cache along with a value that specifies the amount of time the information should remain in the cache before it is discarded. This value is called the *time-to-live* (TTL). Before initiating a full query, the name server looks for the data in its cache.

The name server administrator of the zone that contains the data specifies the TTL value. Larger TTL values can cause the cached data to become outdated; smaller TTL values can ensure that the data is up to date and consistent across all name servers. However, smaller TTL values can cause additional traffic and load on the name servers.

The client (resolver) also caches data it receives and uses the current value of the TTL to determine when it should discard the data.

DNS Configuration and Database Files

The Microsoft DNS server is designed to be compatible with *Berkeley Internet Name Domain* (BIND) servers, the most common DNS server on the Internet. The Microsoft DNS server can import data from BIND configuration files, and it can generate a set of BIND-compatible files if it is necessary to export the data to a BIND server. Although the Microsoft DNS server has a good graphical interface, it is a good idea for you to be familiar with the database files, as well.

BIND DNS systems use a standard set of files to define the DNS system configuration and for the DNS database itself. These files include the boot, database, cache, reverse lookup, and 127 reverse lookup files. This knowledge will be useful if you need to import data to the Microsoft DNS server from existing BIND configuration files.

The BOOT File

The BOOT file provides startup information for the BIND DNS server. Records in the boot file define the zones for which the server is authoritative, as well as whether the server is a primary or a secondary server for the domain. The BOOT file records also declare which files contain the data for each of the zones for which the server is a primary name server.

The Microsoft DNS server does not create a BOOT file. If you are importing data from BIND, the BOOT file is used only once, when the databases are first imported. The BOOT file can contain the following statements:

- **Directory:** On BIND servers, the directory statement specifies the directory in which the server database files are stored. The Microsoft DNS server requires all files to be stored in `\systemroot\system32\dns` and ignores the directory statement.

- **Cache:** This statement specifies the filename of the cache file. Originally, the cache file contained records that were to be loaded into the DNS server's cache at startup. Now the cache file consists only of name servers for the root domain.

- **Primary:** This statement declares a domain for which this is a primary DNS server, along with the name of the database file for the domain.

- **Secondary:** This statement declares a domain for which this is a secondary DNS server. Because the database file resides on another computer, the secondary statement specifies the IP address of the computer that is the source of the zone transfer along with the filename that contains the data for the zone.

The Microsoft DNS server supports all the functions of the BOOT file, doing so graphically.

> **KNOW THIS** **Format of BOOT Files**
> The semicolon (;) character delimits a comment. All characters following the semicolon (;) on a given line are ignored. This convention holds true for all BIND database files.
> When a resource record consists of several fields, as most do, the fields must be separated by at least one white space character—either spaces or tabs. It is common to use multiple spaces or tabs to format the file for legibility.

Database Files and Resource Records

DNS database files are called *zone files* and contain the data for a zone. The zone data definitions take the form of *resource records*. Several types of resource records can appear. For example, address (A) resource records map host names to IP address mappings. A DNS server zone file can contain different types of resource records, depending on the information entered by the DNS administrator. A zone file is created automatically on a Microsoft DNS server using the DNS Manager program. The filename used will be the name of the zone you create with a .dns extension added, for example, quicklearn.com.dns.

If you prefer, you can use the provided file called place.dns as a template when starting to configure the information in a zone file. You can use a text editor to modify the contents of this file, and then use DNS Manager later.

The Microsoft DNS Server database is a set of files containing the host-name-to-IP-address mappings and other DNS information for the computers on your TCP/IP network. These data records are referred to as *resource records* and are contained in the zone, cache, reverse-lookup, and arpa-127 files. The following sections describe the most important resource records in the DNS database.

The *start of authority (SOA) record* defines a number of general operational parameters for the DNS server. The elements of the SOA record are:

- **Name server:** Immediately after the SOA keyword appears the DNS name of the name server that is most authoritative for this domain, in this case dnsserver.alpha.com.

- **Contact:** After the name server appears the e-mail address of the primary contact for this name server. Because the at character (@) has special significance in BIND files, the name is entered with a period in place of the at character. In this example, jsmith.alpha.com indicates an e-mail address of jsmith@alpha.com.

- **Serial number:** This number is a revision number for the file. Each time the file is edited, the administrator should increment this value.

- **Refresh:** This value specifies the frequency in seconds at which a secondary name server refreshes itself from the primary. In this example, the secondary server refreshes itself every three hours.

- **Retry:** This value specifies how many seconds a secondary server waits after a failed zone transfer before it attempts the transfer again. In the example, the secondary server waits one hour.

- **Expire:** This entry specifies how long in seconds a secondary server will retain data without successfully retrieving the data from its source server. Data that is not refreshed within this interval is purged from the server database. In the example, unrefreshed data is retained for one week.

- **Time-to-live (TTL):** The name server applies this TTL value in seconds to all records in the database. Servers that retrieve data from this server are permitted to cache the data for the TTL interval before it must be purged. In this example, the TTL is one day.

Comments are used to make the SOA record more readable. All characters on a line that follow a semicolon (;) are ignored.

> **TEST TRAP**
> For the test, remember that only one SOA record can exist in a database file.

In addition to SOA, a number of other types of records are used in the DNS database:

- **Name server record:** Each name server for the domain is declared in an NS record. The at character (@) means "this domain" as declared in the BOOT file. Each name server must be declared in an A record.
- **Address record:** A (address) records are the heart of the DNS database, providing mappings between host names and their IP addresses. From the NS record, we learn the name of the name server for this domain. From the A record we learn the name server's IP address.
- **Canonical name record:** Canonical name (CNAME) records enable the administrator to establish aliases for some hosts.
- **Mail exchanger record:** Internet mail systems such as Sendmail can work with DNS to discover which hosts are functioning as mail servers for a domain. Mail exchanger (MX) records declare a mail server. The number following the MX keyword establishes the preference for this mail server. If several MX records specify mail servers for a domain, the mail server with the lowest preference number will be preferred by outside systems that wish to deliver mail to this domain. If multiple mail servers have the same priority, they will be used about equally to balance the load.

The Cache File

The cache file contains mappings for the Internet root DNS servers. These mappings enable hosts to resolve queries for hosts located outside of an organization's internal network. When your network is attached to the Internet, you need to configure the cache file to enable your hosts to find the Internet root name server.

When you install Microsoft DNS server, a cache file is installed with the current mappings for Internet root servers. If you do not plan to connect to resources on the Internet, you should modify this file to contain mappings for the DNS servers that are authoritative for the root of your internal network. If you work through the comments, you will find that the file consists of nothing more complicated than NS and A records for the various root name servers. In the NS resource record, the initial . (period) indicates that this record defines a name server for the root domain, which is referred to with a single period. The numbers appearing in the NS and A records are obsolete remnants of early versions of BIND, intended to specify how long the entries should remain in cache. At present, entries are held in cache indefinitely, and this parameter no longer has any effect.

The Reverse Lookup File

The reverse lookup file contains mappings (PTR records) that are used to return the host name when a DNS client has only the IP address of a remote computer. An inverse query occurs when, instead of asking for the IP address of a resource, the DNS client requests a name by supplying the IP address to the DNS name server. The special domain named in-addr.arpa was created on the Internet for just this purpose. The reverse lookup file is often used for security applications or TCP/IP network troubleshooting.

Records in the in-addr.arpa domain are named by their IP addresses instead of their domain names. But because IP addresses are more specific from left to right, as opposed to domain names that are more specific from right to left, IP addresses must be stored in reverse octet order. To find the host name for IP address 172.25.3.7, for example, the resolver would query the DNS server for a pointer record for 7.3.25.172.in-addr.arpa.

> **TEST TIP**
> You might see a question on the test about host names. Remember that you must be careful when specifying host names. Improper use of trailing periods is a frequent source of problems in DNS database files.

Planning a DNS Installation

An organization that uses an Internet service provider (ISP) to connect to the Internet may not need to maintain its own DNS server. For small networks, it is simpler, more efficient, and requires less maintenance to have the DNS client query a DNS name server maintained by the ISP.

If the organization wants to maintain control over its own domain and use the DNS for host name resolution on an internal network, then it may want to have its own DNS servers. In either case, the organization's domain name must be registered with the InterNIC. That is, of course, unless the organization will not be connected to the Internet but still wants to use a DNS server internally.

There are two different approaches to designing a DNS architecture. The first option is to create a single domain for the entire organization. The second option is to create multiple domains that reflect the distribution of management tasks to different entities within an organization.

Single-domain Design

The easiest design option is to create a *single domain* that uses one primary DNS server, and one or more secondary DNS servers. One of the disadvantages of this option is that the secondary DNS servers may cause a great deal of network traffic. In addition, the primary DNS server may have trouble keeping up with all of the polling from the secondary DNS servers for zone transfers. One way to avoid some of the overhead of a zone transfer is to install some caching servers. However, caching servers take time to build up their cache to the point where they can resolve queries without having to forward requests to other DNS servers.

The other disadvantage of using a single domain design is seen when an organization is split into different administrative groups. A single domain approach does not provide the capability to distribute management of portions of the domain to different departmental groups.

Multiple-domain Design

For a large organization that has an internetwork spanning multiple sites, it will probably be necessary to use *multiple domains*. This means creating a root domain with one or more subdomains. The root domain contains a primary DNS server with one or more secondary DNS servers. Each subdomain also contains a primary DNS server with one or more secondary DNS servers.

The advantage of this approach is that each subdomain can be managed separately so that network administration can be distributed to different entities.

Installing and Configuring Microsoft DNS Server

Microsoft DNS Server is an RFC-compliant DNS name server that runs on Windows NT Server version 4.0. DNS server uses the same RFC-compliant text files and resource records used in all DNS implementations. Microsoft DNS Server is also compatible with the Berkeley Internet Name Domain (BIND) implementation of DNS.

One important feature in Microsoft DNS Server not found in other implementations is the tight integration with Microsoft Windows Internet Name Service (WINS). This enables a Windows-based computer to first query a DNS server and if a record is not found, the query can be forwarded to a WINS server. WINS/DNS integration will be discussed later.

Before installing the Microsoft DNS Server, the Windows NT Server should be configured correctly with TCP/IP settings such as the IP

MCSE TCP/IP ACE IT!

address, subnet mask, and IP address of a default gateway. The DNS property page settings should be verified before the DNS server uses the current host name and domain name to create zone information. The DNS server will add an SOA record for the zone, and A and NS records for the server.

If you wish to initialize the server database from BIND database files, copy the BIND files to the \systemroot\system32\dns directory. Review the files carefully to ensure that their data is correct and properly formatted. If BIND files are not found when the server initializes, a default configuration will be established.

> **KNOW THIS**
>
> **Zonename**
>
> Microsoft DNS Server uses different file naming conventions than you are likely to encounter on BIND servers. The Microsoft DNS convention is to name files zone-name.dns, where *zonename* is the name of the zone being defined. BIND files often follow the convention *zonename*.dom or db.*zonename*.

DNS Manager and Manual DNS Administration

The DNS Manager is a graphical administration tool that is installed on a Windows NT server when the DNS service is installed. DNS Manager is used to configure the DNS service and to manage the DNS database.

DNS Manager is started from the Administrative Tools folder. When DNS Manager is first started, it will show the zone information in the left pane and the statistics for the currently highlighted DNS server in the right pane.

However, DNS server does support the use of a BIND boot file to specify DNS configuration settings by modifying DNS text files. The use of a boot file is a BIND-specific implementation of DNS and not a RFC-required component. This feature is provided to easily migrate from BIND-based DNS servers to a Microsoft DNS server.

For normal administration of DNS server, the DNS Manager should be used. If DNS Manager is used to create and administer zone

7: DOMAIN NAME SYSTEM

files, the Boot Method property page under Server properties will read "The DNS Server is currently set to boot from data contained in the registry."

If a boot file was used previously, it will be renamed BOOT.BAK and a message will be written to the boot file indicating that the information has been transferred to the registry.

To use the boot file for locating zone file databases, you must enable the EnableRegistryBoot key in the Windows NT registry using Regedit. The EnableRegistryBoot key is found in the following path:

\HKEY_LOCAL_MACHINE\SYSTEM\CurrentControlSet\Services\DNS\Parameters

A value of 1 indicates that the DNS Manager will be used to create or modify zone information. A value of 0 indicates that the boot file will be used.

All of the DNS server database and configuration files on a Microsoft Windows NT Server are located in the path \SYSTEMROOT\SYSTEM32\DNS. All of these files can be edited manually using a text editor. The DNS service must be stopped and restarted for the changes in the Boot file to take effect.

> **KNOW THIS**
> **Porting DNS Files**
> Microsoft DNS Server can use the DNS database, cache, boot, and other files from any other RFC-compliant DNS server. The files can be ported from another system by copying the files to \SYSTEMROOT\SYSTEM32\DNS and either modifying the Boot file or changing the registry to specify the location and file names of the DNS database files.

Adding a DNS server to DNS Manager

DNS Manager can be used to configure both the local DNS server (the one on which you are running DNS Manager) and remote DNS servers. Before you can begin to use DNS Manager with a DNS server,

173

you must first add the server to the list of DNS servers that can be managed by this DNS Manager.

> **KNOW THIS**
> **Hidden Zones**
> Ordinarily, only the cache zone is displayed in DNS Manager. The other automatically created zones are hidden because they require no administrative attention. To reveal the hidden zones, choose the Preferences command in the Options menu. Check Show Automatically Created Zones, and then press F5 to refresh the display.

Creating a DNS zone

Once you have determined the organization and hierarchy of your DNS domains and zones, you can use DNS Manager to create one or more zones. Remember: Zones are created to organize a domain into administrative groups. All DNS configuration and resource records are stored in a zone file.

When you add a new zone, you must specify whether a primary zone or secondary zone will be created. When a primary zone is created, all configuration settings and resource records are created and stored locally. If a secondary zone will be created, the configuration settings and resource records are obtained from an existing master server through a zone transfer.

You must supply a name for the primary zone. By default, the name you select for the primary zone is also used as the name for creating the zone file. The zone files are created in the *system_root*\Winnt\system32\Dns directory.

At this point, you should also create a reverse lookup zone so that you can use the automatic Create PTR Record option in the Add Host dialog box. For example, a reverse lookup zone that could contain PTR records for addresses 172.25.16.1 through 172.25.16.254 would be named 25.172.in-addr.arpa.

In addition to creating multiple zones to divide a domain, one or more subdomains can be created within a single zone.

POP QUIZ — True or False?

1. A secondary DNS server must get its zones from a primary server.
2. When a DNS server is not present, a HOSTS file can be used to provide hostname resolution.
3. HOSTS files are case sensitive.

Answers: 1. False 2. True 3. False

Adding DNS resource records

After all zones and subdomains have been created and configured, resource records can be added using DNS Manager. Information about computers in the zone is added by selecting either New Host or New Record from the context menu of the zone or subdomain. As you browse, you will notice that several resource records were created automatically. When each zone is established, DNS Manager creates the SOA, NS, and A records for the DNS server.

You must add resource records for hosts yourself. Use the New Host option to add the address (A) and pointer (PTR) records for computers in the zone. The A record is used to map a host name to an IP address in a zone. The PTR record is a counterpart record used to map the IP address to a host name in a DNS reverse zone (in the `in-addr.arpa` DNS domain).

You will use the New Record option to add additional information to the zone. Each type of resource record provides its own dialog box with options that are specific for the type of resource record selected. You can create an alias (`CNAME`) record, a mail server (`MX`) record, and so on.

KNOW THIS — Resource Records

On the test you may be asked about resource records. When you enter a host name in any resource record, as in, for example, the CNAME record For Host DNS Name

Continued

field, be sure to enter the fully qualified domain name of the host and be sure to include a trailing period. The FQDN and trailing period ensure that there is no confusion about the domain in which the name falls, and they prevent the DNS server from improperly appending the domain name to the host name you specify.

The only exception to this practice is the Host name field in the A record, where the DNS server will correctly manage the name if you specify the host name only without the zone name.

Configuring zone properties

You can configure and modify zone information to change the zone from a primary to a secondary zone; modify the TTL values, refresh, and zone transfer intervals; identify secondary servers that should be notified; and configure a zone server to use WINS for host name resolution. Properties you can figure and modify include:

- **General:** These property settings are used to change the server from a primary to a secondary name server or back. If you change it to a secondary name server, you must specify the IP address of at least one name server from which the zone transfer will be performed.
- **SOA Record:** These properties are used to edit settings in the SOA record, as shown in Figure 7-1.
- **Notify:** This tab is used to define secondary name servers that will be notified when changes are made to the database of the primary name server. This causes the secondary name servers to initiate a zone transfer to copy the changed database. You must enter the IP addresses of each secondary name server to be notified. To allow only the specified secondary servers to request zone transfer requests, check Only Allow Access From Secondaries Included on Notify List.

7: DOMAIN NAME SYSTEM

- **WINS Lookup:** This tab is used to set properties for using WINS as a method of host name resolution. If the Use WINS Resolution checkbox is selected, then a special resource record will be added to the zone database to specify that WINS should be used to resolve host names that cannot be resolved by the DNS server. You must also specify the IP address of each WINS server that will be used for name resolution.

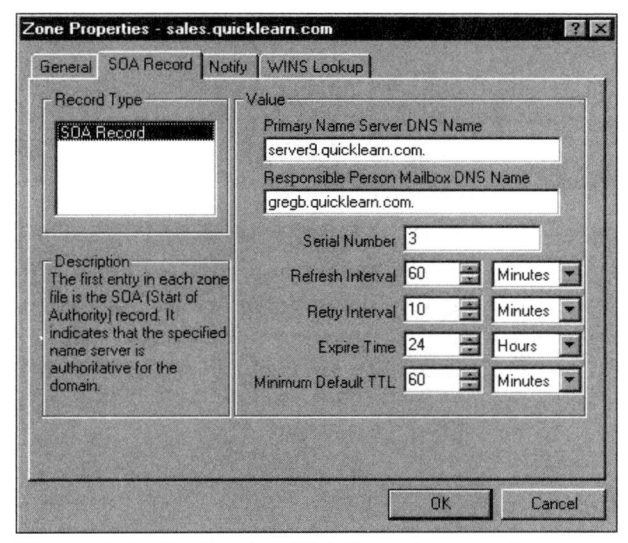

Figure 7-1 *Configuring SOA Record properties*

These settings are summarized as follows:

- **Primary Name Server DNS Name:** The fully qualified domain name (such as `server1.quicklearn.com`) of the server host (computer) that is the original or primary source of data for this DNS zone.

- **Responsible Person Mailbox DNS Name:** A DNS name that specifies the mail address of the person in charge of this DNS zone. The mail address is in standard DNS fully qualified domain name (FQDN) format. For example, the mail address gregb@quicklearn.com would be represented in DNS FQDN format as gregb.quicklearn.com, where you substitute a period (.) for the at character (@).

- **Serial Number:** The trigger that enables DNS zone transfers between primary and secondary DNS name servers. In preparation for a zone transfer, a secondary name server contacts a primary name server and requests the serial number of the primary's zone data. The secondary compares the serial number of its current copy of the zone data with the serial number from the primary. If the primary's is larger (indicating that the secondary's zone data is out of date), the secondary transfers a new copy of the zone data from the primary.
- **Refresh Interval:** Tells the secondary DNS name server(s) how often to check the accuracy of their data.
- **Retry Interval:** If a secondary DNS name server fails to connect to the primary DNS name server after the Refresh Interval has expired, Retry Interval tells the secondary DNS name server how often to try to reconnect. Normally, the Retry Interval is shorter than the Refresh Interval.
- **Expire Time:** If a secondary DNS name server fails to contact the primary DNS name server for Expire Time, the secondary stops responding to queries about the data because the data may be invalid. (The secondary expires the data.)
- **Minimum Default TTL:** When a DNS name server responds to a DNS query, along with the data, the name server supplies a minimum default TTL interval. The TTL interval indicates how long the receiving name server is allowed to cache the data from the query.

7: DOMAIN NAME SYSTEM

> **KNOW THIS**
>
> ### Zone Transfers
>
> Zone transfers normally occur during system startup and periodically as configured by the interval settings described above. For faster response in updating the secondary servers when changes have occurred, the primary server can be configured to notify the secondary servers when changes have occurred. When zone changes have occurred, a notification will be sent to all secondary servers whose IP addresses are specified in the notify list. This can be useful to know for the test when you are asked about ways to make things work more efficiently.

Configuring forwarders and slaves

In nonexclusive mode, when a DNS server receives a request that it cannot process using its local zone files, it passes the request to the first designated forwarder. If the forwarder is unsuccessful in resolving the query, the DNS server that originally received the query can attempt to resolve the query on its own.

In exclusive mode, the same process occurs, except when the forwarder is unsuccessful, the DNS server that originally received the request cannot resolve the query on its own. The requesting DNS server in exclusive mode is called a *slave*. A slave must return a query failure message back to the requesting computer when the forwarder cannot resolve the query.

Using the Nslookup Utility

Nslookup is a useful utility that is used to troubleshoot DNS problems, such as host name resolution, by querying a DNS server for information. When nslookup is started, it will show the host name and IP address of the DNS server that the local host is configured to use, and then display a command prompt.

179

Nslookup command reference

The command syntax for nslookup is as follows:

`nslookup` [-option . . .] [host name | - [server]]

The `nslookup` utility lets you query Internet domain name servers. The utility has two modes: interactive and noninteractive. In interactive mode, you can query name servers for information about various hosts and domains or print a list of hosts in a domain. In noninteractive mode, `nslookup` just prints the name and requested information for a host or domain.

The utility enters interactive mode when:

- No arguments are given (the default name server will be used).
- The first argument is a hyphen (-) and the second argument is the host name or Internet address of a name server.

The utility enters noninteractive mode when the first argument is the name or Internet address of the host to be looked up. The optional second argument specifies the host name or address of a name server.

Interactive commands

Interactive commands can be specified on the command line if they precede the arguments and are prefixed with a hyphen.

To interrupt a command at any time, press Ctrl+C. To exit, press Ctrl+D (end of file) or type `exit`. To treat a built-in command as a host name, place an escape character (\) before the command.

Note that the length of the command line must be less than 256 characters. Any unrecognized command will be interpreted as a host name.

7: DOMAIN NAME SYSTEM

Have You Mastered?

Now it's time to review the concepts in this chapter and apply your knowledge. These questions will test your mastery of material covered in this chapter.

1. Which of the following is a resolver?

- ☐ A. DNS server
- ☐ B. DNS client
- ☐ C. Host computer
- ☐ D. Router

B. A DNS client is known as a resolver. See the "DNS Overview" section.

2. What is the highest-level domain?

- ☐ A. Second-level
- ☐ B. First-level
- ☐ C. Top-level
- ☐ D. Root

D. The top level of a DNS name is the root. See the "Domains" section.

MCSE TCP/IP ACE IT!

3. **Which server is the source of zone information for a secondary server?**

    ☐ A. Primary server
    ☐ B. Secondary server
    ☐ C. Zone server
    ☐ D. Master server

   D. The master server is the source of zone information; it can be either a primary or a secondary server. See the "Zones" section.

4. **Host aliases are established using which record type?**

    ☐ A. Name server
    ☐ B. Address
    ☐ C. CNAME
    ☐ D. MX

   C. CNAME records are used to establish an alias. See the "Database Files and Resource Records" section.

5. **What is a DNS database file known as?**

    ☐ A. Record
    ☐ B. Zone
    ☐ C. BOOT file
    ☐ D. Forwarder

   B. DNS database files are known as zones. See the "Zones" section.

7: DOMAIN NAME SYSTEM

Practice Your Skills

The following exercises provide you with a practical opportunity to apply the knowledge you've gained in this chapter.

1. Implementing Microsoft DNS Server

EXERCISE You are planning to implement Microsoft DNS Server for your organization. Your organization has 500 computers at the company's headquarters and 200 computers each at two remote locations. There is a high-speed communications link between each of the locations. You want to create a single domain to provide DNS services for all locations. What should be the role of the DNS server at the company's headquarters? What should be the role of the DNS servers at the remote locations?

ANALYSIS To create a single domain to provide DNS services for all locations, the DNS server at the company headquarters should be a primary DNS server, and the servers at all remote locations should be secondary servers.

2. Configuring a DNS server that does not perform zone transfers

EXERCISE You want to add an additional DNS server for the existing domain at the company's headquarters. You do not want this server to perform zone transfers with the existing primary DNS server. How should you configure the new DNS server?

ANALYSIS To prevent an additional DNS server from performing zone transfers, you should configure it as a caching-only server.

3. Configuring a DNS server to resolve requests for Internet resources

EXERCISE You are planning to connect your company's network to the Internet. You have installed one primary DNS server and one secondary DNS server. You want to install a new DNS server that will be used to resolve a DNS request for a resource that exists on the Internet. How must you do this? You want to prevent the existing DNS servers from attempting to resolve the DNS request when the new server is unsuccessful. How must you do this? What must be specified on the existing DNS servers to enable them to use the new DNS server configured as a forwarder?

ANALYSIS To install a new DNS server that will resolve a request for a resource that exists on the Internet, configure it as a forwarder. To prevent the existing DNS servers from resolving the DNS request when the new server is unsuccessful, configure each server as a slave (exclusive mode). To enable existing DNS servers to use a new server as a forwarder, the IP address of the new server must be configured as a forwarder.

4. Configuring a secondary DNS server

EXERCISE You currently have a Microsoft DNS server installed on your network. You want to install a second Microsoft DNS server that will be configured as a secondary name server. After installing Microsoft DNS on the second server, how must you configure the server to become a secondary DNS server?

ANALYSIS To configure a new server as a secondary DNS server, you must create a secondary zone and specify the IP address of the name server that this secondary server will use for zone transfers.

5. Configuring the DNS zone transfer frequency

EXERCISE You want to configure your DNS servers so that a secondary name server receives updates as soon as changes have been made to records on the primary name server. How can you do this?

ANALYSIS To allow a secondary server to receive immediate updates of changes to records on the primary name server, you need to configure the primary server to send a notification to all secondary name servers when changes have been made to the primary.

6. Configuring a reverse lookup record

EXERCISE Your company uses an application that requires the resolution of an IP address to a hostname. How can you configure the DNS server to support this?

ANALYSIS To configure the DNS server to support the resolution of an IP address to a hostname, create an associated PTR record for each host record in the zone.

IP Address Resolution

THIS CHAPTER COVERS ADDRESS *resolution* — how a host determines the hardware address for a destination host when all it knows about the destination host is its TCP/IP address. Address resolution occurs using the ARP protocol. Be sure you are familiar with ARP and how it works when two hosts reside on the same subnet, and how it works when two hosts reside on different subnets.

MCSE TCP/IP ACE IT!

Exam Material in This Chapter

Official Word

Based on Microsoft Objectives
- Understand IP address resolution.
- Use the `arp` command.
- Troubleshoot IP resolution issues.

Inside Scoop

Based on Author's Experience
- ARP cache
- Address resolution
- Troubleshooting duplicate addresses
- Troubleshooting subnet masks

8: IP ADDRESS RESOLUTION

Are You Prepared?

Take the following short quiz to test your knowledge of this subject. If you have problems with any of the questions, you'll be able to identify areas where further review is necessary.

1. **What is the command used to view the ARP cache?**

    - ☐ A. `arp`
    - ☐ B. `arp -s`
    - ☐ C. `arp -a`
    - ☐ D. `arp -d`

2. **What is the command used to add a static mapping to the ARP cache?**

    - ☐ A. `arp`
    - ☐ B. `arp -s`
    - ☐ C. `arp -a`
    - ☐ D. `arp -d`

3. **What is the command used to delete a mapping from the ARP cache?**

    - ☐ A. `arp`
    - ☐ B. `arp -s`
    - ☐ C. `arp -a`
    - ☐ D. `arp -d`

Answers:

1. C See the "arp Utility" section.
2. B See the "arp Utility" section.
3. D See the "arp Utility" section.

The Address Resolution Protocol (ARP)

TCP/IP addressing is based on hardware-independent IP addresses. A TCP/IP host can be identified by an IP address regardless of whether it is attached to a token ring, an Ethernet, or an X.25 network. IP addresses uniquely identify hosts and incorporate network IDs that facilitate routing. From the Internet layer, IP addresses provide the mechanism for identifying hosts and for routing data through the network.

At some point, however, data must be delivered through the physical network to the network interface of a destination host. At the network level, hosts are identified not by IP addresses but by hardware addresses, and these hardware addresses provide the mechanism for delivering the data through the network to the target host. Consequently, when IP gets to the point of sending data to the network, it cannot rely entirely on IP addresses. To accomplish delivery, IP must have a way to determine the hardware address of the target host. Hosts do not automatically have access to lists of host hardware addresses. Instead, there must be a procedure for learning hardware addresses from hosts on the network.

The *Address Resolution Protocol* (ARP) enables IP to learn the hardware address of a host associated with a given IP address. The hardware ARP is a required part of any IP implementation.

ARP functions are divided into two tasks: determining the hardware address of a destination host when sending a packet, and answering requests from other hosts requesting a hardware address.

The following sequential events take place when a host attempts to send a datagram:

1. IP calls ARP with a request for the hardware address of the destination host.

2. ARP creates an ARP request frame, which requests the hardware address associated with an IP address. The ARP request frame includes the following information:
   - The sender's hardware address
   - The sender's IP address

191

- The target's IP address

3. The ARP request frame broadcasts the hardware address on the local network.

4. All hosts on the network receive the ARP request frame and attempt to match the IP address in the frame with their own. Hosts with addresses that do not match discard the frame.

5. If a host finds that its IP address matches the IP address in the ARP request frame, it generates an ARP reply frame that incorporates the hardware address of the replying host.

6. The ARP reply frame is sent directly to the host that generated the ARP request. (The ARP reply frame is not broadcast.) The ARP reply includes the following information:

- The sender's hardware address
- The sender's IP address
- The target's hardware address
- The target's IP address

KNOW THIS: ARPing Across Subnets

The destination host must reside on the local network. ARP cannot be used to determine the hardware address of a host on a remote network because broadcasts are not propagated across IP routers. But there is no need for the hardware address of a remote host. If the target host resides on a distant network, IP sends the datagram to a router for forwarding. In that case, IP uses ARP to determine the hardware address of the router that will escort the datagram on its way.

When a destination host resides on a remote network, a datagram cannot be transmitted directly to the host, and the source host does not attempt to discover the hardware address of the remote host. Instead, the source host uses ARP to discover the hardware address of a router that can forward the datagram. The source host then transmits the datagram to the router using the router's hardware address.

8: IP ADDRESS RESOLUTION

TEST TIP
Troubleshooting is an important part of managing a TCP/IP network. Address resolution problems are a common difficulty. The TCP/IP exam includes questions that test your knowledge of how to use troubleshooting tools, such as `arp`, to solve common address resolution problems. You should fully understand how ARP works and how the `arp` utility can be used to help you diagnose problems.

The ARP Cache

Broadcasts are costly because every host on the network must perform some processing to determine whether they should respond to or ignore the broadcast message. To minimize the number of broadcasts necessary to perform address resolution, each host maintains a local table called the *ARP cache*. The ARP cache contains a list of the most recent IP address-to-hardware address mappings. When the source host for an ARP request receives a reply, the address mapping is stored in the host's ARP cache. The replying host also stores an address mapping for the source host, on the assumption that the source host is preparing to communicate and the destination host will need to reply.

ARP always examines its cache for an IP address-to-hardware address mapping before initiating a broadcast to request a hardware address. Because the ARP cache is maintained in temporary memory, it must be dynamically created each time the computer or router is restarted.

ARP Cache Aging

Entries in the ARP cache have a limited lifetime. Different implementations of TCP/IP use different time-out values. Sometimes the time-out value is as short as 30 seconds; another implementation may retain ARP entries for as long as several hours. The shorter the time, the more ARP broadcasts need to occur. Longer cache times can cause problems if the target host has changed its Ethernet address (installed a new network adapter).

For Windows NT computers, the ARP cache entries expire after two minutes if they have not been used. Hosts examine all ARP broadcasts, regardless of which IP address the ARP broadcast was requesting. The mapping is placed in the ARP cache with a *time-to-live* (TTL) value of two minutes. If the mapped entry is not accessed within 2 minutes, it will be purged from the cache.

If ARP references a cached entry within two minutes, the TTL is adjusted so the entry will remain in the cache for ten minutes. When a host uses a cached entry to find the hardware address of a destination host, the TTL is increased to ten minutes. Because the hardware address for the destination host is found in the ARP cache, a datagram can be sent immediately, so an ARP request is not necessary.

If the ARP cache reaches its maximum capacity before an entry expires, the oldest entries are deleted as new ones are added.

ArpCacheLife

For Windows NT computers, a registry parameter, `ArpCacheLife`, enables more administrative control over aging time. In the absence of an `ArpCacheLife` parameter, the default for ARP cache time-outs is a two-minute time-out on unused entries, and a ten-minute time-out on used entries as described above. Adding this parameter and setting a value in seconds overrides both default values. You must add the `ArpCacheLife` to the Registry to affect ARP cache activity. The entry should be placed in the following Registry key:

`HKEY_LOCAL_MACHINE\SYSTEM\CurrentControlSet\Services\Tcpip\Parameters`

Static ARP Entries

When a host computer is making frequent ARP requests to a specific host, it is possible to create a static entry in the ARP cache so that the mapping stays in the cache permanently (does not age). This eliminates the need to perform repetitive broadcasts to the same host. However, problems can occur if an IP address is later changed for a host or a new network adapter is installed.

8: IP ADDRESS RESOLUTION

Static entries remain until one of the following occurs:
- The mapping is deleted manually using the arp utility.
- The host is restarted.
- The host receives a broadcast containing a different hardware address for the static entry that is currently in the cache. When this happens, the new hardware address is updated with the new value and the entry type is changed to dynamic.

The arp Utility

You can view and manage the ARP cache using the arp utility. This diagnostic command displays and modifies the IP address-to-hardware address translation tables used by ARP. The arp utility can be used to view and modify the ARP cache only on the local computer. The arp command syntax is as follows:

arp -a [*inet_addr*] [**-N** [*if_addr*]]
arp -d *inet_addr* [*if_addr*]
arp -s *inet_addr phys_addr* [*if_addr*]

The fields are defined as follows:

-a	Displays current ARP entries in the ARP cache. If *inet_addr* is specified, only the IP and hardware addresses for the specified computer are displayed.
-d	Deletes from the ARP cache the entry specified by *inet_addr*.
-s	Adds an entry in the ARP cache to associate the IP address *inet_addr* with the hardware address *ether_addr*. The hardware address is specified as six hexadecimal bytes and must be separated by hyphens. The IP address must be specified using dotted decimal notation. This creates a permanent entry; that is, it will not be automatically removed from the ARP cache after the time-out expires.

195

-N [if_addr]	Displays the ARP entries for the network interface specified by if_addr. This is used to view ARP entries on a specific network interface for computers with multiple network interfaces (multihomed computers).
phys_addr	Specifies a hardware address. A hardware address must be entered in hexadecimal form and must contain hyphens between the bytes, for example, 0A-11-3B-12-44-AC.
if_addr	Specifies, if necessary, the IP address of the specific interface for which the address translation table is to be modified. If an address is not specified, the first applicable interface will be used.
inet_addr	Specifies an IP address using dotted decimal notation.

Hardware Address Resolution Methods

The method ARP uses to resolve an IP address to a hardware address differs slightly, depending on whether the destination host resides on the same subnet (local resolution) or a different subnet (remote resolution).

TEST TIP Understanding the steps required to resolve an IP address for both local and remote hosts is important for troubleshooting and configuring TCP/IP. You will find several questions related to this topic on the exam.

Local IP Address Resolution

ARP works to resolve an IP address on a local subnet using the following process:

1. **Check local cache.** When attempting to determine the hardware address of a destination host on the same subnet, ARP first checks the local ARP cache to see if it contains an IP address-to-hardware address mapping for the destination host.

   If it does, it extracts the hardware address for the destination host and places the data directly into a frame for transmission. No ARP broadcasts are required because the hardware address had been cached from a previous session.

2. **Send an ARP request for the destination host.** If the mapping is not found in the ARP cache, the host must broadcast an ARP request and wait for a reply. The ARP request contains the sender's IP address and hardware address. The ARP request also contains the IP address of the host with which the sender wants to communicate.

   Broadcasting an ARP request to find an address mapping can become complex. ARP broadcasts cannot directly pass through a router and are subject to delays due to network traffic or the destination host may be too busy to accept the request.

3. **Cache the ARP request.** Because the ARP request is a broadcast on the subnet, each host on the network accepts the packet and compares its configured IP address to the IP address specified in the ARP request. If the requested hardware address does not match the hardware address of the receiving host, the ARP request is ignored; if the requested hardware address does match the receiving host's hardware address, the receiving host updates its local ARP cache.

4. **ARP response is sent to source host.** If an exact match occurs during the ARP request, the destination host sends back an ARP reply to the sending host (not a broadcast because the hardware address of the sender is now known).

5. **Source host updates its ARP cache.** The source host updates its own cache to include the IP address-to-hardware address mapping for the destination host. At this point, ARP has

performed all resolution steps and communications can now be established between the two host computers.

Remote IP Address Resolution

If the destination host resides on a different subnet than the source host, the method of address resolution is slightly different. This is because ARP broadcasts do not pass through routers. When there are several routers between the source and destination hosts, ARP must resolve the IP address for each successive hop (router) hat the IP datagram passes through.

For any datagram that is to be sent to a remote subnet, ARP at the source host must determine the hardware address of the default gateway (router).

When the IP datagram reaches the router, the router determines if the destination host resides on a locally attached subnet or a remote subnet. If the destination hosts resides on a local subnet, an ARP request is used to determine the hardware address of the destination host.

If the destination host resides on a subnet remote to the router, a series of ARP requests and replies continue on each subnet until the datagram reaches the destination host. Keep in mind that ARP requests are sent as broadcasts and ARP replies are sent directly back to the source host because its hardware address was contained in the broadcast.

The following process shows how a remote IP address is resolved:

1. **Check local cache.** When attempting to determine the hardware address of a destination host on a remote subnet, ARP first checks the local ARP cache to see if it contains a mapping for the default gateway (Router Port A).

   If it does, it extracts the hardware address for the router port and places the data directly into a frame for transmission. In other words, no ARP broadcasts need to occur to resolve the known IP address (assuming a default gateway address was configured on the host) because the hardware address had been cached from a previous session. The hosts on a subnet

8: IP ADDRESS RESOLUTION

will often already have a cached entry for the default gateway if the router is being used regularly.

2. **Send ARP request for the default gateway.** If the mapping for the router is not found in the ARP cache, the host must broadcast an ARP request for the default gateway and wait for a reply. The ARP request contains the sender's IP address and hardware address, as well as the IP address of the default gateway on the subnet.

3. **Caching the ARP request.** Because the ARP request is a broadcast on the subnet, each host on the network accepts the packet and compares its configured IP address to the IP address specified in the ARP request. If the requested IP address does not match the host's configured IP address, the ARP request is ignored. If the host's IP address (the router in this case) does match the requested IP address, the host updates its local ARP cache.

The router, just like any other host, will also cache a mapping for the source host. But because the router has multiple network adapter ports, the cache is maintained separately for each port.

4. **ARP response is sent to the source host.** The router sends back an ARP response to the sending host (not a broadcast because the hardware address of the sender is now known).

5. **The source host updates its ARP cache.** The source host updates its own cache to include the IP address-to-hardware address mapping for the router. At this point ARP has performed all resolution steps in order for the host to communicate with the router. But the connection to the FTP server has not been completed. Next, the router must be able to communicate with the host computer on the remote Subnet B.

6. **The datagram is routed to Subnet B.** Now that the datagram containing the `ftp` command is sent to the router, the router needs to determine the interface through which it passes the message — in this case, the interface connected to Subnet B. The router determines the interface by looking at the IP address for the destination host computer in the IP packet.

199

7. **Send ARP request for the destination host.** If the mapping for the destination host is not found in the ARP cache on the router, the router must broadcast an ARP request and wait for a reply. The ARP request contains the router's IP address and hardware address, as well as the IP address for the destination host.

8. **All hosts receive the ARP request.** Because the ARP request is a broadcast on the Subnet B, each host on the network accepts the packet and compares its configured IP address to the IP address specified in the ARP request. If a hardware address does not match, the host discards the ARP request; if the hardware address does match, the host discards the ARP request and takes no further action.

9. **ARP response is sent to the router.** The target host sends back an ARP response to the router (not a broadcast because the hardware address of the router is now known). After receiving the response, the router updates its cache to include the mapping for the destination computer on Subnet B.

10. **The datagram is routed to the source host.** Finally, the datagram originating from the remote host is sent by the router to the source host. At this point, ARP has performed all resolution steps and communications can now be established between the two host computers.

Troubleshooting Address Resolution Problems

The most common problems associated with address resolution are duplicate IP addresses, invalid subnet masks, and invalid static ARP entries.

TEST TIP The exam includes a number of questions relating to troubleshooting. You should be familiar with the methods and tools used to diagnose and solve address resolution problems.

Duplicate IP Addresses

When a duplicate IP address exists on the network, hosts may respond to an ARP broadcast that causes an incorrect IP address-to-hardware address mapping to be added to the ARP cache. This will prevent two hosts from communicating and can cause them to *hang* (stop responding). A duplicate address can be especially critical if the duplicate address is that of a router. This may prevent any communications outside of the subnet.

Duplicate IP address detection is an important and valuable feature of ARP. When the TCP/IP protocols are first initialized on a Windows NT computer, an ARP request is broadcast for the IP address(es) of the local host. If another computer replies, this indicates that the IP address is already in use.

When this happens, the Windows NT computer will still start; however, TCP/IP will be disabled, a system log will be generated, and an error message will be displayed, as shown in Figure 8-1. If the computer "defending" its IP address (attempting to protect its IP address from being used by another host) is also a Windows NT computer, a message will also be displayed there. The defending computer will also send an ARP request for its own address so that other hosts will be updated to contain the correct mapping in their ARP cache.

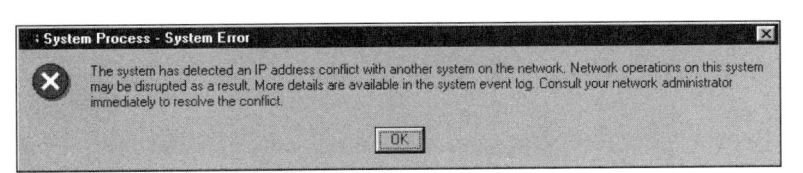

> **System Process - System Error**
> The system has detected an IP address conflict with another system on the network. Network operations on this system may be disrupted as a result. More details are available in the system event log. Consult your network administrator immediately to resolve the conflict.
> [OK]

Figure 8-1 *Detecting a duplicate IP address*

On each Windows NT computer, ARP attempts to prevent duplicate IP addresses by challenging any ARP request that would result in a duplicate address. Figure 8-2 shows a sample of an event log entry.

MCSE TCP/IP ACE IT!

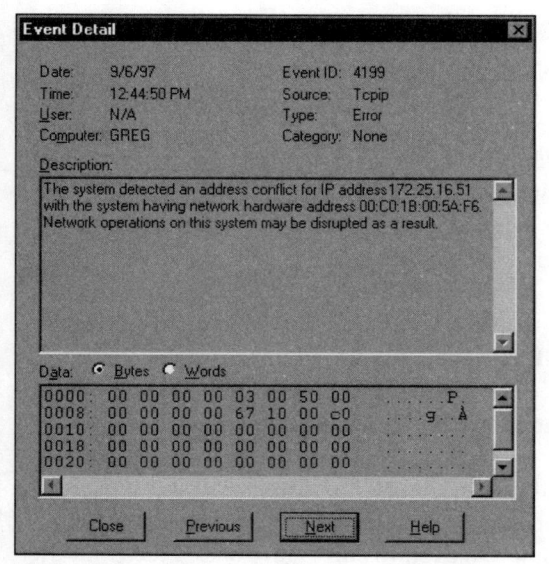

Figure 8-2 *Duplicate address error as shown in the event log*

POP QUIZ **True or False?**

1. ARP is used to resolve host names.
2. DNS and ARP can work together to ensure delivery of data using IP.
3. The ARP cache is cleared when the computer is rebooted.

Answers: 1. False 2. True 3. True

Invalid Subnet Masks

As described in Chapter 3, TCP/IP software uses the subnet mask to determine if the two IP addresses exist on the same or different subnets. If the subnet mask has been configured incorrectly on a host, that host may think a destination host exists on the same subnet, when it actually exists on a different subnet. This can result in excessive broadcasts as the host unsuccessfully attempts to discover the hardware address of the destination host.

If many hosts are attempting to send broadcasts at the same time, a broadcast storm can occur. Broadcast storms can decrease performance and cause hosts to stop responding.

Often, such problems will not be noticeable without the use of a network monitoring tool, such as Microsoft's Network Monitor.

Invalid Static ARP Entries

By creating a static entry in the ARP cache, you can speed up performance to heavily used IP resources, such as routers and servers located on the same subnet. If the hardware address of the destination host has changed, however, you will not be able to connect to that host. An invalid ARP mapping would create "Request timed out" errors when using the `ping` command. However, the entry would be corrected the next time an ARP broadcast is sent from the destination host.

Troubleshooting Tools

The `Ipconfig` utility, the `arp` utility, and the `ping` utility can help you solve address resolutions problems. Use `Ipconfig` to verify TCP/IP configuration settings; use the `arp` utility to view the current ARP cache entries; and use `ping` to verify communications between two hosts.

MCSE TCP/IP ACE IT!

Have You Mastered?

Now it's time to review the concepts in this chapter and apply your knowledge. These questions will test your mastery of material covered in this chapter.

1. **When an ARP request locates the destination on the local subnet, where is the reply frame sent?**

    ☐ A. To the router
    ☐ B. To the sender
    ☐ C. To the target
    ☐ D. To the server

    B. Reply frames are sent to the sender of the ARP request. See the "Address Resolution Protocol (ARP)" section.

2. **Which of the following is not included in the ARP reply information?**

    ☐ A. The sender's IP address
    ☐ B. The sender's gateway
    ☐ C. The sender's hardware address
    ☐ D. The target's hardware address

    B. The sender's gateway is not included in the ARP reply information. See the "Address Resolution Protocol (ARP)" section.

8: IP ADDRESS RESOLUTION

3. **When computer A pings computer B, what does ARP do first to resolve the IP address?**
   - ☐ A. Checks the local cache
   - ☐ B. Sends an ARP request to the destination
   - ☐ C. Caches the request
   - ☐ D. Sends an ARP request to the local gateway

A. Regardless of whether the destination is on the local or remote subnet, ARP checks the local cache first. See the "Troubleshooting Tools" section.

MCSE TCP/IP ACE IT!

Practice Your Skills

The following exercises provide you with a practical opportunity to apply the knowledge you've gained in this chapter.

1. Using ARP to resolve an IP address for a host on a local subnet

EXERCISE You are working on a Windows NT workstation computer. You use Windows NT Explorer to connect to a Windows NT server computer on the same subnet. The TCP/IP address of the server is resolved to a hardware address. How many ARP broadcasts will be required before you can connect to the server? Suppose you are unable to connect to the server. All other users on the subnet can connect successfully. Using Network Monitor, you determine that the workstation is sending an ARP request to the default gateway instead of the server. Why might this be happening?

ANALYSIS One ARP broadcast is required, which is used to resolve the IP address of the server. The IP address of the server is not within the range of addresses for the same subnet as the workstation. This is normally caused by an incorrect subnet mask on the workstation.

8: IP ADDRESS RESOLUTION

2. Using ARP to resolve an IP address for a host on a remote subnet

EXERCISE Your network consists of two subnets. You are working on a Windows NT workstation computer. You use Windows NT Explorer to connect to a Windows NT server computer on the remote subnet. The TCP/IP address of the server is resolved to a hardware address. How many ARP broadcasts will be required before you can connect to the server? In which case would an ARP broadcast not be necessary in order for the workstation to communicate with the server? How can you determine which ARP entries are currently cached on the workstation? Suppose you want to prevent your workstation from having to send out an ARP broadcast every time you need to communicate with the default gateway. How can you do this?

ANALYSIS Two ARP broadcasts are required. First, your computer needs to resolve the hardware address of the default gateway (router). Second, the router on the remote subnet needs to resolve the hardware address of the server. The broadcast would not be necessary when the ARP cache already contains the resolved IP address from a previous ARP request. Determine which ARP entries are cached by typing `arp -a` from a command line. You can prevent your workstation from having to send out an ARP broadcast every time by adding a static entry to the ARP cache by using the `arp -a` command.

9

NetBIOS Name Resolution

THE DOTTED DECIMAL NOTATION described in previous chapters is the method used to uniquely identify all networking devices on a TCP/IP network. However, it is not the most user-friendly way of referring to network servers and peer computers; *NetBIOS* is. This chapter describes how NetBIOS works to provide name registration and name resolution for Microsoft-based clients.

MCSE TCP/IP ACE IT!

Exam Material in This Chapter

Official Word

Based on Microsoft Objectives
- Configure HOSTS and LMHOSTS files.

Inside Scoop

Based on Author's Experience
- NetBIOS
- NetBIOS name resolution
- b-node name resolution
- p-node name resolution
- m-node name resolution
- h-node name resolution
- LMHOSTS file
- Nbtstat

Are You Prepared?

Test your knowledge with the following questions, which will reveal if you're prepared for the material covered in this chapter, or if you should review problem areas.

1. **Which resolution method uses only broadcasts to resolve NetBIOS names?**

    - ☐ A. b-node
    - ☐ B. p-node
    - ☐ C. m-node
    - ☐ D. h-node

2. **Which resolution method uses broadcast first and then a name server to resolve NetBIOS names?**

    - ☐ A. b-node
    - ☐ B. p-node
    - ☐ C. m-node
    - ☐ D. h-node

3. **Which resolution method uses a name server first and then broadcast to resolve NetBIOS names?**

    - ☐ A. b-node
    - ☐ B. p-node
    - ☐ C. m-node
    - ☐ D. h-node

Answers:

1. A   *See the "Standard NetBT Name Resolution Modes" section.*
2. C   *See the "Standard NetBT Name Resolution Modes" section.*
3. D   *See the "Standard NetBT Name Resolution Modes" section.*

What Is NetBIOS?

NetBIOS was designed to provide services that applications could use to communicate over a network. NetBIOS was eventually included as a standard or optional component in almost every network operating system. Thousands of user applications and many of the core components of networking operating systems, including Microsoft operating systems, have been designed to use NetBIOS services.

One of the important features of NetBIOS is its capability to use "friendly" names with which people can connect to network resources. It is the networking components running in the background on a client computer that are responsible for dealing with the complex numbering systems used at the lowest layers of network communications. NetBIOS enables users to connect to computers using names such as Server1, Accounting, or Sales.

NetBIOS Components

NetBIOS consists of two major components:

- **The NetBIOS interface:** Provides a standard *applications programming interface* (API) that applications can use to communicate with the underlying network protocol. The API enables applications to register and use names over the network, to manage sessions between two computers, and to send datagrams to one or more computers that are listening to a registered name.

- **The NetBIOS protocol:** Specifies a method of passing network I/O requests to underlying protocols such as TCP/IP. The Windows NT implementation of NetBIOS over TCP/IP is referred to as *NetBT* (and sometimes as NBT).

NetBIOS Naming Services

To remain compatible with the many network services and applications in use today, NetBIOS support is an important requirement in

Windows-based operating systems. Windows NT services, such as Workstation, Server, Browser, Messenger, and Netlogon services, use NetBIOS.

Each Windows NT computer running NetBT on a network requires a unique IP address and a unique computer name (also called the *NetBIOS name*). Mechanisms must be available on a TCP/IP network to match a computer name to an IP address. These mechanisms are called *NetBIOS name resolution services*.

The NetBIOS interface is responsible for establishing logical names on the network, establishing connections (called *sessions*) between two logical names on the network, and supporting reliable data transfer between computers that have established a session. The most important aspects of naming activities are:

- NetBIOS name registration
- NetBIOS name resolution
- NetBIOS name release

TEST TIP
NetBIOS name resolution problems are typically the result of configuration errors. The TCP/IP exam will test your knowledge of the NetBIOS name resolution process and the methods and tools used to diagnose problems.

NetBIOS name registration

NetBIOS services use special names to identify themselves on a network. Each service registers a unique name consisting of 1 to 16 characters (no other workstation on the network may have the same name as another computer, domain, or workgroup). The user or an administrator specifies the first 15 characters of a NetBIOS name on a computer to assign it a unique *computer name*. The sixteenth character of the NetBIOS name contains a hexadecimal value that is used to indicate the type of NetBIOS name.

TEST TRAP NetBIOS names (also known as *computer names*) should not be confused with DNS or host names. The two types of naming systems are independent of one another. Understanding this will help avoid confusion when taking the test.

The two main classes of NetBIOS name types are *unique names* and *group names*. NetBIOS names that are registered as unique belong to one owner. NetBIOS names that are registered as group names belong to multiple owners.

KNOW THIS **Checking Name Registration**
To see which names a Windows 95 or Windows NT computer has registered over NetBT, go to a command prompt and type `nbtstat -n`.

When a NetBIOS over TCP/IP client computer starts, it registers its NetBIOS name using a special *name registration request*. The name registration request either occurs as a broadcast or is directed to a NetBIOS name server, such as WINS.

NetBIOS name resolution

During the registration process, it may be discovered that another host has already registered the same NetBIOS name. In that case, the computer attempting to register the duplicate NetBIOS name receives a negative name registration response and fails to load any services that require the NetBIOS name.

NetBIOS name resolution is the process of successfully mapping a computer's NetBIOS name to an IP address. When a Windows-based computer wants to communicate with another computer, it uses a NetBIOS name query request to locate the other destination computer.

With Windows NT, Microsoft has introduced a NetBIOS name resolution service that automatically maintains a name-to-IP address mappings database that can be consulted by Microsoft network clients. This name service, the *Windows Internet Name Service* (WINS), greatly simplifies the task of supporting NetBIOS name resolution.

NetBIOS name release

When a NetBIOS application or service stops working (the computer shuts down or the service is stopped), the computer will no longer respond with a *negative name registration response* to requests from other computers that attempt to register the same name. The NetBIOS name is said to be *released* and available to be used by another computer.

Windows NetBIOS Name Resolution

Beginning with Windows NT 4.0, Microsoft has significantly enhanced the NetBIOS name resolution methods that are available to Windows-based computers. Microsoft TCP/IP now supports additional methods of resolving NetBIOS computer names.

Standard NetBT Name Resolution Modes

NetBIOS name resolution order depends on the node type and computer configuration. The node types in Table 9-1 are supported.

TABLE 9-1 NetBIOS node types

NetBIOS name resolution node type	Description
b-node	Uses an IP broadcast to register and resolve NetBIOS names to IP addresses. Windows-based computers use *modified b-node* name resolution, which also includes the capability to use a local LMHOSTS file that contains NetBIOS-to-IP-address mappings.
p-node	Uses point-to-point communications with a NetBIOS name server (a WINS, server for example) to register and resolve computer names to IP addresses.

9: NETBIOS NAME RESOLUTION

NetBIOS name resolution node type	Description
m-node	Uses a combination of b-node and p-node communications to register and resolve NetBIOS names. M-node first attempts to use b-node; then, if that is unsuccessful, it attempts p-node. M-node is usually not recommended for larger networks because its preference for b-node broadcasts increases network traffic.
h-node	Uses a combination of b-node and p-node. When a client has been configured to use h-node, it always tries p-node first and uses b-node *only* after p-node fails. When a Windows NT-based computer is configured as a WINS client, it will be configured by default as h-node.

b-node name resolution

The b-node (broadcast) mode relies on broadcast messages for name registration and resolution. The b-node resolution method works like this:

1. If a computer named Wksta1 wants to communicate with a server named Server1, Wksta1 first checks its local cache to see if it already has an address mapping for the NetBIOS name. This helps to reduce broadcasts on the network if the two devices communicate regularly.

2. If the NetBIOS name is not found in the cache, the Wksta1 broadcasts a name query on the network for the computer named Server1.

3. All computers on the subnet receive the broadcast request, but only the computer with the matching NetBIOS name will respond.

4. Once the IP address of Server1 is known, Wksta1 can take the additional steps necessary to resolve the IP address to a physical address using ARP.

The two major disadvantages of b-node are:

- On large networks, b-node loads the network with many broadcast messages.
- Routers do not forward broadcast messages, so computers on different subnets will never hear the requests. Consequently, b-node name resolution works only on networks consisting of a single network segment.

Microsoft uses an enhanced version of b-node to resolve NetBIOS names to IP addresses. In the previous example, after Step 3, if the broadcast attempt for `Server1` fails, the local LMHOSTS file is checked for a matching NetBIOS name. If a mapping is found in LMHOSTS, resolution is successful and the process of resolving the IP address to a physical address is carried out.

> **TEST TRAP**
>
> For the test, remember: To use the LMHOSTS file with Windows NT 4.0, the Enable LMHOSTS Lookup checkbox on the WINS Address property page must be selected. This is enabled by default.

p-node name resolution

The use of p-node (point-to-point) mode solves most of the problems that occur with b-node; p-node does not create or respond to broadcast messages. All computers register with a WINS server when they start. The WINS server is responsible for keeping track of all NetBIOS names and their corresponding IP addresses. WINS servers also ensure that no duplicate NetBIOS names exist on the network.

P-node hosts consult the WINS server for all NetBIOS name resolution (assuming the local NetBIOS name cache does not already contain the mapped entry). Because broadcast messages are not used, and because the IP address of the source computer is received by the target computer, computers on different subnets can communicate with each other.

The two major disadvantages of p-node are:

- All computers must be configured (typically through DHCP) to know the address of the WINS server.

- If the WINS server is down, computers that rely on p-node to resolve addresses cannot get to any other systems on the network. Because of this limitation, h-node is a preferred node type.

m-node name resolution

The m-node (modified) mode is a combination of b-node and p-node. In an m-node environment, a computer first attempts registration and resolution using b-node. If the broadcast fails, the computer then attempts to resolve the NetBIOS name using WINS.

The advantages of m-node are as follows:

- Because b-node is always tried first, computers on the same side of a router continue to operate as usual if the WINS server is down.

- If the broadcast fails to resolve the NetBIOS name, m-node can cross routers in order to use a WINS server.

- In some cases, m-node can increase LAN performance by eliminating the need to cross routers to resolve every NetBIOS name.

h-node name resolution

The h-node (hybrid) mode solves many of the problems associated with broadcast methods of NetBIOS registration and resolution. Like m-node, h-node mode is also a hybrid between b-node and p-node. However, p-node is always the primary method of name resolution. NetBIOS name resolution requests are always sent to a *NetBIOS Name Server* (NBNS), such as WINS, first. Broadcast messages are used only as a last resort.

If a WINS server is down, broadcast messages can be used to resolve the NetBIOS name. However, a computer will periodically attempt to poll the WINS server so that when it can be reached again, the system returns to using p-node as the primary method of name resolution.

MCSE TCP/IP ACE IT!

> **KNOW THIS**
>
> **Default Name Resolution Modes**
>
> Windows 95 and Windows NT TCP/IP clients default to b-node name resolution unless they are configured to use WINS. Clients that are configured to use WINS for name resolution default to h-node. The node type can be specified for DHCP clients by configuring the WINS/NBT Node Type option.

Other Name Resolution Methods

The other methods Windows NT 4.0 supports for resolving NetBIOS names on a TCP/IP network fall into two general categories: NetBT and *Domain Name System* (DNS). The method and order of NetBIOS name resolution for a Windows NT computer are configurable. The methods include:

- NetBIOS name cache
- NetBIOS name server (WINS)
- IP subnet broadcasts
- Static LMHOSTS files
- Static HOST files
- DNS servers

When a computer has been configured to support more than one method of name resolution, each of these methods is attempted until the NetBIOS name is resolved. If none of the methods works to resolve the NetBIOS name, name resolution fails.

> **KNOW THIS**
>
> **Restrictions on NetBIOS Names**
>
> If the name to be resolved is more than 15 characters, Windows NT assumes the name to be a host name and issues a request to a DNS server.

LMHOSTS File

An LMHOSTS file is commonly used if a WINS server is not available on the network. The LMHOSTS file is a local text file that maps IP addresses to NetBIOS names for remote computers that you want to communicate with over a TCP/IP network. The LMHOSTS file should list all the names and IP addresses of the servers you regularly access. Each entry in an LMHOSTS file consists of an IP address and a NetBIOS name.

Table 9-2 describes the supported LMHOSTS file keywords.

TABLE 9-2 LMHOSTS file keywords

Keyword	Meaning
#PRE	This is added after an entry and causes the entry to be preloaded into the name cache. Entries are not preloaded into the name cache by default. #PRE must be appended for entries also appearing in #INCLUDE statements; otherwise, the #INCLUDE entry is ignored.
#DOM:*domain*	This is appended after an entry and specifies that it refers to a special group name for the specified domain name. In routed TCP/IP environments, this keyword affects how the Browser and Logon services behave. To pre-load a #DOM entry, add the #PRE keyword to the line.
#INCLUDE *filename*	This forces the system to seek the specified *filename* and to parse it as local. Specifying a Universal Naming Convention (UNC) *filename* lets you use a centralized LMHOSTS file on a server. A mapping for the server is required before its entry in the #INCLUDE section. You must also append #PRE to ensure that it is preloaded (otherwise, the #INCLUDE will be ignored).
#BEGIN_ALTERNATE	This is used to designate multiple #INCLUDE statements.

Continued

TABLE 9-2 Continued

Keyword	Meaning
#END_ALTERNATE	This is used to designate the end of an #INCLUDE grouping.
\0x*nn*	Gives support for nonprinting characters in NetBIOS names. Bracket the NetBIOS name in double quotation marks and use \0x*nn* hexadecimal notation to assign a hexadecimal value to the character. This allows custom applications using special names to function correctly across subnets. Note that the hexadecimal notation applies to only one character in the name. The name should be padded with spaces so that the special character is last in the string (character 16).

Included LMHOSTS files are processed only while the host is initializing its TCP/IP configuration. Therefore, entries in included files must include the #PRE keyword, forcing the entries to be loaded into cache memory.

When a name resolution request is executed, entries in the LMHOSTS file are examined sequentially from beginning to end. Therefore, you should place the most commonly referenced names at the beginning of the file. Any #INCLUDE or #PRE statements should appear later in the file because these statements are processed only when the client is initializing its TCP/IP configuration.

POP QUIZ — True or False?

1. NetBIOS can function over TCP/IP.
2. LMHOSTS files are case sensitive.
3. HOSTS files can be used to resolve NetBIOS names.

Answers: 1. True 2. False 3. True

The nbtstat command

The `nbtstat` is a useful tool for troubleshooting problems with NetBIOS name resolution. The `nbstat` command allows for viewing, removing, or correcting dynamic and static entries in the NetBIOS name cache.

The `nbstat` command syntax is as follows:

nbtstat [-a *remotename*] [-A *IPaddress*] [-c] [-n] [-R] [-r] [-S] [-s] [*interval*]

The following details the different parameters and how they function:

- -a *remotename*: Lists the contents of the remote computer's name table using the computer's name.
- -A *Ipaddress*: Lists the contents of the remote computer's name table using the computer's IP address.
- -c: Lists the contents of the NetBIOS name cache, showing the IP address of each name.
- -n: Lists the local NetBIOS names.
- -R: Purges all names from the NetBIOS name cache and reloads the LMHOSTS file.
- -r: Lists name resolution statistics. Returns the number of names resolved and registered via broadcast or via WINS.
- -S: Displays both workstation and server sessions, listing all of the remote computers by IP address only.
- -s: Displays both workstation and server sessions. It attempts to resolve the remote computer IP address to a name by using the name resolution services.
- Interval: Redisplays selected statistics, pausing at the specified interval between each display.

The column headings generated by the `nbtstat` utility are defined in Table 9-3.

TABLE 9-3 Output generated by the `nbtstat` utility

Column Headings	Definitions
`In`	Number of bytes received.
`Out`	Number of bytes sent.
`In/Out`	Indicates whether the connection is from the computer (outbound) or from another computer (inbound).
`Life`	The time remaining for the name table cache entry before it will be purged.
`Local Name`	The NetBIOS name associated with the connection.
`Remote Host`	The name or IP address associated with the remote computer.
`Type`	Indicates the type of name. A name can either be a unique name or a group name.
`<03>`	Each NetBIOS name is 16 characters long. The last byte is always used to indicate a specific NetBIOS application that identifies itself by using the NetBIOS computer name. (The <> notation is the last byte converted to a hexadecimal value.)
`State`	The state of NetBIOS connections.

The possible states are shown in Table 9-4.

TABLE 9-4 State of a NetBIOS connection

State	Meaning
`Connected`	The session has been established.
`Associated`	A connection has been created and is associated with an IP address.
`Listening`	This endpoint is available for an inbound connection.
`Idle`	This endpoint has been opened but cannot receive connections.

State	Meaning
Connecting	The session is in the connecting phase where the name-to-IP address mapping of the destination is being resolved.
Accepting	An inbound session is currently being accepted and will be connected shortly.
Reconnecting	A session is trying to reconnect if it failed to connect on the first attempt.
Outbound	A session is in the connecting phase where the TCP connection is currently being created.
Inbound	An inbound session is in the connecting phase.
Disconnecting	A session is in the process of disconnecting.
Disconnected	The local computer has issued a disconnect, and it is waiting for confirmation from the remote computer.

MCSE TCP/IP ACE IT!

Have You Mastered?

Now it's time to review the concepts in this chapter and apply your knowledge. These questions will test your mastery of material covered in this chapter.

1. **Which resolution method do WINS clients use?**

    ☐ A. b-node
    ☐ B. p-node
    ☐ C. m-node
    ☐ D. h-node

    D. WINS clients use h-node name resolution, which first checks the WINS server and then uses broadcast to attempt name resolution. See the "Standard NetBT Name Resolution Modes" section.

2. **Which resolution method does not work on networks connected using routers?**

    ☐ A. b-node
    ☐ B. p-node
    ☐ C. m-node
    ☐ D. h-node

    A. B-node resolution uses broadcasts that are not passed across a router. This makes b-node a bad choice for networks connected using a router. See the "Standard NetBT Name Resolution Modes" section.

9: NETBIOS NAME RESOLUTION

3. Where is the LMHOSTS file stored?

- ☐ A. \Systemroot\SYSTEM32\DRIVERS\ETC
- ☐ B. \Systemroot\SYSTEM32
- ☐ C. \Systemroot\SYSTEM32\TCP
- ☐ D. \Systemroot\TCP

A. The location of the LMHOSTS file is \WINNT\SYSTEM32\DRIVERS\ETC. See the "LMHOSTS File" section.

4. What keyword is required in the LMHOSTS file to load an entry into the name cache?

- ☐ A. #DOM
- ☐ B. #INCLUDE
- ☐ C. #CACHE
- ☐ D. #PRE

D. The #PRE tag loads the LMHOSTS entry into the name cache. See the "LMHOSTS File" section.

5. What switch is used with the nbtstat command to display the name cache?

- ☐ A. -n
- ☐ B. -c
- ☐ C. -s
- ☐ D. -r

B. Nbtstat -c displays the name cache. See the "nbtstat command" section.

MCSE TCP/IP ACE IT!

Practice Your Skills

The following exercises provide you with a practical opportunity to apply the knowledge you've gained in this chapter.

1. NetBIOS name resolution for a host on a local subnet

EXERCISE Your network consists of a single subnet. You do not have a WINS Server on your network. You are working on a Windows NT Workstation computer. You use Windows NT Explorer to connect to a Windows NT Server computer. Which method of NetBIOS name resolution will the workstation use first to resolve the computer name of the server to an IP address? In which case can the workstation resolve the computer name to an IP address without needing to use a broadcast?

ANALYSIS The Workstation will use a NetBIOS broadcast first to resolve the computer name of the server. The workstation can resolve the computer name without a broadcast when the NetBIOS name-to-IP address mapping already exists in the NetBIOS name cache.

2. NetBIOS name resolution for a host on a remote subnet

EXERCISE Your network consists of two subnets. You do not use WINS or DNS on your network. Windows NT Workstation computers on one subnet need to connect to a Windows NT Server that is on a different subnet. How can you configure the workstations so they can resolve the NetBIOS name of the server to an IP address? What is contained in an LMHOSTS file? After creating an LMHOSTS file with the appropriate mapping entries on a workstation, what else must you do before the workstation will use the LMHOSTS file to resolve NetBIOS names?

ANALYSIS Configure an LMHOSTS file or a HOSTS file on each of the workstations so they can resolve the NetBIOS name of the server. LMHOSTS files contain IP address-to-NetBIOS name mappings. After creating an LMHOSTS file, you must enable LMHOSTS lookup by modifying the WINS TCP/IP properties using the Network option in Control Panel.

10

Host Name Resolution

NAME RESOLUTION IS AN important function on the TCP/IP network. This chapter covers host name resolution using DNS and HOSTS files. It is essential that you understand the different methods of resolving host names to IP addresses before taking the test. The exercises in this chapter will help you determine whether you are prepared for this portion of the test.

Exam Material in This Chapter

Official Word

Based on Microsoft Objectives
- Configure HOSTS files.
- Provide connectivity to UNIX hosts.

Inside Scoop

Based on Author's Experience
- Understand the role of HOSTS files.
- Understand how name resolution occurs using HOSTS files.
- Understand how name resolution occurs using DNS.
- Configure host name resolution to occur using WINS and LMHOSTS files.

10: HOST NAME RESOLUTION

Are You Prepared?

Test your knowledge with the following questions. Then you'll know if you're prepared for the material in this chapter or if you should review problem areas.

1. **What is the maximum character length of a host name?**

    - ☐ A. 8
    - ☐ B. 16
    - ☐ C. 32
    - ☐ D. 256

2. **What is the IP address of the loopback address?**

    - ☐ A. 0.0.0.0
    - ☐ B. 255.255.255.255
    - ☐ C. 127.0.0.1
    - ☐ D. 0.0.0.1

3. **Which of the following is not a cause of host names being resolved incorrectly?**

    - ☐ A. The computer is turned off.
    - ☐ B. There are duplicate entries for the host name in the HOSTS file.
    - ☐ C. The HOSTS entry has an incorrect IP address.
    - ☐ D. The host name was typed incorrectly.

MCSE TCP/IP ACE IT!

Answers:

1. D   *See the "What Is a Host Name" section.*
2. C   *See the "Resolving Names Using a HOSTS File" section.*
3. A   *See the "Host Name Resolution Methods" section.*

What Is a Host Name?

The naming conventions supported in all TCP/IP systems use host names. One advantage of using host names on a TCP/IP network is that virtually all implementations of TCP/IP support the *Domain Name System* (DNS). DNS acts as a distributed database for resolving host names to IP addresses. Windows-based computers support the use of both NetBIOS computer names and TCP/IP host names.

Host names provide a method of assigning an alias to a computer so a user does not need to remember the host address. A host name can be as long as 256 characters. Computers can even be assigned multiple host names.

The host name can be any combination of the letters A through Z, the numerals 0 through 9, and the hyphen (-), with the period (.) character used as a separator. By default, this value is the Microsoft networking computer name, but an administrator can assign a different host name without affecting the computer name. The default host name is also set to lowercase, so that a Windows NT computer with a NetBIOS name of *MARKETING* becomes *marketing*.

> **KNOW THIS** **DNS Case Sensitivity**
> By convention, DNS names are stored in lowercase characters. When users come to use a TCP/IP host name, however, the case doesn't matter. They can enter the name in upper-, lower-, or mixed case, and DNS will resolve the name appropriately.

A *fully qualified domain name* (FQDN) is a host name that conforms to the multipart naming scheme used by DNS. An FQDN is formed when a host name, such as accounting, is added to a DNS domain name, such as quicklearn.com. The resulting FQDN becomes accounting.quicklearn.com. The use of FQDN assumes that a DNS server is available with an entry for each host name. FQDNs are widely used on the Internet to identify a specific TCP/IP host.

Host names are most commonly used with TCP/IP utilities such as ping or FTP. This enables a user to type **ping ftp.quicklearn.com**

235

instead of `ping 131.107.3.11`. This works because the local TCP/IP software has a method of determining the corresponding IP address for the host name. Microsoft networking supports several different methods of host name resolution, including the use of a local HOSTS file and the use of a database on a DNS or WINS server.

The host name utility will display the host name assigned to a computer. By default, the host name is the computer name of a computer running Windows NT or Windows.

Host Name Resolution Methods

Host name resolution is the process of determining the IP address associated with a host name. Ultimately, hosts communicate with one another using hardware addresses. However, before the IP address can be resolved to a hardware address, the host name must be resolved to an IP address. Microsoft TCP/IP supports several different methods of host name resolution, including:

- HOSTS file
- Domain Name Server (DNS)
- Windows Internet Naming Service (WINS)
- Local broadcasts
- LMHOSTS file

TEST TIP You should understand the different methods of host name resolution supported by Microsoft TCP/IP. You should also know what happens next when one method of host resolution fails.

Resolving Names Using a HOSTS File

The HOSTS file is a text file maintained on a local host. The HOSTS file provides compatibility with the UNIX HOSTS file. The HOSTS file contains entries consisting of an IP address corresponding to one or more host names. The HOSTS file on a Windows NT computer must reside in the *system_root*\system32\drivers\etc directory.

Host names in the HOSTS file are not case sensitive and are conventionally entered in lowercase. If desired, more than one name can be included, which enables you to define alias names for select hosts.

In the HOSTS file, any characters following a # character are treated as comments and are ignored when the file is processed. Therefore, host names cannot contain # characters.

> **KNOW THIS**
>
> **HOSTS File Entries**
>
> Entries in the HOSTS file are checked from top to bottom until a match is found. If duplicate entries for a host name exist, only the first entry is used. This can prevent communications with the desired host computer if the first address map is incorrect or obsolete. Also, entries that are most commonly used should be placed at the top of the file for best performance.
>
> In a typical HOSTS file, you will see an entry for IP address 127.0.0.1. It is conventional to include an entry for the loopback address to facilitate testing.

To resolve a host name using a HOSTS file, follow these steps:

1. When using a TCP/IP program, a user types a command using a host name (for example, **ping hostb**). The Windows-based computer checks to see if the host name specified is the same as the local host's name. If the two names are the same, the local host can resolve the host name directly.

MCSE TCP/IP ACE IT!

2. If the host name specified is different from the local host name, the local HOSTS file is checked to see if there is an entry for the requested host name. If the host name is found, it is resolved to an IP address. If the host name cannot be resolved, the resolution process terminates with an error message unless the computer has been configured to use WINS, DNS, or an LMHOSTS file.

3. If the IP address of the destination host exists on the same subnet, ARP is used to resolve the IP address of the destination host to a physical address. ARP does this by first attempting to obtain the physical address from the local ARP cache. If the mapping is not found, ARP sends a broadcast using the destination host's IP address.

4. If the IP address of the destination host exists on a different subnet, ARP is used to resolve the IP address of the default gateway (which has been set on the host). ARP does this by first attempting to obtain the physical address for the router from the local ARP cache. If the mapping is not found, ARP sends a broadcast using the router's IP address.

5. The router then uses ARP to resolve the IP address of the destination host. ARP does this by first attempting to obtain the physical address for the destination host from the local ARP cache. If the mapping is not found, ARP sends a broadcast using the destination host's IP address, which was passed to the router from the source host.

Communication problems between two hosts can occur because of errors in the HOSTS file. Common problems include:

- The HOSTS file is not located in the correct directory on the Windows NT computer. The HOSTS file must exist in the *Systemroot*\System32\Drivers\Etc directory.
- The HOSTS file does not contain the particular host name.
- The host name in the HOSTS file or specified in the command is misspelled.
- An invalid IP address is entered for the host name in the HOSTS file.

10: HOST NAME RESOLUTION

- The HOSTS file contains multiple entries for the same host name on separate lines. The first entry is used in this case.

POP QUIZ — True or False?
1. The HOSTS file is case sensitive.
2. The LMHOSTS file can be used to resolve host names.
3. The # character is a reserved character that cannot be used in a host name.

Answers: 1. False 2. True 3. True

Resolving Names Using Domain Name System (DNS)

The *Domain Name System* (DNS) provides an online database for resolving host names to IP addresses. The database contains a listing of names that are each mapped to an IP address. The names that are managed by the DNS are called domain names. DNS domains form a logical grouping of TCP/IP hosts in an organization. Larger organizations further divide their domains into subdomains for manageability. DNS relies on a distributed network of DNS servers to resolve host names on other networks.

KNOW THIS — DNS Domains vs. NT Domains
DNS domain names are totally different from Windows NT domain names that make up the Windows NT directory services. NT domains are used to group computers and provide security on the network. One company may have several NT domains and only one DNS domain.

The process of resolving a host name using a DNS server works as follows:

1. A user types a command using a domain name (a host name or an FQDN) when using a TCP/IP program (for example, `ping HostB.quicklearn.com`). A DNS server is contacted to look up the requested name.
2. The IP address is returned to the source host. If DNS does not respond after several attempts, the resolution process terminates with an error unless the computer has been configured to use WINS or an LMHOSTS file.
3. After the host name has been resolved to an IP address, the Address Resolution Protocol (ARP) is used to resolve the IP address of the destination host to a hardware address.

The process of resolving the IP address to the hardware address for a host on a remote subnet is identical to the process described previously in Steps 4 and 5 when using a HOSTS file.

Resolving Names Using Microsoft Host Name Methods

Windows NT can be configured to use additional methods of host name resolution. This allows for redundancy in case other methods fail. Microsoft host name resolution works as follows:

1. The local HOSTS file is scanned for a match to the requested host name.
2. If no match is found in the local HOSTS file, a request is sent to a DNS server.
3. If DNS cannot resolve the name, the local host uses NetBIOS methods of name resolution to resolve the host name. The host first checks its local NetBIOS name cache before sending the request to a WINS server.

4. If the WINS server cannot resolve the name, a b-node broadcast is sent onto the local subnet.

5. If a broadcast cannot resolve the name, the local LMHOSTS file is scanned for a matching name.

If none of these methods works, the IP address of the remote host will need to be specified.

MCSE TCP/IP ACE IT!

Have You Mastered?

Now it's time to review the concepts in this chapter and apply your knowledge. These questions will test your mastery of material covered in this chapter.

1. **Which of the following uses broadcasts to resolve IP addresses?**

    ☐ A. HOSTS file
    ☐ B. LMHOSTS file
    ☐ C. ARP
    ☐ D. DNS server

    C. ARP is used to resolve IP addresses. HOSTS, LMHOSTS, and DNS are used for name resolution. Be sure you understand the difference between the various resolution methods before taking the exam. See the "Resolving Names Using a HOSTS File" section.

2. **What is the correct location of the HOSTS file on Windows NT?**

    ☐ A. `\Systemroot\System32`
    ☐ B. `\Systemroot\System32\IP`
    ☐ C. `\Systemroot`
    ☐ D. `\system_root\system32\drivers\etc`

    D. The HOSTS file must be located in the path `\system_root\system32\drivers\etc`. The location of this file is very important. If the file is not located in this directory, it will not be used for name resolution. See the "Resolving Names Using a HOSTS File" section.

10: HOST NAME RESOLUTION

3. **UNIX computers are capable of using which of the following for host name resolution?**

    ☐ A. LMHOSTS
    ☐ B. WINS
    ☐ C. HOSTS
    ☐ D. Host names

    C. UNIX computers use HOSTS files for host name resolution. UNIX computers use host names and have the capability to use both DNS and HOSTS files. They are not capable of using NetBIOS names and therefore do not use LMHOSTS or WINS for name resolution. See the "Resolving Names Using a HOSTS File" section.

4. **Which of the following services cannot be used for host name resolution on a Microsoft network?**

    ☐ A. HOSTS
    ☐ B. DNS
    ☐ C. WINS
    ☐ D. LMHOSTS
    ☐ E. All of the above

    E. All of these methods can be used to resolve host names on a Microsoft network. Although LMHOSTS and WINS are meant for NetBIOS name resolution, they can be used for DNS resolution by Microsoft clients. This eases the administrative burden by requiring the names to be registered automatically in WINS. See the "Host Name Resolution Methods" section.

5. How many characters can a host name contain?

- ☐ A. 16
- ☐ B. 8
- ☐ C. 256
- ☐ D. 12

C. Host names can contain up to 256 characters. If NetBIOS names are longer than 16 characters, they are assumed to be host names and are resolved using host name resolution. See the "What Is a Host Name?" section.

… **10: HOST NAME RESOLUTION**

Practice Your Skills

The following exercise will give you a chance to use your knowledge of host name resolution. Successful completion of these exercises is a must before taking the exam.

1. Configuring a HOSTS file for host name resolution

EXERCISE You use a HOSTS file to provide host name resolution on a Windows NT Workstation computer. The HOSTS file will be used so that the workstation can connect to UNIX computers that are located on a different subnet. What must be specified in the HOSTS file? When resolving a host name to an IP address using a HOSTS file, how can you provide the best performance for the hosts to which you connect most frequently? You notice when you attempt to connect to a host by using its host name that a different IP address is returned from the one you just entered. Why is this happening?

ANALYSIS You should specify IP-address-to-host-name mappings in the HOSTS file. You can provide the best performance for the most frequently used host names by placing them at the top of the list in the HOSTS file. If there is a duplicate mapping entry higher up in the HOSTS file, a different IP address is returned from the one you just entered when you connect to a host using its host name.

245

11

Internetworking and Connectivity

MICROSOFT TCP/IP ENABLES Windows-based computers to connect to and operate with many types of hosts by using a variety of utilities that can be run on Windows-based computers. This chapter will explain different methods of managing print devices on a network and look at how UNIX-based printers can be used and monitored using utilities provided with Windows NT. Also explained in this chapter is how Microsoft's Computer Browser service works and how to configure browsing to work over an internetwork.

MCSE TCP/IP ACE IT!

Exam Material in This Chapter

Official Word

Based on Microsoft Objectives

- Configure a Windows NT Server to support TCP/IP printing.
- Given a scenario, identify which utility to use to connect to a TCP/IP-based UNIX host.
- Configure and support browsing in a multiple-domain routed network.
- Configure a RAS server and dial-up network for use on a TCP/IP network.

Inside Scoop

Based on Author's Experience

- Understand what must be done to integrate UNIX computers into a Microsoft network.
- Know how to use the remote connectivity tools for TCP/IP.
- Know the different components of TCP/IP printing and how they work together.
- Understand what capabilities are included with Microsoft clients and servers.

11: INTERNETWORKING AND CONNECTIVITY

Are You Prepared?

Test your knowledge with the following questions. Then you'll know if you're prepared for the material in this chapter or if you should review problem areas.

1. Which utility is not included with Windows NT?

- ☐ A. LPD
- ☐ B. FTP
- ☐ C. LPR
- ☐ D. Syslog

2. Which protocol is used to print over TCP/IP?

- ☐ A. LPR
- ☐ B. FTP
- ☐ C. InetD
- ☐ D. DLC

3. Which type of computer may become a browser if needed?

- ☐ A. Master browser
- ☐ B. Backup browser
- ☐ C. Potential browser
- ☐ D. Idle browser

MCSE TCP/IP ACE IT!

4. Which file is used to resolve NetBIOS names to IP addresses?

   ☐ A. HOSTS
   ☐ B. LMHOSTS
   ☐ C. RESOLVE
   ☐ D. ADDRESS

5. Which tag is used in the LMHOSTS file to have the computer precache that entry?

   ☐ A. DOM
   ☐ B. CACHE
   ☐ C. STORE
   ☐ D. PRE

Answers:

1. **D**   *Syslog is not included with Windows NT. See the "Microsoft TCP/IP Connectivity" section.*
2. **A**   *LPR is used to print over TCP/IP. See the "TCP/IP Printing" section.*
3. **C**   *Potential browsers are capable of becoming browsers if they are needed. See the "Computer Roles" section.*
4. **B**   *LMHOSTS files are used to resolve NetBIOS names. HOSTS files are used to resolve TCP/IP domain names. See the "Using LMHOSTS" section.*
5. **D**   *The PRE tag tells the computer to cache that entry into memory to help speed things up. See the "Using LMHOSTS" section.*

Microsoft TCP/IP Connectivity

One of the biggest benefits of using TCP/IP is that it provides the capability to operate with many types of host computers. Communication between two computers requires the following:

- A common networking protocol, such as TCP/IP
- A common networking application, such as FTP, which is typically configured with a client and a server component

Protocol Differences

Computers running Microsoft operating systems, such as any Windows-based computers, use a specialized protocol called *Server Message Blocks* (SMB) as a file sharing protocol. SMBs are used when a client computer attempts to connect to a remote computer by using Windows NT Explorer or File Manager or when a `net use` command is entered from the command line. Because most other non-Microsoft operating systems, such as UNIX, do not support the SMB protocols, Windows-based computers cannot connect to these other operating systems when using Explorer or File Manager.

However, most foreign hosts (non-Microsoft operating systems) provide different client-server applications and standard high-level protocols that allow other systems to communicate with them. Microsoft TCP/IP includes the client-side versions of these tools for communicating with UNIX computers. For example, a number of standard utilities are provided for *terminal emulation* (telnet), *file transfer protocol* (FTP), and browsing the *World Wide Web* (WWW).

In some cases, Microsoft provides TCP/IP services, as well. The Microsoft Internet Information Server includes World Wide Web, FTP, and Gopher servers. Third-party products support other common TCP/IP services, such as SMTP electronic mail and *Network File System* (NFS), but these server-side applications aren't the subject of this book.

Table 11-1 summarizes the TCP/IP utilities that are included with Windows NT.

Table 11-1 TCP/IP Utilities Included with Windows NT

Utility	Description	Security Support
FTP	File Transfer Protocol. Copies files to and from computers running FTP server application.	User/password authentication
LPD	Line printer daemon. Receives print jobs from LPR clients and forwards them to printing devices	User/password authentication
LPQ	Line printer queue. Used to examine contents of LPD print job queues.	User/password authentication
LPR	Line printer. Directs print jobs to LPD servers.	User/password authentication
RCP	Remote copy. Copies files to and from computers running the RCP daemon. Logon is not required.	None
REXEC	Remote execution. Executes processes on remote hosts running REXEC server application.	Password
RSH	Remote shell. Executes processes on remote hosts without logging on.	User name
Telnet	Terminal emulation. Terminal emulation access to hosts running.	Telnet server applications

11: INTERNETWORKING AND CONNECTIVITY

Utility	Description	Security Support
TFTP	Trivial File Transfer Protocol. A UDP-based protocol that provides unauthenticated transfer of files to and from computers running.	TFTP server applications

> **KNOW THIS — UNIX Daemons**
>
> UNIX background processes are called *daemons*. The name of a daemon process often includes a terminal letter *d*. For example, `rexecd` is the `rexec` daemon, which is the server component of `rexec`.

TCP/IP Connectivity Utilities

Microsoft TCP/IP connectivity utilities are provided to perform file transfer and terminal emulation on foreign hosts. The connectivity utilities enable users to interact with and use resources on non-Microsoft hosts such as UNIX workstations.

Remote Execution Utilities

The remote execution utilities can be used on remote hosts that are running the corresponding service required by the utility. For example, a client computer uses a command line utility called `rsh` to connect to a computer running the rsh daemon. The remote execution utilities include:

- RSH
- REXEC
- Telnet

253

The remote shell connectivity command runs commands on remote hosts running the `rsh` service. To use `rsh` to connect to an `rsh` server, the user must have an entry in the `.rhosts` on the UNIX host. The `.rhosts` file includes a list of authorized remote user names. However, `rsh` does not use passwords to authenticate users.

Syntax for the `rsh` command is as follows:

RSH *host* [**-l** username] [**-n**] command

Following are the parameters used with the RSH command:

- `host` specifies which remote host to run the command on.
- `-l username` specifies the user name to use on the remote host. If it is omitted, the logged-on user name is used.
- `-n` redirects the input of `rsh` to NUL.
- `Command` specifies which command to run.

The Remote Execute connectivity command runs commands on remote hosts running the `rexecd` service. Rexec authenticates the user name on the remote host by using a password, before executing the specified command.

The command syntax for the `rexec` command is as follows:

REXEC *host* [**-l** username] [**-n**] command

Following are the parameters used with the REXEC command:

- `host` specifies which remote host to run command on.
- `-l username` specifies the user name to use on the remote host. If it is omitted, the logged-on user name is used.
- `-n` redirects the input of `rexec` to NUL.
- `command` specifies which command to run.

The Telnet connectivity command starts terminal emulation with a remote host running a Telnet server service (a Telnet *daemon*). Telnet provides DECVT 100, DEC VT 52, or TTY emulation, using the connection-based services of TCP. When the Telnet command is started, you will be asked for a login name and password.

11: INTERNETWORKING AND CONNECTIVITY

The Telnet client can be started by selecting Telnet from the Accessories program group or by using the command prompt.

> **KNOW THIS** — **Telnet Servers**
> Windows NT Server and Windows NT Workstation provide the `telnet` client utility, but they do not provide a Telnet server service (`telnetd`), also referred to as the *Telnet daemon*.

The syntax for the `telnet` command is as follows:

TELNET [*host* [*port*]]

Following are the parameters used with the TELNET utility:

- `host` specifies the remote host you want to connect with.
- `Port` specifies the remote port you want to connect to. The default value is determined by the telnet entry in the Services file. If no entry exists in the Services file, the default connection port value is decimal 23.

Data Transfer Utilities

The date transfer utilities are used to transfer data across the network. FTP and HTTP are the most commonly used utilities but you should be familiar with them all as listed here:

- RCP
- FTP
- TFTP
- HTTP

The *Remote Copy Protocol* (RCP) connectivity command copies files between an RCP computer and a computer running `rshd`, the remote shell server service or daemon.

Syntax for the `rshd` command is as follows:

255

    rcp [-a | -b] [-h] [-r] source1 source2 ... sourceN
    destination

Following are the parameters used with the RCP utility:

- **-a** specifies ASCII transfer mode, converts the carriage return/line feed characters to carriage returns on outgoing files, and line feed characters to carriage return/line feeds on incoming files. It is the default transfer mode.
- **-b** specifies binary image transfer mode. Carriage return/line feed conversion is not performed.
- **-h** transfers source files that are marked with the hidden attribute on the Windows NT-based computer. If this option is not used, specifying a hidden file on the **rcp** command line has the same effect as if the file did not exist.
- **-r** recursively copies the contents of all the subdirectories of the source to the destination. Both the *source* and *destination* must be directories.
- *source* and *destination* must have the form *[host[.user]:]filename*. If the *[host[.user]:]* section is omitted, the host is assumed to be the local computer. If the *user* section is omitted, the currently logged-on Windows NT user name is used. If a fully qualified host name, which contains the period (.) separators, is used, the *[.user]* must be included. Otherwise, the last part of the host name is taken as the user name. If multiple source files are specified, the *destination* is required to be a directory.

If the filename does not begin with a forward slash (/) for UNIX computers or a backward slash (\ ) for Windows NT-based computers, it is assumed to be relative to the current working directory. Under Windows NT, this is the directory from which the command is issued. On the remote computer, it is the logon directory for the remote user. A period (.) means the current directory. Use the escape characters (\ , ", or ') in remote paths to use wildcard characters on the remote host.

11: INTERNETWORKING AND CONNECTIVITY

The *File Transfer Protocol* (FTP) is used to transfer files to and from a host running an FTP server service. FTP commands can be entered from a command prompt or by processing FTP commands in ASCII text files.

Syntax for the `FTP` command is as follows:

`ftp [-v] [-n] [-i] [-d] [-g] [-s: filename] [hostname]`

Following are the parameters used with the FTP utility:

- `-v` suppresses the display of remote server responses.
- `-n` suppresses autologon upon first connection.
- `-i` turns off interactive prompting while multiple file transfers are in progress.
- `-d` enables debugging, showing all FTP commands transferred between the client and server.
- `-g` disables filename globbing. Globbing permits the use of wildcard characters in local file and path names.
- `-s: filename` specifies a text file containing FTP commands; the commands run automatically after FTP starts. Use this switch instead of redirection (>).
- `hostname` specifies the host name or IP address of the remote host to which to connect. If specified, the host must be the last parameter on the line.

When you connect with FTP, you must log on and initiate a session. Once a session is started, FTP works very much like a command-line interface for a file system. You use commands to change and view directories and to send and receive files. Different FTP servers support different commands.

Following are some of the commands used with the FTP utility:

- `ascii` changes the file transfer mode from raw binary to ASCII. In ASCII mode, text files copied between UNIX and DOS environments are changed into the appropriate local format conventions.
- `binary` changes the file transfer mode from ASCII to raw binary. Files are captured verbatim.
- `cd` changes the directory on the FTP server.

- bye or quit ends the FTP session.
- dir generates a detailed listing of a remote directory.
- get retrieves a file from the FTP server.
- lcd changes the directory on the local computer.
- ls lists the contents of a directory.
- open opens a connection to a new host.
- put sends a file to the FTP server.

> **KNOW THIS — FTP Help**
> You can list all of the available FTP commands by typing **help** or **?** from an ftp prompt. You can also get help about a specific command by typing **help** *command*.

The *Trivial File Transfer Protocol* (TFTP) is run from a command line and is used to transfer files to and from a remote computer running the TFTP service. TFTP file transfers use the *User Datagram Protocol* (UDP). The TFTP utility is similar to FTP, but it does not provide user authentication, although the files require read and write UNIX permissions. The TFTP utility can be used only for unidirectional transfer of files. Because TFTP does not support user authentication, it can access only files that can be read by all users (called *world readable* files).

Syntax for the TFTP command is as follows:

tftp [**-i**] *host* [**get** | **put**] *source* [*destination*]

Following are the parameters used with the TFTP utility:

- **-i** specifies binary image transfer mode (also called *octet*). The file is moved byte by byte in binary image mode. Use this mode when transferring binary files. If **-i** is omitted, the file is transferred in ASCII mode, the default transfer mode. This mode converts the end-of-line (EOL) characters to a carriage return for UNIX and to a carriage return/line feed for PCs. Use this mode when transferring text files. The data rate is displayed if a file transfer is successful.

- *host* specifies the local or remote host.
- *get* transfers *destination* on the remote computer to *source* on the local computer.
- *put* transfers *source* on the local computer to *destination* on the remote computer.
- *source* specifies the file to transfer.
- *destination* specifies where to transfer the file.

The *Hypertext Transport Protocol* (HTTP) is a client/server protocol used to transfer information on the World Wide Web. The WWW provides the easiest way to access information on the Internet or a company's internetwork. HTTP supports the transfer of many different data types such as text, graphics, sound, and video. To access resources using HTTP, a client uses a WWW browser, such as Microsoft's Internet Explorer or Netscape Navigator, to access a WWW server.

Microsoft TCP/IP Printing

Microsoft TCP/IP provides services and utilities that enable users to send documents to print devices that are connected to a UNIX computer or that are connected directly to the network using a network adapter.

It is possible to configure only the Windows NT Server computer with TCP/IP to communicate with TCP/IP-based print devices. The server becomes a print server, also called a *print gateway*, for all other client computers on the network.

> **TEST TRAP**
>
> In Microsoft Windows NT terminology, a *printing device* is the physical printer attached to a computer or connected directly to the network. The term *printer* is the software interface that defines printer characteristics and parameters, such as the specific device driver used, and optional settings, such as paper trays and font cartridges. Keeping this terminology in mind will help avoid confusion on the test.

259

TCP/IP Printing

Line printer (LPR) defines a standard print server protocol for sending documents between computers over the Internet or over an internetwork. Using the LPR protocol, a client computer can send a document to a print spooler service, known as the *line printer daemon* (LPD), running on another computer. RFC 1179 describes the print server protocol that is widely used on the Internet.

Windows NT provides both the LPR and the LPD services for printing on a TCP/IP network. The LPR service provided with Windows NT is installed as a print monitor to forward documents to LPD-based printers. The LPD service is installed with Microsoft TCP/IP Printing service.

Methods of Connecting Printers

Windows NT computers support several different methods for connecting to print devices. The following methods offer different advantages and disadvantages depending on how a network is designed:

- **Direct connection:** A printing device can be directly connected to a Windows NT computer via the serial (COM) or parallel (LPT) port. This provides the easiest method of connecting and configuring a printer for use on the network. However, there are usually distance limitations as to how far the print device can be located away from the Windows NT computer. Also, there is a limit to the number of print devices that can be physically attached to a Windows NT computer without purchasing additional hardware.

- **Network interface printer:** Many manufacturers of high-end print devices now include, or offer as an option, a network adapter installed in the print device. Also, the manufacturer often includes firmware or software that enables the printer to be configured as an LPD print device. This enables the printer to be directly connected anywhere on the network and lets users send documents directly to these printers using the `lpr` utility. Also, a Windows NT Server computer can be configured with the LPR port monitor, which forwards locally spooled print jobs to LPD-based printers.

> **KNOW THIS**
>
> **Configuring IP Printers**
>
> It is normally preferable to require all users to send their documents to a Windows NT Server computer (acting as a print gateway) so that print jobs can be managed centrally by an administrator. A printer (remember, a printer is a software interface) is configured on the Windows NT Server to forward documents that it has received to the LPD-based network printer.

- **UNIX host printer:** A print device also may be attached to a UNIX-based computer running the LPD service. Just as with a network interface printer, when the Microsoft TCP/IP Printing service has been installed on a Windows NT computer, a printer can be defined with the LPR Port monitor to forward all print jobs to the UNIX computer. Users can also send documents directly to this print device using the `lpr` utility. However, this would prevent you from managing print jobs from the Windows NT computer.

Microsoft TCP/IP Printing Service

Microsoft TCP/IP provides an optional service called *Microsoft TCP/IP Printing*. Microsoft TCP/IP Printing is an LPD service and is compliant with RFC 1179. The LPD service receives print jobs from clients running LPR software. Most UNIX systems include LPR software, and Windows-based computers include a command line `lpr` utility called `lpr.exe`.

Line Printer Port Monitor

The purpose of a *port monitor* is to control the communications between the computer and the print device. Windows NT computers include support for several different types of port monitors used to communicate with different types of print devices. For example, there are several types of port monitors provided for network-based printers manufactured by different companies.

In addition to port monitors provided for these proprietary printers, you can install the *line printer port monitor* (also called the *LPR port print monitor*). The LPR port print monitor enables a Windows NT computer to forward documents to an LPD-based print device (UNIX computer or network interface printer configured with the LPD service). To use the LPR port print monitor, the Windows NT Printing service must be installed.

Windows-based clients connect and send documents to the Windows NT print server by simply connecting to a shared printer that has been configured with the LPR port print monitor. The client does not need to know where the print server is located or how the print server communicates with the print device. All this happens in the background, making it transparent to the client. In fact, the client can be running any network protocol. The only requirement is that the client be able to communicate with the server configured with the LPR port print monitor.

TCP/IP Printing Utilities

Windows-based computers can use TCP/IP utilities to use and monitor print jobs to an LPD-based printing device.

The lpr utility

The `lpr` connectivity utility is used to print a file to a host running the LPD service. To use the `lpr` command from the Windows NT command prompt, you must first install the Microsoft TCP/IP Printing service. Syntax for the `lpr` utility is as follows:

```
lpr -SServer -PPrinter [-oOptions] [-CClass] [-JJobname]
[-o option] [-x] [-d] filename
```

Following are the parameters used by the `lpr` utility:

- `-S`*Server* specifies the name of the host that has the printer attached.
- `-P`*Printer* specifies the name of the printer for the desired queue.
- `-C`*Class* specifies the content of the banner page for the class.
- `-J`*Jobname* specifies the name of this job.
- `-o option` indicates the type of the file. By default, a text file is assumed. Use `-o l` for binary PostScript files.
- `-x` indicates compatibility with SunOS version 4.1.*x* and earlier.
- `-d` sends data file first.
- *filename* is the name of the file to be printed.

The lpq utility

The *line printer query* (`lpq`) utility is used to obtain the status of a print queue on a host running the LPD server. To use the `lpq` command from the Windows NT command prompt, you must first install the Microsoft TCP/IP Printing service. Syntax for the `lpq` command is as follows:

`lpq -S`*Server* `-P`*Printer* `[-l]`

Following are the parameters used by the `lpq` utility:

- `-S`*Server* specifies the name of the host that has the printer attached.
- `-P`*Printer* specifies the name of the printer for the desired queue.
- `-l` specifies that a detailed status be given.

Internetwork Browsing

Microsoft's Computer Browser service enables users to see what domains and servers are accessible from their local computers. When properly configured, the Computer Browser service enables users to easily connect to shared folders and directories on remote servers regardless of where these computers are located. Network Neighborhood on any Windows 95 computer or Windows NT computer can be used to browse the network from any client computer.

Computer Roles

The Computer Browser service works by managing lists (called the browse list) of all available domains and servers (any computer that has been configured to share resources) on the network. The browse lists are distributed by computers that have been specially assigned to perform browsing functions for the benefit of all client computers on the network.

There are five types of computers in the browser system:

- **Domain master browser:** The primary domain controller always becomes the master browser for a domain. If necessary, the domain master browser distributes the browse list to master browsers for the same domain that are located on different subnets.
- **Master browser:** This is the machine that collects and maintains the master list of all available servers on the LAN group.
- **Backup browser:** This browser receives a copy of the network resource browse list from the master browser. The backup browser distributes the list upon request to the computers in the LAN group.
- **Potential browser:** This is a computer that is not currently acting as a browser but can be elected to become one by the master browser.
- **Non-browser:** This is a computer that has been configured so that it cannot maintain a browse list. This is

done to eliminate the processing overhead for browsing tasks or to prevent browsing services from running on computers that are shut down regularly (typically client computers).

How Browsing Works

There are three different processes performed by the browsing services: collecting browse lists, distributing browse lists, and servicing browser client requests.

> **TEST TRAP**
> For the test, remember: A *LAN group* is a logical grouping of computers and can be either a domain or a workgroup.

Collecting browse lists

After starting, every computer that runs the browser service registers with the master browser by sending its computer name. The master browser adds that computer name to the browse list. This process is repeated periodically (every 12 minutes) when the client sends an announcement message to the master browser. If the master browser hasn't heard from the client after three announcement periods (36 minutes), the client is dropped from the browse list.

The master browser also communicates with other master browsers in different LAN groups. Only the names of the LAN groups are collected (not the servers from those LAN groups).

> **POP QUIZ** **True or False?**
> 1. Windows NT can run both LPD and LPR.
> 2. The utility used to run programs remotely is Telnet.
> 3. WINS requests cannot be routed.
>
> *Answers: 1. True 2. True 3. False*

Distributing browse lists

The backup browser contacts the master browser periodically (every 15 minutes) to receive the current copy of the browse list. The list includes the list of servers from within the LAN group and the list of other LAN groups that have been collected by the master browser.

If the master browser is unavailable when a backup browser attempts to connect to it, the backup browser will force an election to occur so that a new master browser can be selected. The computer that wins the election depends on the type of operating system.

The following list summarizes the priority of which computer can win the election:

- Windows NT Server
- Windows NT Workstation
- Windows 95 computer
- Windows for Workgroups

Within these categories, the latest version of the computer's operating system has a higher priority. For example, Windows NT Server version 4.0 would win the election over a computer running Windows NT Server version 3.51.

Servicing client browser requests

In addition to announcing itself to the master browser upon startup, a browser client requests a list of all available backup browsers on the network. The master browser returns this list to the client, and the client randomly selects one of the backup browsers. From this point on, the client will contact the backup browser for a list of servers within the LAN group.

The client connects directly to a server by selecting it from the list. The server will then return a list of shared resources directly to the client. If permissions have been granted to the user working at the client computer, the client computer can then connect to one of the shared resources.

Instead of selecting a server from the local LAN group, a client can select a different LAN group. In this case, the master browser for the remote LAN group is contacted and a list of backup browsers is returned to the client for that LAN group. The client can then connect to a server in a remote LAN group.

Browsing an Internetwork

All browsing announcements rely on a series of broadcast packets for announcements, elections, and client requests. But broadcasts are not forwarded between subnets. Fortunately, there are a couple of Windows NT solutions that enable browsing to work over an internetwork. The easiest solution is to use WINS. If your network does not use WINS, however, it's possible to create special LMHOSTS entries to facilitate the distribution of browsing information.

Using WINS

Each subnet requires a master browser to support browsing services for clients on that subnet. When a domain spans a subnet, each subnet functions as an independent browsing entity with its own master browser and backup browser. When all computers on the network register with WINS, the master browsers query WINS for the computer that has registered itself as the domain master browser (the PDC). This enables the master browser to contact and exchange browse lists with the domain master browser.

> **KNOW THIS** **Master Browsers**
> Master browsers in different subnets can never communicate with each other directly to exchange browse lists. If the domain master browser goes offline, the master browsers will eventually drop any browse lists for the other subnets. This will prevent any client computer from browsing computers outside of its own subnet.

When multiple domains are separated by subnets, each of the domain master browsers registers with the WINS Server. This way, the domain master browsers can identify each other and exchange browse lists.

Using LMHOSTS

WINS definitely simplifies the process of updating the browse lists between subnets. But if you don't use WINS on your network, you can always use the LMHOSTS file to enable a master browser to locate the domain master browser. This requires that you create an LMHOSTS file with special tags on the master browser and the domain master browser.

The LMHOSTS file on each master browser must contain an entry for the domain master browser. For example:

```
172.25.16.71  domain_master_browser      #PRE
#DOM:domain_name
```

The entries in the LMHOSTS file include:

- IP address of the domain master browser
- The computer name of the domain master browser
- #PRE tag — tells TCP/IP to preload the entry into the NetBIOS name cache
- #DOM tag — tells TCP/IP the entry references a domain controller

The LMHOSTS file on each domain master browser must contain a similar entry for each of the master browsers with which it will exchange browse lists.

> **KNOW THIS**
>
> ### Preparing for Promotion of Domain Controller
>
> It is a good idea to add the entries of all domain controllers on each master browser in case a backup domain controller is promoted to a primary domain controller.

11: INTERNETWORKING AND CONNECTIVITY

Have You Mastered?

Now it's time to review the concepts in this chapter and apply your knowledge. These questions will test your mastery of material covered in this chapter.

1. What are background processes called in UNIX?

- ☐ A. Services
- ☐ B. Applets
- ☐ C. Daemons
- ☐ D. TSR

C. Background processes in UNIX are referred to as *daemons*. See the "Protocol Differences" section.

2. Which utility provides terminal emulation to remote hosts?

- ☐ A. RSH
- ☐ B. REXEC
- ☐ C. TELNET
- ☐ D. NNTP

C. Telnet allows you to open a terminal emulation session to remote hosts. See the "Remote Execution Utilities" section.

3. **Which utility is normally used to transfer files to/from remote hosts?**

    ☐ A. TELNET
    ☐ B. SMTP
    ☐ C. SNMP
    ☐ D. FTP

    D. FTP is used to transfer files between hosts. See the "Data Transfer Utilities" section.

4. **Which FTP command is used to retrieve a file from a remote host?**

    ☐ A. PUT
    ☐ B. GET
    ☐ C. BINARY
    ☐ D. DOWNLOAD

    B. GET is used to tell the FTP server to send you a file. See the "Data Transfer Utilities" section.

5. **Which protocol does TFTP use?**

    ☐ A. TCP
    ☐ B. IP
    ☐ C. UDP
    ☐ D. SMB

    C. TFTP uses the UDP protocol and is therefore not as reliable as FTP. See the "Data Transfer Utilities" section.

11: INTERNETWORKING AND CONNECTIVITY

6. **What is the daemon called that provides printing capabilities on a UNIX print server?**

    - ☐ A. LPR
    - ☐ B. LPD
    - ☐ C. PrintD
    - ☐ D. Spooler

    B. LPD is the daemon that runs on the UNIX server that allows it to share printers to the network. See the "TCP/IP Printing" section.

7. **Which utility is used to print a file from the command line to a TCP/IP printer?**

    - ☐ A. LPD
    - ☐ B. FTP
    - ☐ C. LPR
    - ☐ D. Print

    C. You can use LPR to print text files to a remote printer from the command prompt. See the "lpr utility" section.

8. **How many master browsers can there be on each subnet?**

    - ☐ A. 1
    - ☐ B. 2
    - ☐ C. 8
    - ☐ D. 16

    A. There is only one Master Browser per subnet. See the "Computer Roles" section.

MCSE TCP/IP ACE IT!

Practice Your Skills

The Practice Your Skills labs will provide you with an opportunity to apply the knowledge you've gained in this chapter about TCP/IP internetworking and connectivity.

1. Copying files from UNIX computer

EXERCISE Your organization has seven different UNIX computers that are used to store common data files. Three of the servers run the rshd daemon so that files are available to all users on the network. Which utility included with Windows NT can be used by the Windows NT computers to copy files from these UNIX computers?

ANALYSIS Windows NT computers can use the `rcp` (remote copy utility) utility to copy files from UNIX computers running the `rshd` daemon.

2. Copying files from an FTP server

EXERCISE Four of the remaining UNIX computers run the ftp daemon so that files are available to users on the network. Which utility included with Windows NT can be used by the Windows NT computers to copy files from these UNIX computers?

11: INTERNETWORKING AND CONNECTIVITY

ANALYSIS Windows NT computers can use the File Transfer Protocol (ftp) utility to copy files from UNIX computers running the ftp daemon.

3. Configuring a TCP/IP printer that is managed by a Windows NT Server computer

EXERCISE You have installed a printer that is attached directly to your TCP/IP network. You want this computer to be available to all users on the network. You want the printer to be managed by a single Windows NT Server computer. What service must be running on the TCP/IP printer so that it can receive print documents from the Windows NT Server computer? What service must be installed on the Windows NT Server computer so that it can forward print documents to the TCP/IP printer?

ANALYSIS You must run the line printer daemon (LPD) on the TCP/IP printer and the Microsoft TCP/IP Printing service on the Windows NT Server.

4. Printing directly to a TCP/IP printer

EXERCISE Occasionally you want to be able to bypass the Windows NT Server computer and send print documents directly to the TCP/IP printer. How can you do this?

ANALYSIS Use the `lpr` utility to bypass the server.

5. Configuring internetwork browsing

EXERCISE Your network consists of a single Windows NT Server domain that is spread across three different subnets. Subnet A contains the PDC (primary domain controller). Subnet B and Subnet C each contain a BDC (backup domain controller). You want all Windows-based client computers to be able to see the browse list for computers on any subnet. Which two methods can be used to allow the browse lists to be exchanged between subnets? If the BDC on Subnet C goes offline, how will computers on each of the different subnets be affected? If the PDC on Subnet A goes offline, how will computers on each of the different subnets be affected?

ANALYSIS To enable Windows-based clients to see the browse list, configure all domain controllers to use WINS. Alternately, you can configure all domain controllers with an LMHOSTS file, and create entries in the LMHOSTS file on each domain controller for the other domain controllers. If the BDC on Subnet C goes offline, a new master browser will be elected on Subnet C, and the browse lists will continue to be exchanged without interruption. If the PDC on Subnet A goes offline, eventually the browse list for each subnet will be modified so that it contains only computers that reside on that subnet. This will continue to be the case until the PDC is restarted or a BDC is promoted to a PDC.

12

Setting Up the SNMP Service

THE *SIMPLE NETWORK MANAGEMENT Protocol* (SNMP) is a set of protocols and services that enable a network administrator to query and set values on a remote device that has been configured with an SNMP agent. Windows NT computers can be configured with the SNMP service, which is an SNMP agent. This chapter explains how SNMP works and how to configure a Windows NT computer to use SNMP. Network management generally refers to the ability to perform specific administration tasks from a central computer, which runs *SNMP manager*.

MCSE TCP/IP ACE IT!

Exam Material in This Chapter

Official Word

Based on Microsoft Objectives
- Configure SNMP.

Inside Scoop

Based on Author's Experience
- Understand the components of SNMP.
- Know what SNMP capabilities are included with NT.
- Understand the different configuration options for SNMP, such as communities.

12: SETTING UP THE SNMP SERVICE

Are You Prepared?

Test your knowledge with the following questions. Then you'll know if you're prepared for the material in this chapter or if you should review problem areas.

1. Where are traps sent from?

- ☐ A. SNMP managers
- ☐ B. SNMP agents
- ☐ C. MIB
- ☐ D. RFC

2. What requirement must a variable meet in order to be set using the SNMP manager set command?

- ☐ A. archived
- ☐ B. read access
- ☐ C. write access
- ☐ D. read/write access

3. Which of the following is not a counter added to Performance Monitor by the SNMP service?

- ☐ A. ICMP
- ☐ B. IP
- ☐ C. UDP
- ☐ D. MIB

Answers:

1. B   SNMP traps are sent by SNMP agents. See the "SNMP Communities and Traps" section.
2. D   A variable must be set for read/write access to be changed using the SNMP set command. See the "Managing SNMP" section.
3. D   MIB is not a counter in Performance Monitor. See the "Managing SNMP" section.

How SNMP Works

SNMP (Simple Network Management Protocol) is a network management system that includes software and protocols for monitoring and managing computers and other devices connected to a network. Most network management systems use either a *polling-based* method for collecting information or an *interrupt-based* method of reporting information. When an SNMP management station needs to poll a managed station, it uses a `get` command to obtain required information.

Using an interrupt-based approach, managed devices provide immediate notification by sending a message to a network management station when a specified event occurs. An event can be designated as a significant error condition or when a certain threshold has been reached (for example, low disk space or excessive network traffic). SNMP supports both polling-based and interrupt-based methods. SNMP stations send *traps* to notify SNMP management stations of network events.

SNMP is a well-defined public standard that is used widely in the Internet community. While SNMP is predominately used on TCP/IP networks, it should be noted that SNMP is protocol-independent. It can be used over IPX, AppleTalk, and OSI protocols. As part of the Internet TCP/IP protocol suite, SNMP is defined in RFCs 1155, 1157, and 1213.

SNMP Components

An *SNMP manager* is software that runs on a computer called an SNMP management station, which is configured to collect information from an SNMP agent. The *SNMP agent* is the counterpart software to the SNMP manager that runs on a managed computer or device. The SNMP agent reports events or responds to requests that originate from an SNMP manager. An SNMP agent can be installed on many different types of devices including printers, routers, hubs, servers, and client computers. The SNMP manager collects information on other computers and the network itself, including:

- Network protocol information and statistics
- Discovery and identification of computers that have attached to the network
- Hardware and software configuration data
- Computer performance and usage statistics
- Computer system events and error reporting
- Services and applications usage statistics

The SNMP manager is configured to query an agent at regular intervals. The results of the queries are passed on to a software program that enables the information obtained to be made available to a network administrator in a textual or graphical format on a console.

The SNMP manager sends specially formatted messages to an SNMP agent. These messages define one of three different operations: get, get-next, and set.

- The get operation retrieves a specific value about a managed object, such as available hard disk space.
- The get-next operation returns the next value when there are multiple values that need to be collected from a table of objects (for example, all of the NetBIOS names registered by a client.)
- The set operation changes the value of a managed-object variable. Only variables whose object definitions allow read/write access can be set.

KNOW THIS: SNMP Managers

The SNMP service is an SNMP agent that can be installed on Windows NT computers. Microsoft does not provide the software for an SNMP manager. Several third-party vendors provide SNMP managers, including Hewlett Packard's Open View and Sun Microsystem's SunNet Manager.

The SNMP agent is special software or firmware (integrated into the hardware) that contains a database of information about a specific network computer or device. The agent returns information contained in the database when requested to do so by the SNMP manager. The agent can also be configured to send a message called a `trap` to a manager when a specified event occurs. A trap operation is the only type of message that can be initiated by an agent.

- A `get` response is used to respond to a get request message.
- A `trap` is an SNMP message that originates from the agent to a predetermined manager. Traps are used to report errors or important events back to the manager. Typical usage of traps is notification of a service starting or stopping and notification of serious error conditions.

Designed as a polling protocol, SNMP uses a simple set of commands to set and retrieve values of objects in management information bases (MIBs). SNMP messages that are sent by a manager are encapsulated within a UDP (connection-less protocol) datagram and routed via IP. This enables the agent and the manager to reside on different subnets and still be able to communicate with each other.

Management Information Base (MIB)

A *Management Information Base* (MIB) is a database that represents the set of manageable objects for a specific device or service. Each host that is to be managed by SNMP must have a MIB that describes the manageable objects on the host. All MIBs are defined using a precise organizational structure. The SNMP manager uses the information from the MIB when connecting to the agent to identify how the information contained on the agent is organized. Because of the flexible nature of the MIB format and the way the manager and the agents communicate, new and updated MIBs can work with management consoles that were written years ago.

The name space for a MIB file is a hierarchical (tree-like) database of manageable objects. A MIB is structured very similarly to the multi-level organization found in the Windows NT registry. Each individual type of MIB is a subtree of a structure that is defined by the *International Standards Organization* (ISO), as shown in Figure 12-1. This structure enables each manageable object to be assigned a globally unique name.

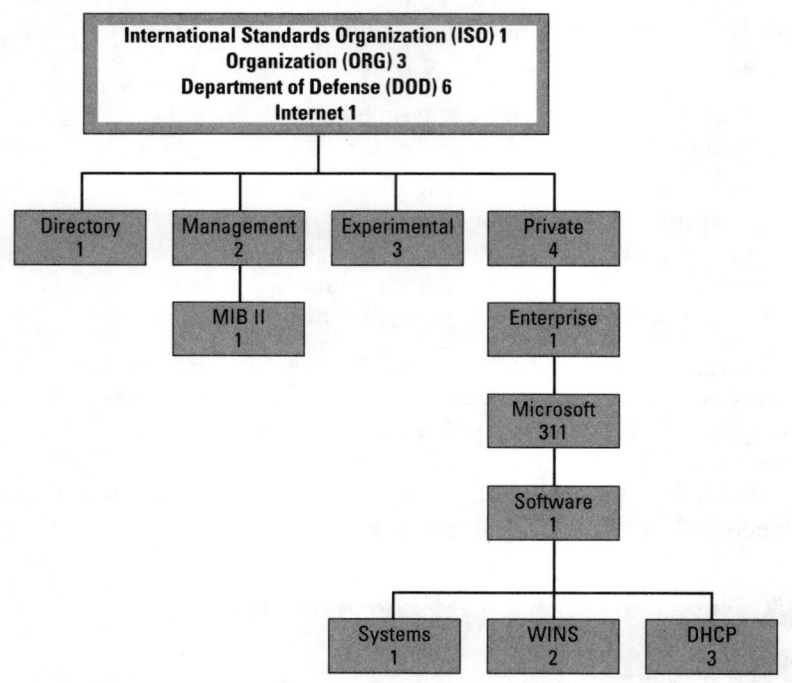

Figure 12-1 *A MIB is a hierarchical database of manageable objects that conforms to a structure defined by the International Standards Organization (ISO).*

RFC 1213 defines an industry-standard SNMP MIB format referred to as *MIB-II*. Authority for parts of the name space (global naming format for MIB objects) is also assigned to individual organizations. Vendors such as Microsoft can define additional MIBs to support unique hardware or software services that can be monitored and managed by SNMP managers.

Object identifier and definition

Each SNMP host has one or many MIBs that contain information about the managed-objects on that computer. A unique label referred to as an object-identifier (OID) identifies each object in a MIB. For example, the object-identifier for the name space assigned to Microsoft is 1.3.6.1.4.1.311. Microsoft has the authority to assign names to objects anywhere below that name space. As shown in Figure 12-1, Windows NT Server services such as WINS and DHCP have uniquely identifiable OIDs assigned to them. For example:

Object Name	Object Number
Iso.org.dod.internet. private.enterprise. microsoft.software.wins	1.3.6.1.4.1.311.1.2
Iso.org.dod.internet. private.enterprise. microsoft.software.dhcp	1.3.6.1.4.1.311.1.3

Table 12-1 shows the object identifier and description of each of the MIBs used in Windows NT.

Table 12-1 MIB objects included with Windows NT Server

MIB	Object name	Object number	Contents
Internet MIB-II	iso.org.dod. internet.mgmt. mib-2	1.3.6.1.2.1	Defines objects that are essential either for configuration or fault analysis. Internal MIB II is defined in RFC 1213.
Lan Manager MIB-II	iso.org.dod. internet. private. enterprise. lanmanager	1.3.6.1.4 .1.77	Defines objects that include items such as statistical, share, session, user, and logon information.

Continued

Table 12-1 *Continued*

MIB	Object name	Object number	Contents
Microsoft WINS Server MIB	iso.org.dod. internet. private. enterprise. microsoft. software.wins	1.3.6.1.4.1. 311.1.2	Contains information for the WINS server, including statistics, database information, and push and pull data.
Microsoft DHCP server MIB	iso.org.dod. internet. private. enterprise. microsoft. software.dhcp	1.3.6.1.4.1 .311.1.3	Contains statistics for the DHCP server and DHCP scope information.
Microsoft Internet Information Server MIB	iso.org.dod. internet. private. enterprise. microsoft. software.iis	1.3.6.1.4. 1.311.1.7	Comprises several MIBs that branch from the base object for FTP server, HTTP server, and gopher server.

The contents of a MIB database include a definition of each object that the SNMP can report on. The following is just one example out of the hundreds of different objects that can be contained in a MIB:

```
The Domain Group
domPrimaryDomain  OBJECT-TYPE
    SYNTAX   DisplayString (SIZE (1..15))
    ACCESS   read-only
    STATUS   mandatory
    DESCRIPTION "The name of the primary domain to which
this machine belongs."
    ::= { domain 1 }
```

SNMP Communities and Traps

SNMP provides a basic level of security to authenticate SNMP messages sent between an SNMP manager and an SNMP agent. Authentication works by adding a group identifier to each SNMP message that is sent. This identifier is called an SNMP *community name*. A community name is a string of characters that serve as a shared password for a group of managers and agents.

All SNMP messages must include a community name. An agent that receives an SNMP message compares the community name in the message with the community name that has been set on the agent. If the message contains a community name that matches one configured on the host, the message is processed; otherwise, the message is rejected. Community names are not encrypted, however, and travel in clear text through the network. Therefore, community names should be regarded as management conveniences—limiting communication to desired hosts—rather than as security restrictions.

An agent can be a member of multiple communities at the same time. This enables multiple managers to send SNMP messages to a single agent. The default community name that is set on a Windows NT computer when SNMP is installed is `public`. If all community names are deleted on a Windows NT computer, then the SNMP agent will successfully authenticate and process all SNMP messages.

An SNMP agent can generate a message, called a *trap*, when some prespecified event occurs on a host. These events are internally defined by the agent and cannot be changed by the user. However, the destination of the traps can be configured so that trap messages can be sent to the host name or IP address of one or more SNMP managers.

An *authentication trap* is a trap message that is sent to an SNMP manager when an agent receives a message that contains a community name that has not been defined on the agent. The trap message notifies the manager that a message authentication failure has occurred on that host.

285

The Microsoft SNMP Service

The SNMP service is an optional service that can be installed after TCP/IP is installed on a Windows NT computer. After the SNMP service is installed on a computer, it automatically starts each time the computer is started. The SNMP service provides an SNMP agent that enables remote, centralized SNMP management of the following:

- Windows NT Server computers
- Windows NT Workstation computers
- Windows NT-based WINS server computers
- Windows NT-based DHCP server computers
- Windows NT-based Internet Information Server computers
- LAN Manager server computers

Much of the SNMP object values come directly from the registry on a Windows NT computer. The registry contains most of the information that is identified in the MIB. The Microsoft SNMP service accesses the registry and converts the information into a format that can be used by an SNMP manager.

TEST TRAP Because SNMP is an optional TCP/IP service, the TCP/IP exam has very few questions covering SNMP topics. However, you should, at the very least, know how to install and configure the SNMP agent as covered in this section.

Installing and Configuring the SNMP Service

The SNMP service can be installed on any Windows NT computer that has TCP/IP installed.

Configure the following information for SNMP traps:

12: SETTING UP THE SNMP SERVICE

- **Community Name:** To identify each community to which you want this computer to send traps. Typically, all hosts belong to `public`, which is the standard name for the common community of all hosts. To delete an entry in the list, select it, and then choose the Remove button. Community names are case sensitive.
- **Trap Destination:** To specify the host name(s) or IP address(es) to which traps should be sent.

SNMP trap information is entered by selecting the Traps tab on the SNMP Properties dialog box.

Configuring SNMP security

Click the Security tab in the Microsoft SNMP properties dialog box to configure the following information for SNMP security:

- **Send Authentication Trap (checkbox):** To send a trap for a failed authentication. This happens when a message is sent to the SNMP agent with a different community name than has been configured on the agent.
- **Accepted Community Names:** The community names from which the SNMP agent will accept requests. A host must belong to a community that appears on this list for the SNMP agent to accept requests from that host. Normally, all hosts belong to `public`, which is the standard name for the common community of all hosts.
- **Accept SNMP Packets From Any Host:** If this option is selected, no SNMP packets are rejected on the basis of source host ID. The list of hosts under Only Accept SNMP Packets From These Hosts has no effect.
- **Only Accept SNMP Packets From These Hosts:** If this option is selected, SNMP packets will be accepted only from the hosts listed. A host can be specified by using a host name or an IP address.

SNMP security settings are entered by selecting the Security tab in the SNMP Properties dialog box.

287

Configuring SNMP agent services

Click the Agent tab in the Microsoft SNMP properties dialog box to configure the following information for SNMP agent services:

- **Contact:** The name of the person to contact, such as the network administrator or person who uses the computer.
- **Location:** Location of the contact or the location of this computer.
- **Service: Physical:** Select this option if this Windows NT computer manages any physical TCP/IP device, such as a repeater.
- **Service: Applications:** Select this option if this Windows NT computer includes any applications that use TCP/IP, such as e-mail. This option should be selected for all Windows NT installations (default).
- **Service: Datalink/Subnetwork:** Select this option if this Windows NT computer manages a TCP/IP subnetwork or datalink, such as a bridge.
- **Service: Internet:** Select this option if this Windows NT computer acts as an IP gateway (default).
- **Service: End-to-End:** Select this option if this Windows NT computer acts as an IP host. This option should be selected for all Windows NT installations (default).

SNMP agent services are entered by selecting the Agent tab on the SNMP Properties dialog box.

Managing SNMP

After the SNMP service has been installed and configured on a Windows NT computer, a network administrator using a third-party SNMP manager can do the following:

- View and change parameters in the LAN Manager and MIB-II MIBs
- Monitor and configure parameters for any WINS servers on the network
- Monitor DHCP servers

12: SETTING UP THE SNMP SERVICE

Additional counters for TCP/IP activity will be available for viewing in Performance Monitor. The SNMP service adds the following TCP/IP counters:

- ICMP
- IP
- Network Interface
- TCP
- UDP
- DHCP
- FTP
- WINS
- Internet Information Server performance counters

Also, the Windows NT Server Resource Kit software includes a utility called PERF2MIB.EXE, which is used to create a MIB file that can be used by an SNMP manager to request current values for any Windows NT Performance Monitor counter. The PERF2MIB utility works by exposing the HKEY_PERFORMANCE_DATA Registry key.

The syntax for PERF2MIB.EXE is as follows:

perf2mib MIBfilename INIfilename [ObjectName MIBIndex MIBPrefix [...]]

The following are parameters for the PERF2MIB utility:

- *MIBfilename:* The name of the MIB file to be created
- *INIfilename*: The name of the generated configuration file, used by the Windows NT SNMP extension agent to map performance counters to MIB variables
- *ObjectName:* The name of the performance object whose counters are to be exposed (such as Processor or Memory)
- *MIBIndex:* The numeric ID of the MIB branch where the particular object's data should be placed
- *MIBPrefix:* The abbreviation to be placed before counter names belonging to this object (such as mem for Memory counters or proc for Processor counters)

> **KNOW THIS**
>
> **MIB Parameters**
> The last three parameters can be repeated to map multiple object types with one call. If multiple object types are specified, the resulting MIB and MIB agent configuration information is combined into one MIB file.
> Example: `perf2mib counter.mib counter.ini Memory 1 mem Processor 2 proc System 3 sys`

Whenever the SNMP service is started and whenever an error occurs with the SNMP service, an entry is recorded to the event log. You can use the Event Viewer to display the System log for any suspected problems.

The Windows NT Resource Kit also includes a utility called `SNMPUTIL.EXE` that can be used to communicate problems with the SNMP agent. The `SNMPUTIL` can be used to simulate the messages that are generated from an SNMP manager.

The syntax for `SNMPUTIL.EXE` is as follows:

snmputil [get|getnext|walk] *agent community oid* [*oid*]

or

snmputil trap

The following are parameters for the SNMPUTIL utility:

- **get:** Gets the current value of the designated *oid*(s).
- **getnext:** Gets the current value of the item in the MIB that follows the one whose *oid* is specified.
- **walk:** Steps through the MIB and brings back the values of all items in the branch of the MIB designated by *oid*.
- *agent:* Specifies the computer to query. This can be an IP address, an IPX address, or a host name.
- *community:* Specifies a community name, used to group computers together into management groups.

12: SETTING UP THE SNMP SERVICE

- *oid:* The ASN.1 name of the variable being queried, of the form .N.N.N.N (a string of numbers or names separated by periods).
- trap: Instructs SNMPUTIL to listen for traps.

POP QUIZ — True or False?

1. An SNMP agent can be a member of multiple communities.
2. Windows NT includes SNMP management and agent capabilities.
3. The SNMP service must be installed before IP counters are available in Performance Monitor.

Answers: 1. True   2. False   3. True

MCSE TCP/IP ACE IT!

Have You Mastered?

Now it's time to review the concepts in this chapter and apply your knowledge. These questions will test your mastery of material covered in this chapter.

1. Which of the following is not a component of SNMP?

- ☐ A. Managers
- ☐ B. Agents
- ☐ C. Communities
- ☐ D. Monitors

D. SNMP utilizes managers, agents, and communities. See the "SNMP Components" section.

2. Where are the SNMP object values stored on a Windows NT computer?

- ☐ A. `Win.ini`
- ☐ B. `System.ini`
- ☐ C. Registry
- ☐ D. `SNMP.ini`

C. SNMP values are stored in the Registry. See the "Microsoft SNMP Service" section.

12: SETTING UP THE SNMP SERVICE

3. **Which of the following instructs the SNMPUTIL to listen for traps?**

    ☐ A. Trap
    ☐ B. Get
    ☐ C. Getnext
    ☐ D. Walk

    A. Trap is used to instruct SNMPUTIL to listen for SNMP traps. See the "Managing SNMP" section.

4. **Which SNMP agent service should be configured on a Windows NT computer acting as an IP router?**

    ☐ A. Location
    ☐ B. Physical
    ☐ C. Internet
    ☐ D. End-to-end

    C. Internet is the SNMP agent service used on a computer functioning as an IP gateway. See the "Managing SNMP" section.

5. **If SNMP fails, where would you look to discover the cause?**

    ☐ A. Registry
    ☐ B. Event Log
    ☐ C. SNMP.log
    ☐ D. Errors.log

    B. SNMP errors are stored in the Event Viewer. See the "Managing SNMP" section.

MCSE TCP/IP ACE IT!

Practice Your Skills

The Practice Your Skills labs will provide you with an opportunity to apply the knowledge you've gained in this chapter about the Microsoft SNMP service.

1. Implementing Simple Network Management Protocol (SNMP)

EXERCISE   You want to use SNMP to monitor and manage Windows NT Server computers on your network. You currently use a third-party SNMP manager to manage other types of devices on your network. What must be installed on a Windows NT Server computer before it can participate on the SNMP-managed network? What must be installed on the SNMP manager so that information about the managed objects on that computer can be determined? What type of message is generated by an SNMP agent?

ANALYSIS   The SNMP agent (also called the SNMP service) must be installed on a Windows NT Server computer. One or more MIBs must be installed on the SNMP manager so that you can determine information about the managed objects on the computer. An SNMP trap is generated by an SNMP agent.

12: SETTING UP THE SNMP SERVICE

2. Configuring SNMP for Windows NT computers

EXERCISE You have installed the SNMP agent on your Windows NT Server computers. You want to configure SNMP security for these computers. You want to configure the Windows NT Server computers so they can send trap messages only to the SNMP manager you use. How can you do this? How can you be notified when any of the Windows NT Server computers receives a message from an unauthorized SNMP manager? How can you configure the SNMP agent to send trap messages to multiple SNMP managers?

ANALYSIS If you want to configure a Windows NT Server computer to send trap messages to a specific SNMP manager, you should define an SNMP community name that will be used by the SNMP agent and the SNMP manager. You can be notified when a Windows NT Server computer receives a message from an unauthorized SNMP manager by configuring the SNMP agent to send an authentication trap. You can configure the SNMP agent to send trap messages to multiple SNMP managers by specifying the IP addresses of the SNMP managers that should receive trap messages.

3. Diagnosing SNMP problems

EXERCISE One of the Windows NT Server computers is not generating any trap messages or responding to requests from an SNMP manager. You verify that the SNMP manager is running and configured correctly. Where should you look for possible problems with the SNMP agent? Which utility can you use to diagnose problems with the SNMP agent?

ANALYSIS Use Event Viewer to view the contents of the system log. You can use the `SNMPUTIL.EXE` utility to diagnose problems with the SNMP agent.

295

13

Installing and Configuring TCP/IP

THE FOLLOWING CHAPTER ON setting up a TCP/IP network combines all of the information that we have reviewed thus far. It covers how to configure the options on the client that you have specified on your network. This information is a small part of the test that relies on everything you have learned so far and ties it together. Review this chapter carefully because it will help strengthen your understanding of topics covered in previous chapters.

MCSE TCP/IP ACE IT!

Exam Material in this Chapter

Official Word

Based on Microsoft Objectives
- Identify valid network configurations.
- Select the appropriate services to install when using Microsoft TCP/IP on a Microsoft network.

Inside Scoop

Based on Author's Experience
- Understand how to configure the TCP/IP services for use on the client.
- Know the function of each service.
- Be able to identify which service to use in a given situation.

13: INSTALLING AND CONFIGURING TCP/IP

Are You Prepared?

Test your knowledge with the following questions. Then you'll know if you're prepared for the material in this chapter or if you should review problem areas.

1. Which of the following is used with Windows 95 to view IP configuration information?

    ☐ A. DNS
    ☐ B. DHCP
    ☐ C. ipconfig
    ☐ D. winipcfg

2. Which of the following is used with a Windows NT workstation to view the IP configuration information?

    ☐ A. DNS
    ☐ B. DHCP
    ☐ C. ipconfig
    ☐ D. winipcfg

3. Which of the following is used with Windows NT server to view the IP configuration information?

    ☐ A. DNS
    ☐ B. DHCP
    ☐ C. ipconfig
    ☐ D. winipcfg

Answers:

1. D *See the "Troubleshooting Your TCP/IP Configuration" section.*
2. C *See the "Troubleshooting Your TCP/IP Configuration" section.*
3. C *See the "Troubleshooting Your TCP/IP Configuration" section.*

13: INSTALLING AND CONFIGURING TCP/IP

Planning Your TCP/IP Installation

TCP/IP protocols are normally selected during the installation of the Windows 95 or Windows NT operating system. During the installation, you can select the different options that must be set for various network client configurations and services. You can always add the TCP/IP protocols and change the options later, but this may require a great deal of effort if many clients need to be reconfigured after they have been installed.

The following questions will help you to determine how to proceed with your installation:

- How will clients be assigned a TCP/IP address (static or dynamic)?
- What subnet mask should be specified?
- Which routers will be used for connecting to hosts that reside on other networks?
- What method of name resolution will be used?

TEST TIP There are a number of questions on the exam that test your knowledge of how to properly install, configure, and test TCP/IP address settings. You will also be tested on how to configure TCP/IP settings for special situations, such as multiple addresses and multiple network adapters.

Assigning IP Addresses on Your Network

Each client computer needs a unique IP address to communicate on the network. With *manual addressing*, an administrator must configure the IP addresses for each computer on the network. Manual addressing must be used when there is no *Dynamic Host Configuration Protocol*

301

(DHCP) server on the network, and for the Windows NT Server computer that is a DHCP server. *Automatic addressing* requires DHCP to assign IP addresses to computers. Addresses are automatically assigned when the computer is turned on or is moved to a different location (subnet) on the network. A client configured for dynamic addressing can request an IP address from computers running the DHCP service.

All computers must be configured with a subnet mask. You can use the default subnet mask when your network consists of a single segment (one subnet). Regardless of whether you use a custom subnet mask or a default subnet mask, all computers on the same subnet should have the same subnet mask in order to communicate with one another.

Using subnets, an organization can divide a single large network into multiple logical networks and connect them together with routers. You can then create a custom subnet mask to define multiple subnets.

When a host prepares to send a message to another host, the source host (sender) includes its own address and the address of the destination host in the IP packet. The source host checks the network ID of the destination host and compares it against a local routing table. If the destination network ID is determined to reside on a remote subnet, the sending host forwards the packet to the default gateway (a router) for delivery onto a different network.

A default gateway address is not required for a host computer. However, if you do not specify a default gateway address, communications will be limited to the local network for that host.

Windows networks rely on NetBIOS names to identify computers. *NetBIOS naming* is a fairly automatic system that depends on broadcast messages, which are not forwarded through routers on TCP/IP networks. Therefore, on TCP/IP networks that include routers, you must take special steps to ensure that NetBIOS names are distributed and can be resolved throughout the entire network. To use WINS, each client computer must be configured with the address of at least one WINS server. To configure WINS on a network client, you must supply the IP address of at least one, but preferably two, WINS servers. During client configuration, you should provide the following information:

13: INSTALLING AND CONFIGURING TCP/IP

- **Primary WINS server address:** This is the IP address of the WINS server that the client will register its name and IP address with.
- **Secondary WINS server address:** This is the WINS server that the client will register with and that will be used if the primary WINS server is unavailable.

The *Domain Name System* (DNS) is a hierarchical, client/server database management system used to identify hosts on the Internet. The purpose of the DNS database is to resolve host names to IP addresses. DNS is the standard way of supporting naming on TCP/IP networks. While DNS serves much the same purpose as NetBIOS naming, DNS differs from NetBIOS in that DNS does not update its database dynamically as computers log on and off the network. The network administrator must manually maintain the DNS database.

You need to determine whether client computers will be configured to use DNS. You will likely need to use DNS if you are using TCP/IP to communicate over the Internet, or if your organization uses DNS to resolve host names on your internal network. If you choose to use DNS, you must configure each computer with the IP address of a primary DNS server and optionally a backup DNS server.

In addition to the typical TCP/IP configuration settings, there may be special cases where multiple IP addresses need to be assigned to a computer. It is possible to configure a Windows NT computer with multiple IP addresses for a single network adapter card. This can be useful for a computer connected to one physical network that contains multiple logical IP networks.

It is also possible to configure a Windows NT computer with multiple network adapters, each connected to a separate subnet. A computer configured this way is called a multihomed host, and provides simultaneous access to multiple subnets. You must configure a multihomed computer so that each adapter has its own IP address, subnet mask, and default gateway address. All other TCP/IP settings apply system-wide.

Installing and Configuring TCP/IP on a Windows NT Computer

During installation of Windows NT Workstation or Windows NT Server, the TCP/IP protocol and connectivity utilities are installed by default. During the installation process you can choose to install and configure other optional TCP/IP components.

> **KNOW THIS** **Administrative Privileges**
> To change TCP/IP configuration settings on a Windows NT computer, you must be a member of the local administrators group.

If DHCP is used to automatically configure IP address settings, then you should not set the WINS address settings. Instead, you should configure your DHCP server to provide the addresses of the WINS servers on your network. If a WINS server is available but DHCP is not used, you must enable WINS resolution by typing the IP addresses of the primary and secondary WINS servers used on your network.

Enabling DNS for Windows resolution causes the computer to use a DNS server to resolve any NetBIOS name references. Enabling LMHOSTS lookup causes the computer to use a local mapping file as one method of resolving a NetBIOS name.

The scope ID option in the TCP/IP configuration provides a way to isolate a group of computers that only communicate with each other. The scope ID consists of one or more characters that are appended to the NetBIOS name and are used for all NetBIOS over TCP/IP communications from that computer. Other computers configured with an identical scope ID are able to communicate with this computer, while all clients with a different scope ID disregard packets from any other scope ID.

You should not change the scope ID on any computers on your network unless you really want to isolate a specific group for security reasons. Keep in mind that once you change the scope ID on one computer, that computer will not be able to communicate with any other computer unless it has the same scope ID. Also, changing the scope ID has no effect on network traffic, as all packets are still accepted and processed by a computer but disregarded at the NetBIOS level.

It might appear that scope IDs enhance security by restricting communication to specific hosts. But like the NetBIOS name, the scope ID is transmitted in clear text on the network, so anyone who is snooping the network (for example, with the network monitor that is included with NT Server 4.0) can learn your scope. Because Scope ID scans really complicate things, Microsoft recommends you avoid using them whenever possible.

If you will use DNS on your network, you must configure how the computer will use DNS. The DNS configuration settings are global for all network adapters installed on a computer. If DHCP is used for automatic configuration, the DHCP server can be configured to provide these parameters. In the Microsoft TCP/IP properties dialog box, click the DNS tab. The dialog box displays the configuration settings for DNS. The host name is used to create an Internet-compatible name for this host. By default the host name is set to the computer name.

> **KNOW THIS** **Host names and Computer names**
>
> The host name can be any combination of the letters A through Z, the numerals 0 through 9, and the hyphen (-), plus the period (.) character used as a separator. By default, this value is the Microsoft networking computer name, but an administrator can assign a different host name without affecting the computer name.

The host name and domain that are set on a computer are used to create a fully qualified domain name (FQDN) for the computer. The FQDN is the host name followed by a period (.), followed by the domain name. For example, this could be `gregb.quicklearn.com`, where *gregb* is the host name and *quicklearn.com* is the domain name. When querying the DNS server for the IP address of *gregb*, the domain name is appended to the short name, and the DNS server is actually asked to resolve the FQDN of `gregb.quicklearn.com`.

You can add up to three IP addresses for DNS servers. For any given DNS query, the client computer attempts to get DNS information from the first IP address in the list. If no response is received, the computer goes to the second server in the list, and so on.

> **KNOW THIS** **Multiple DNS Servers**
> If you have multiple servers listed in the TCP/IP Properties dialog box, the client computer checks the next server only if no response is received from the previous server. If the client computer attempts to check a host name with a DNS server and receives a message that the host name is not recognized, the system does not try the next DNS server.

The *domain suffix search order* specifies the DNS domain suffixes that will be appended to host names during name resolution. You can add up to six domain suffixes. Domain suffixes are placed in the list in alphabetic order. When attempting to resolve a *fully qualified domain name* (FQDN) from a short name, a client computer will use the domain suffix list to create additional FQDNs and query DNS servers in the order listed.

Installing and Configuring TCP/IP on a Windows 95 Computer

You will find that installing TCP/IP on a Windows 95 computer appears to be identical to installing TCP/IP on a Windows NT computer. However, there are some subtle differences that you may notice as you work with the TCP/IP configuration dialog boxes in Windows 95.

13: INSTALLING AND CONFIGURING TCP/IP

When TCP/IP is installed on Windows 95 computers, DHCP is automatically enabled so an IP address will be obtained from a DHCP server. If you cannot use DHCP for automatic configuration, this option can be disabled using the Network option in Control Panel. However, this means you will need to obtain IP configuration parameters from your site administrator.

> **KNOW THIS — Configuring Multiple Adapters**
> If your computer has multiple network adapters, the list will include an instance of TCP/IP for each network adapter you have installed. You must configure each adapter with its own IP address, subnet mask, and gateway. All other settings apply system-wide.

The first IP address that you add will be used as the default gateway. The IP addresses are used in order, starting at the top of the list. Windows 95 will attempt to connect to other gateways only if the default gateway becomes unavailable. You can prioritize the gateway addresses by dragging the IP address in the list to a different position.

> **KNOW THIS — Adding and Removing Networking Components**
> In the Bindings dialog box, you can select or remove the network components that can be used with TCP/IP by clearing the checkmark next to the client name. You might want to do this, for instance, if you want to prevent someone from using TCP/IP to connect to your computer from the network. In this case, you would clear the checkbox for File and Print Sharing for Microsoft Networks. The computer can still use TCP/IP for all outgoing connections; however, because file and print sharing have been removed, users will not be able to use resources on this computer.

If you plan to use WINS for NetBIOS name registration and resolution, each Windows 95 computer must be configured with the IP addresses of the WINS servers. If DHCP is used for automatic configuration of IP address settings, then you should select Use DHCP for WINS Resolution on the WINS Configuration tab and configure your DHCP server to provide the addresses of the WINS servers on your network. If a WINS server is available, but not a DHCP server, then select Enable WINS Resolution and type the IP addresses of the primary and secondary WINS servers that are located on your network. The following instructions are for manually configuring Windows 95 computers with the IP addresses of the WINS servers (when no DHCP server is available).

If you plan to use DNS on your network, you must configure how the computer will use DNS and the HOSTS file. DNS configuration settings are global for all network adapters installed on a computer. If DHCP is used for automatic configuration, the DHCP server can be configured to provide these parameters. The host name is used to create an Internet-compatible name for this host.

TEST TRAP When computers are configured with different host and computer names, remember to be careful with how they are accessed. You won't be able to ping a computer by its computer name because that uses the hostname. Remembering this can avoid confusion on the test.

The domain name is used with the host name to create a fully qualified domain name (FQDN) for the computer. The FQDN is the host name followed by a period (.), followed by the domain name. For example, this could be gregb.quicklearn.com, where *gregb* is the host name and *quicklearn.com* is the domain name.

When querying the DNS server for the IP address of *gregb*, the domain name is appended to the short name, and the DNS server is actually asked to resolve the FQDN of gregb.quicklearn.com. You can add up to three IP addresses for DNS servers. For any given DNS query, the client computer attempts to get DNS information from the first IP address in the list. If no response is received, the computer goes to the second server in the list, and so on.

13: INSTALLING AND CONFIGURING TCP/IP

KNOW THIS **Issues with DNS and Multiple Servers**
If you have multiple servers listed in the TCP/IP Properties dialog box, the client computer checks the next server only if no response is received from the previous server. If the client computer attempts to check a host name with a DNS server and receives a message that the host name is not recognized, the system does not try the next DNS server.

Troubleshooting Your TCP/IP Configuration

Before you begin to troubleshoot your TCP/IP configuration, remember that a large number of network problems are due to incorrect settings on the network adapter. Verify that the I/O address, *interrupt request number* (IRQ), and memory addresses of the network adapter do not conflict with other components you have installed in the computer.

You may need to check your computer's BIOS setup configuration by using the Windows NT Diagnostics program or the Windows 95 Device manager to assist you in identifying hardware conflicts on your system.

Using the Ipconfig and Winipcfg Utilities

The `ipconfig` diagnostic command displays all current TCP/IP network configuration values when run on a particular host. Ipconfig is particularly useful on systems running DHCP, since all TCP/IP parameters are assigned to a host transparently by a DHCP server. With no parameters, `ipconfig` displays all of the current TCP/IP configuration values, including IP address, subnet mask, and WINS and DNS configuration on a Windows NT computer, as shown in this example:

```
C:\>ipconfig
Windows NT IP Configuration
Ethernet adapter NE20001:
IP Address. . . . . . . . . : 172.25.16.51
Subnet Mask . . . . . . . . : 255.255.0.0
Default Gateway . . . . . . : 172.25.16.1
```

If DHCP is used by the client and the DHCP server is unavailable, all of the addresses will appear as 0.0.0.0. If a duplicate address is assigned to the host, the IP address appears as configured, but the subnet mask appears as 0.0.0.0.

TEST TIP There are many situations where `ipconfig` (or `winipcfg`) can be used to help you identify TCP/IP configuration problems. You will be expected to know how to use these utilities and identify the information that they provide.

On a Windows 95 computer, the equivalent of the `ipconfig` utility is called `winipcfg`. The output from `winipcfg` will be shown in a dialog box instead of a command prompt.

POP QUIZ True or False?

1. Gateway and router are terms that can be used interchangeably.
2. WINS clients use h-node name resolution.
3. Master servers provide zone information to primary DNS servers.

Answers: 1. True 2. True 3. False

Testing Your TCP/IP Configuration Using Ping

You can use the *ping* utility to isolate network hardware problems and incompatible configurations. Ping enables you to verify a physical connection to a gateway or remote computer. Ping uses the *Internet Control Message Protocol* (ICMP) *echo request* and *echo reply* messages to determine if a particular remote host is available on the network. As shown in Figure 13-1, when using ping, you should start by checking the configuration of the local computer, then the default gateway, and finally the remote host to which you want to connect.

TEST TIP Troubleshooting problems is an important part of managing a network of TCP/IP computers. The TCP/IP exam includes a number of troubleshooting questions that test your knowledge on how to properly use the ping utility to diagnose network problems.

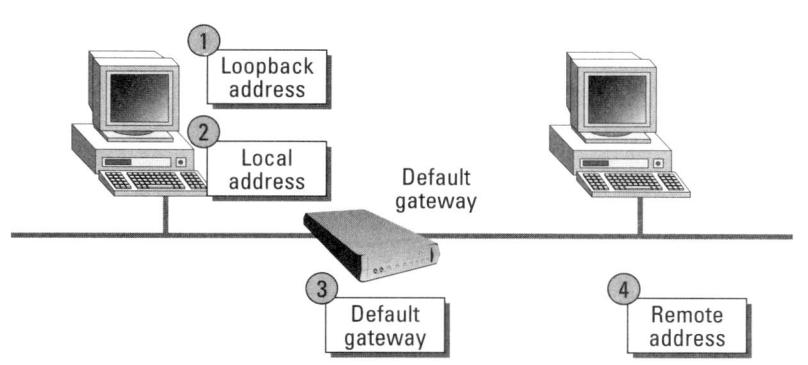

Figure 13-1 *Using* ping *to test the TCP/IP configuration*

> **KNOW THIS** **The Loopback Address**
> To test TCP/IP on your computer, you can use the IP address `127.0.0.1`. This address is known as the *loopback address* for your computer. The loopback address uses *loopback drivers* to reroute outgoing packets back to the source computer. By going through the loopback drivers, the packets can bypass the network adapter card completely and be returned directly to the computer that is performing the test.

If you cannot use `ping` successfully at any point, check the following:

- The computer was restarted after TCP/IP was installed and configured.
- The local computer's IP address is valid and appears correctly in the TCP/IP Configuration dialog box.
- The IP addresses of the default gateway and remote host are correct.
- The link between routers is operational.

If you can use `ping` to communicate with other Windows-based computers on a different subnet but cannot connect using Explorer or by typing **net use *servername**sharename*** from a command line, check the following:

- If the network includes WINS servers, is the local host WINS-enabled?
- Are the WINS server addresses correct, and are the WINS servers functioning?
- Is the correct computer name being used?

- Does the target host use NetBIOS? If not, you must use FTP or Telnet to make a connection; in this case, the target host must be configured with the FTP daemon or Telnet daemon, and you must have correct permissions on the target host.
- Is the scope ID on the target host the same as on the local computer?
- Is there a local LMHOSTS file that contains correct entries so that the remote computer name can be resolved?

> **TEST TIP**
> The TCP/IP exam includes a number of questions that test your knowledge on how to install, configure, and test TCP/IP configuration settings on both Windows NT computers and Windows 95 computers. You will also be tested on the methods of verifying that the computer has been configured properly with TCP/IP.

MCSE TCP/IP ACE IT!

Have You Mastered?

Now it's time to review the concepts in this chapter and apply your knowledge. These questions will test your mastery of the material in this chapter.

1. Where is the domain suffix search order specified?

- ☐ A. WINS tab
- ☐ B. HOSTS tab
- ☐ C. DNS tab
- ☐ D. General tab

C. Domain suffix search order is specified on the DNS tab. See the "Installing and Configuring TCP/IP on a Windows NT Computer" section.

2. A successful ping from which address verifies that TCP/IP is configured properly without testing the network adapter?

- ☐ A. Local address
- ☐ B. Gateway address
- ☐ C. Loopback address
- ☐ D. Address on remote subnet

C. Pinging the loopback address tests the TCP/IP configuration and bypasses the network adapter. See the "Troubleshooting Your TCP/IP Configuration" section.

13: INSTALLING AND CONFIGURING TCP/IP

3. **A successful ping from which address verifies that TCP/IP is configured properly and tests the network adapter?**

   ☐ A. Local address
   ☐ B. Gateway address
   ☐ C. Loopback address
   ☐ D. Address on remote subnet

   A. Pinging the local address tests the TCP/IP configuration and the network adapter. See the "Troubleshooting Your TCP/IP Configuration" section.

4. **A successful ping from which address verifies that TCP/IP is configured properly and there are no problems with the network?**

   ☐ A. Local address
   ☐ B. Gateway address
   ☐ C. Loopback address
   ☐ D. Address on remote subnet

   D. A successful ping of computers on the remote subnet shows a properly functioning network. See the "Troubleshooting Your TCP/IP Configuration" section.

5. **A successful ping from which address verifies that TCP/IP is configured properly on the local computer and that the problem is with the router?**

   ☐ A. Local address
   ☐ B. Gateway address
   ☐ C. Loopback address
   ☐ D. Address on remote subnet

   B. If you are able to successfully ping the gateway but no remote systems, the problem is with the routing table on the router. See the "Troubleshooting Your TCP/IP Configuration" section.

Practice Your Skills

The following exercises provide you with an opportunity to apply the knowledge you've gained in this chapter about configuring TCP/IP.

1. Testing the TCP/IP configuration settings on a Windows NT computer

EXERCISE You have just installed TCP/IP on a Windows NT Workstation computer. After rebooting the computer, you want to test whether the TCP/IP software has properly initialized for the computer. How should you use `ping` to verify the workstation's configuration? How should you use `ping` to determine whether the workstation can communicate on the network?

ANALYSIS To verify the workstation's configuration, run the `ping` command with the loopback address by typing **ping 127.0.0.1** from a command line. To determine if the workstation can communicate on the network, run the `ping` command using the IP address of the computer by typing **ping ip_address** (use the actual IP address of the computer) from a command line.

13: INSTALLING AND CONFIGURING TCP/IP

2. Testing TCP/IP connectivity to a computer on a remote subnet

EXERCISE After installing TCP/IP on a Windows NT Workstation computer, you want to determine whether the workstation can communicate with a Windows NT Server computer located on a different subnet. How should you test to determine whether the workstation can communicate outside of its local subnet? How should you test whether the workstation can communicate with the server on the remote subnet?

ANALYSIS To see if the workstation can communicate outside of its local subnet, run the `ping` command using the IP address of the workstation's default gateway (router). Type `ping gateway_ip_address` (use the actual IP address of the default gateway). To see if the workstation can communicate with the server on the remote subnet, run the `ping` command using the IP address of the server. Type `ping server_ip_address` (use the actual IP address of the remote server).

3. Configuring a computer to automatically receive a TCP/IP address

EXERCISE You have just installed TCP/IP on a Windows NT Workstation computer. You want this workstation to automatically receive its TCP/IP address settings. This workstation will also need to communicate with a Windows NT Server computer on a remote subnet. What service must be installed on a Windows NT Server computer to enable the workstation to receive IP address settings automatically? In addition to the TCP/IP address, which two TCP/IP configuration settings must be set on the workstation?

ANALYSIS DHCP Server must be installed on the Windows NT Server computer to enable the workstation to receive IP address settings automatically. The IP address of a default gateway and a subnet mask must be set on the workstation.

4. Configuring a Windows NT Workstation as a multihomed computer

EXERCISE You want to configure a Windows NT Workstation computer so it can communicate simultaneously on two different subnets. What hardware must be installed on the workstation in order to do this? How must you specify the TCP/IP settings for a multihomed computer?

ANALYSIS The computer must have two network adapter cards installed. Each network adapter must be configured with a unique IP address. You must also specify a subnet mask and a default gateway for each adapter. All other TCP/IP settings, such as WINS and DNS, apply system-wide.

5. Diagnosing TCP/IP configuration problems

EXERCISE A Windows NT Workstation computer has been configured to use DHCP to receive all TCP/IP configuration settings. The workstation has been started and TCP/IP has been initialized. How can you determine what IP address settings have been assigned to this workstation? Why would the TCP/IP address appear as 0.0.0.0 on the workstation after it has been started?

13: INSTALLING AND CONFIGURING TCP/IP

ANALYSIS To determine what IP settings have been assigned, run the `ipconfig` utility from a command line by typing **ipconfig**. The TCP/IP address would appear as 0.0.0.0 if the workstation could not contact a DHCP server.

14

TCP/IP Performance Monitoring

PERFORMANCE MONITORING AND TROUBLESHOOTING are important parts of the test that some people overlook; at least they do the first time they take the test. There is a lot of important information covered in this chapter, so be sure you are comfortable with this material before taking the test.

MCSE TCP/IP ACE IT!

Exam Material in this Chapter

Official Word

Based on Microsoft Objectives
- Diagnose and resolve IP addressing problems.
- Identify which utilities to use to diagnose IP configuration problems.

Inside Scoop

Based on Author's Experience
- Be very familiar with the capabilities of Performance Monitor and Network Monitor.
- Understand the advantages of each of the different troubleshooting tools.
- Understand which utilities provide network information and which provide machine information.
- Familiarize yourself with how to use each of the utilities.

14: TCP/IP PERFORMANCE MONITORING

Are You Prepared?

Test your knowledge with the following questions. Then you'll know if you're prepared for the material in this chapter or if you should review problem areas.

1. Which utility does not show IP statistics?

- ☐ A. Netstat
- ☐ B. Performance monitor
- ☐ C. Network monitor
- ☐ D. Nbtstat

2. Which utility is used to view the path of an IP packet?

- ☐ A. Netstat
- ☐ B. Nbtstat
- ☐ C. Tracert
- ☐ D. Ping

3. Which switch allows `netstat` to display the routing table?

- ☐ A. -a
- ☐ B. -e
- ☐ C. -s
- ☐ D. -r

MCSE TCP/IP ACE IT!

Answers:

1. D *See the "Monitoring TCP/IP Activity" section.*
2. C *See the "Monitoring TCP/IP Activity" section.*
3. D *See the "Monitoring TCP/IP Activity" section.*

Improving Network Performance

With each successive version of a Microsoft network operating system, there are fewer parameters provided for tuning system performance. Microsoft expended considerable effort in designing adaptive algorithms into the operating system for detecting current operating conditions and automatically adjusting parameters.

This holds true for the protocols, as well. Not only has Microsoft fine-tuned the code for Microsoft TCP/IP, but there are many new RFCs that describe methods for dynamically allocating TCP window sizes, timing delays, and other performance-related algorithms. Because of this, manual tuning of TCP/IP protocols' performance parameters is often unnecessary.

The good news is a network administrator is not required to know a lot of detail about protocol parameters and can instead focus on the typical causes of network performance problems.

Network performance is measured by analyzing the speed at which two hosts on a network communicate. Performance problems usually become apparent when a user notices changes in response time. However, there are a number of tools that can be used to monitor and evaluate network performance.

Two of the most typical performance problems on a TCP/IP network are having inadequate network hardware and excessive network traffic.

Hardware Performance

While moving data across the media is one factor to consider (we discuss network traffic next), a bigger hardware problem is usually how fast devices can process the information moving across the media.

If a network is large or spans multiple locations, there are probably a few routers connecting the subnets together. Routers must quickly examine the contents of a packet header and then pass the packet to the appropriate interface. An inadequate CPU (processor) or lack of memory (RAM) can cause routers to drop packets. This causes the sender to retransmit, which increases network traffic even further.

While the networking components on a Windows NT computer are just one of the potential performance bottlenecks on a Windows NT computer, they are an important factor that can affect throughput. A slow performing or defective network adapter can cause performance problems on the computer itself or even the entire network.

Network Traffic

On a busy network there are always periods of peak activity and possibly certain times when network traffic is minimal. It is important to analyze network activity over a period of time to get a good picture of traffic patterns on a network.

Analyzing traffic on a busy network may help identify ways to improve network performance. Unnecessary protocols and applications, such as terminal emulation programs or file transfer programs, may be causing a higher percentage of network traffic.

Many of the problems associated with network traffic may be hard to pinpoint. Fortunately, there are a number of simple diagnostics tools that can be used to help isolate problems relating to hardware or TCP/IP protocols.

Monitoring TCP/IP Activity

Once you know that a TCP/IP host is communicating on the network, you may want to know how well it is communicating. Microsoft TCP/IP provides several tools that can be used to help you monitor TCP/IP.

TCP/IP Connections and Statistics

Netstat is a utility designed to display statistics about TCP/IP protocols. Netstat can be used to display the current TCP/IP connections one host has to another computer and the information about the amount of data and number of packets that have been sent by the different protocols, such as TCP, UDP, IP, and ICMP. The command line for `netstat` may include a numeric value which sets the number of seconds between interactions. Thus, `netstat 5` produces the report every five seconds. Here is the command syntax for using `netstat`:

netstat [-a] [-ens] [-p *protocol***] [-r] [***interval***]**

Following are the parameters used with the netstat utility:

-a shows all connections; server connections are usually not shown.

-e shows Ethernet statistics. This option may be used jointly with the -s option.

-n shows addresses and port numbers in numerical form (avoids name lookups).

-s shows per-protocol statistics. Default statistics shown are TCP, UDP, ICMP, and IP; the -p option may be used to specify a subset of the default.

-p *protocol* shows connections for the protocol specified by *protocol*; *protocol*, either tcp or udp. If paired with the -s option to display per-protocol statistics, *protocol* may be tcp, udp, icmp, or ip.

-r shows the contents of the routing table.

interval reshows selected statistics, pausing *interval* seconds between each display. Press CTRL+C to stop reshowing statistics. Without this parameter, netstat prints the current configuration information once.

Performance Monitor

In addition to the many operating system-related counters that can be monitored, the Windows NT Performance Monitor can be used to view many different TCP/IP-related counters. To view the network counters in Performance Monitor, the *Simple Network Management Protocol* (SNMP) service must be installed on all Windows NT computers that are to be monitored. This is true for any remote Windows NT computer, as well as the computer on which you may be running Performance Monitor. This is because one of the features of Performance Monitor is that it enables counters from various systems to be monitored from a single computer.

> **KNOW THIS**
>
> **SNMP**
>
> SNMP is not automatically installed when you install TCP/IP. It must be installed before the TCP/IP counters will appear in Performance Monitor.

The SNMP service acts as an agent to collect all TCP/IP statistics on a Windows NT computer. When the SNMP service is installed, TCP/IP-related counters are added to Performance Monitor. The following list describes the information that is collected in each object category:

- **Network Interface:** Indicates the rates and statistics at which bytes and packets are received and sent over a network TCP/IP connection; also includes error counts for that connection.

- **ICMP:** The ICMP object type includes counters that describe the rates at which *Internet Control Message Protocol* (ICMP) messages are sent and received by an entity using the ICMP protocol. It also gives various error counts for the ICMP protocol.

- **IP:** The IP object type includes counters that describe the rates at which *Internet Protocol* (IP) datagrams are sent and received by a computer using the IP protocol. It also gives various error counts for the IP protocol.

- **TCP:** The TCP object type includes counters that describe the rates at which *Transmission Control Protocol* (TCP) segments are sent and received by an entity using the TCP protocol. It also gives the number of TCP connections in each possible TCP connection state.

- **UDP:** The UDP object type includes counters that describe the rates at which *User Datagram Protocol* (UDP) datagrams are sent and received by a certain entity using the UDP protocol. It also gives various error counts for the UDP protocol.

- **NBT Connection:** The WINS object counters are automatically installed with the installation of WINS service on a Windows NT Server computer. The WINS object counters include rates and statistics for name registrations and name resolution on a WINS server.
- **DHCP, WINS, and FTP Servers:** The FTP Server object counters are automatically installed with the installation of Internet Information Service on a Windows NT Server computer. The FTP Server counters include rates and statistics for FTP Server logons and file transfer activity. Each time you start and stop the FTP Server service, the FTP Server performance counters are cleared.

Network Monitor

A protocol analyzer is a tool that captures, filters, and analyzes network traffic. The Microsoft Network Monitor is a software-based traffic analysis tool. Using Network Monitor you can:

- Capture frames (packets) directly from the network
- Display and filter captured frames
- Edit captured frames and transmit them on the network

Network Monitor is useful for diagnosing hardware and software problems when two or more computers cannot communicate. You can also use it to capture network activity and then send the capture file to professional network analysts or support organizations.

Full version versus limited version

A limited version (also called the simple version) of Network Monitor comes with Windows NT Server 4.0. The full version comes with Microsoft *Systems Management Server* (SMS). The biggest difference between the full version and the limited version is the limited version can only capture traffic being sent to or from the computer on which Network Monitor is running. The full version enables you to capture traffic from any device on the subnet and provides these other additional benefits:

- View statistics on devices and protocols that are generating the most network traffic
- Identify which devices are configured as routers
- Store a list of device names for easy identification
- Edit and retransmit a frame
- Installable on any Windows-based computer

Previous versions of Network Monitor required an adapter that could be placed in *promiscuous mode* (capable of accepting all packets regardless of the destination address). Promiscuous mode places the network adapter in a state so that it accepts all frames on the network cable regardless of the destination address. The problem with promiscuous mode is it is very CPU intensive, so that it places greater demands on a computer.

The newer *Network Device Interface Specification* (NDIS) that comes with Windows NT 4.0 allows Network Monitor to capture network traffic in a new mode called "local only." This mode allows for capturing packets without requiring the network adapter to be placed in promiscuous mode.

How does Network Monitor work?

Network Monitor works by setting the network adapter in a mode that allows it to capture network traffic by monitoring the *data stream*, which consists of all information transferred over a network at any given time.

Capture filters can be used so that only desired frames will be saved for analysis. This is useful not only for readability but also because the capture buffer can fill up quickly, preventing new packets from being captured. The capture buffer can only be as large as the available system memory on the capture computer. *Display filters* can be used to further narrow down the focus of captured frames. Display filters work on the data that has been already captured so that Network Monitor only shows you those frames that you need to view to help you isolate a problem.

The Network Monitor Capture window, shown in Figure 14-1, displays statistical and captured data in four different views (or panes).

14: TCP/IP PERFORMANCE MONITORING

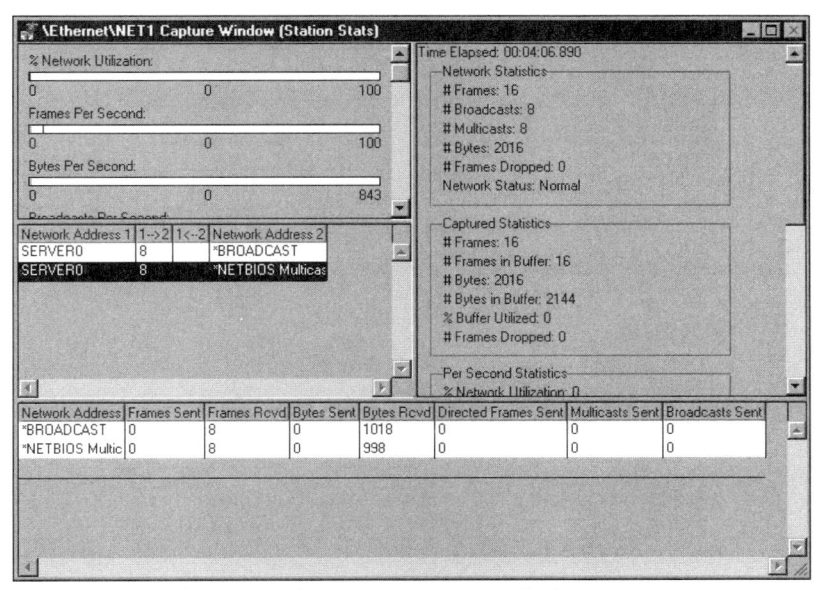

Figure 14-1 *The Network Monitor Capture window*

The four panes displayed in the Capture window are:

- **Graph:** A graphical picture of current network activity
- **Session Statistics:** Statistics about current individual sessions on the network
- **Station Statistics:** Statistics about the sessions in which the computer running Network Monitor participated
- **Total Statistics:** Summary statistics about network activity detected since the beginning of the capture process

Once data has been captured, Network Monitor parses (interprets the protocol data contents) and formats the data for viewing in the *Capture Summary* window, as shown in Figure 14-2. A protocol parser is a *dynamic-link library* (DLL) that identifies the protocols used within a frame. For each protocol that Network Monitor supports, there is a corresponding parser.

MCSE TCP/IP ACE IT!

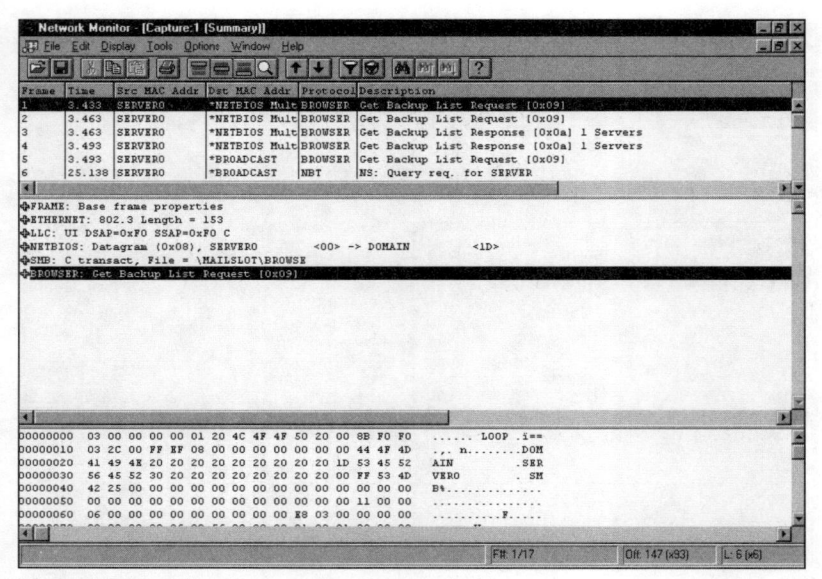

Figure 14-2 *The Capture Summary window*

The three panes displayed in the Capture Summary window are:

- **Detail:** Protocol information about the currently highlighted frame in the Summary pane
- **Hex:** A hexadecimal and ASCII representation of captured data for the information that is currently highlighted in the Detail pane
- **Summary:** General information about captured frames (in the order of their capture)

Using Network Monitor Agent

Network Monitor Agent is a software driver that must be installed in order for a computer to capture network traffic for use in Network Monitor. It also adds the Network Segment object, which adds additional network counters for use with Performance Monitor.

Also, Network Monitor Agent can be installed on a computer on a remote subnet, which can then act as an agent for collecting network traffic for that subnet. The collected data is then sent over the network to the subnet containing the computer running the Network Monitor program.

Troubleshooting TCP/IP Problems

Even the most experienced persons cannot possibly retain the knowledge and skills necessary to solve all problems that surface. Because of this, possibly the second most important asset to problem solving, after personal experience, is having access to troubleshooting resources and tools. Some of the more valuable resources are discussed in the following section.

Resources

Microsoft TechNet is a series of compact discs containing a complete set of online Microsoft Resource Kits and a collection of technical support documents known as the Microsoft KnowledgeBase. The discs, published monthly and available by subscription, also include drivers and patches to Microsoft applications and operating systems.

Microsoft also offers an Internet site that includes online support resources such as frequently asked questions about technical products, references to special focus newsgroups, and technical support chat sessions with Microsoft support engineers and guests.

The newsgroups are especially valuable because they are used by thousands of professionals. You may find someone who may have already solved some of the very problems you are experiencing.

Diagnosing TCP/IP Problems

Most TCP/IP problems can be grouped into one of the categories in the following list:

- **Hardware:** TCP/IP cannot initialize.
- **Configuration:** TCP/IP cannot initialize, TCP/IP-related service cannot start.
- **Subnet addressing:** You can ping your workstation, but not any other local or remote host.

- **Address Resolution:** You can ping your workstation, but not any other hosts.
- **NetBIOS name resolution:** You can access a host by its IP address but not using a NetBIOS name.
- **Host name resolution:** You can access a host by its IP address but not using its host name.

When attempting to isolate the source of a TCP/IP problem, you should begin at the network interface layer and work from there to the application layer, as shown in Figure 14-3. After testing the network adapter and its connection to the network, you should test the protocols at the next layer and verify that the protocols at that layer can communicate with the layers above and below it.

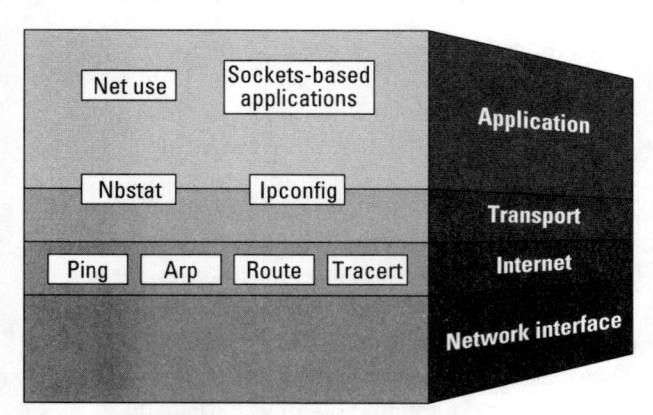

Figure 14-3 *Diagnosing TCP/IP problems*

Before you dig into your arsenal of software troubleshooting tools and protocol analyzer programs, you should check to see if your problems are the result of faulty hardware or hardware configuration problems.

If any kind of hardware was recently introduced to the computer, you should check for resource conflicts with the current interrupt and I/O address setting on the network adapter. Try running the ping command using the loopback address by typing: `ping 127.0.0.1` from a command line. If the ping is successful, then everything up through the network interface is working. At this point, you should check the network adapter's connection to the network cabling.

In the case of any system problems, including TCP/IP communications, you should first view the contents of the *system log* using Event Viewer. If the problem is related to the network adapter or the failure of a TCP/IP related service, it will be logged in the system log file. You should specifically look for critical errors (those with the red stop sign), but do not completely overlook warning error messages that may provide a clue to a more serious problem somewhere else in the list. You can see the details for a specific error message by double-clicking the error message in Event Viewer.

TCP/IP services problems

On a Windows NT Server computer, the failure of a service such as DHCP, WINS, or DNS may be caused by a dependency service (a service that is required to load successfully in order for other services to load) or the failure of TCP/IP protocols to initialize on the server. Select the Services program in Control Panel to verify that none of the required TCP/IP services have been disabled or have failed to start for any reason. Use the following diagnostic tools to assist you:

- `ipconfig`: Check to see if the TCP/IP has been initialized on this computer. An error message or missing IP address is an indication of a problem.

- **Event Viewer:** To view the contents of the system log, select Event Viewer from the Administration Tools menu. Error messages preceded by a red stop sign are indications of a severe failure. The event list is sorted by date with the newest messages first. You may need to check one of the older messages to discover a problem affecting the severe error condition.

`Ping` is a useful tool to help diagnose connection problems on an internetwork. `Ping` is used to verify that one host can communicate with another host. The `ping` command works by sending an ICMP echo request to a destination host by specifying its IP address or host name.

As shown in Figure 14-4, you should use the following steps when using `ping` to diagnose connection problems.

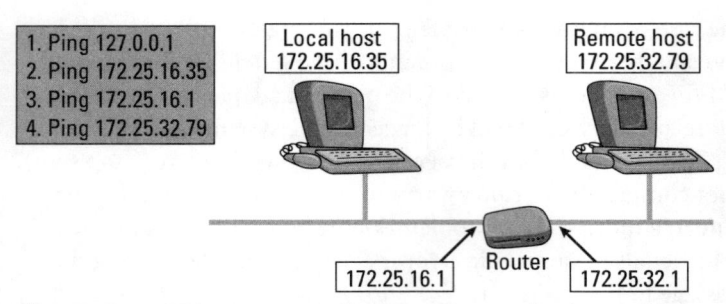

Figure 14-4 *Using* `ping` *to diagnose communication problems*

IP address resolution problems

Incorrect IP address configuration settings are a common source of TCP/IP communication problems. The following scenarios characterize IP addressing problems:

- The computer cannot communicate with any other host.
- The computer can communicate only with hosts on the same subnet.
- The computer can communicate only with hosts on other subnets.

Common causes of these IP addressing problems are invalid IP addresses and invalid subnet masks.

Windows NT computers will attempt to detect duplicate IP addresses automatically by sending an ARP request when they initialize TCP/IP during startup. If another computer using the same IP address has started and is not currently attached to the network, however, the conflicting address will not be detected. Later, when the computer has reattached to the network, the duplicate address condition will be detected the first time that computer ARPs for another IP address. An error message will be displayed indicating that a duplicate address was found.

The computer detecting the conflict will display an error message and an entry will be written to the Event Viewer system log. The fact that error messages are easily removed from a computer's display is another reason you should view the event log first when TCP/IP problems occur.

14: TCP/IP PERFORMANCE MONITORING

Subnets enable you to partition a single network address into multiple subnets for use on your organization's internal network. One of the jobs in subnetting is to define a subnet mask and then identify the range of addresses that can be used for any given subnet. A common source of IP addressing problems is using an IP address that is not within the range of allowable IP addresses on a specific subnet, or when the subnet mask does not match the subnet mask of other computers on that subnet.

For example, if a company uses a Class B network address of 172.25.0.0 and a subnet mask of 255.255.224.0, this provides for six different subnets that can use the range of IP addresses in Table 14-1.

TABLE 14-1 Valid subnet address ranges

Subnet	Range of addresses		
1	172.25.32.1	through	172.25.63.254
2	172.25.64.1	through	172.25.95.254
3	172.25.96.1	through	172.25.127.254
4	172.25.128.1	through	172.25.159.254
5	172.25.160.1	through	172.25.191.254
6	172.25.192.1	through	172.25.223.254

If an attempt is made to assign an IP address of 172.25.64.11 to a computer located on Subnet 1, that computer will not be able to communicate with any other computer on Subnet 1. Any attempts this computer makes to connect to a computer on the same subnet will cause the connection request to be forwarded to the default gateway. This is true of any host that resides on a subnet with an address that is out of range for that subnet.

Use the following diagnostic tools to assist you:

- **ipconfig**: Check the current TCP/IP configuration settings on the computer. Verify the IP address subnet mask and default gateway.

- **ping**: Attempt to ping another host on the local subnet by its IP address. If there is no response, try pinging the IP address of the default gateway on your subnet.

- **arp:** Check the ARP cache by typing `arp -a` on a command line after attempting to ping another host on the local subnet. If the ARP cache shows a different IP address-to-physical address mapping for a target host, then two possible problems are:
  - The network adapter has been changed recently on the target host.
  - A static mapping was created on the source that is incorrect.

> **TEST TIP** Familiarize yourself with the types and causes of IP addressing problems. They are covered heavily in the exam.

Host name resolution problems

The following examples are typical of the kinds of problems that can occur with host name resolution:

- The HOSTS file is not located in the correct directory on the Windows NT computer. The HOSTS file must exist in the \Systemroot\System32\Drivers\Etc directory.
- The HOSTS file or DNS does not contain the particular host name.
- An invalid IP address is entered for the host name in the HOSTS file or DNS.
- The client computer has been configured with an invalid IP address for the DNS server.
- The HOSTS file contains multiple entries for the same host name on separate lines. The first entry is used in this case.

Many types of host name resolution problems that occur when using a HOSTS file are the result of incorrect entries or formatting problems with information in the HOSTS file. Also, the host file may not be located in the correct directory.

14: TCP/IP PERFORMANCE MONITORING

NetBIOS name resolution problems

Troubleshooting NetBIOS name resolution problems can be a bit more complicated because there are several methods that can be used to resolve NetBIOS computer names. Keep in mind the order the Windows-based computers use when attempting to resolve names. The order will also depend on the mode (or node type, such as b-node, m-node, p-node, and so on) that is used to resolve computer names.

Use `ipconfig` to determine the node type used to resolve computer names. To determine the mode, type **ipconfig /all** on a command line. **Nbtstat** is a useful tool for troubleshooting problems with NetBIOS name resolution. The **nbtstat** command allows for viewing, removing, or correcting dynamic and static entries in the NetBIOS name cache. The command syntax is as follows:

nbtstat [**-a** *remotename*] [**-A** *IPaddress*] [**-c**] [**-n**] [**-R**] [**-r**] [**-S**] [**-s**] [*interval*]

- **-a** *remotename*: Using the computer's name, lists the remote computer's name table.

- **-A** *IPaddress*: Using the computer's IP address, lists the remote computer's name table.

- **-c**: Giving the IP address of each name, lists the contents of the NetBIOS name cache.

- **-n**: Lists local NetBIOS names.

- **-R**: After purging all names from the NetBIOS name cache, reloads the LMHOSTS file. Available if LMHOSTS LOOKUP is enabled on the computer. (Check Enable LMHOSTS LOOKUP on the WINS Address tab on the TCP/IP Properties page.)

- **-r**: Lists name resolution statistics for Windows networking. This option returns the number of names resolved and registered over broadcast or over WINS on a Windows NT-based computer configured to use WINS.

- **-S**: Displays both workstation and server sessions. Remote computers are listed by IP address only.

- **-s**: Shows both workstation and server sessions. It tries to resolve the remote computer IP address to a name using

339

the name resolution services (including, but not limited to, HOSTS FILE LOOKUP) configured on the computer.

Interval: Reshows selected statistics, pausing *interval* seconds between each display. Press CTRL+C to stop redisplaying statistics. If this parameter is omitted, `nbtstat` prints the current configuration information once.

The column headings generated by the `nbtstat` utility have the meanings given as follows:

- **In:** Number of bytes received.
- **Out:** Number of bytes sent.
- **In/Out:** Tells if the connection is from the computer (outbound) or from another computer to the local computer (inbound).
- **Life:** Remaining time that a name table cache entry will live before it's purged
- **Local Name:** The local NetBIOS name associated with the connection.
- **Remote Host:** The name or IP address associated with the remote computer.
- **Type:** The type of name, either a unique name or a group name.
- **<03>:** Each NetBIOS name is 16 characters long. The last byte is used to indicate specific NetBIOS applications that identify themselves using the NetBIOS computer name. (<> notes the last byte converted to a hexadecimal value.)
- **State:** The state of NetBIOS connections.

The possible states are as follows:

- **Connected:** Session has been established.
- **Associated:** Connection endpoint has been created and associated with an IP address.
- **Listening:** Endpoint is available for an inbound connection.

- **Idle:** Endpoint has been opened but is not able to receive connections.
- **Connecting:** The session is in the connecting phase; the name-to-IP address mapping of the destination is being resolved.
- **Accepting:** An inbound session is now being accepted and will be connected shortly.
- **Reconnecting:** A session is attempting to reconnect if it failed on the first attempt.
- **Outbound:** A session is in the connecting phase; the TCP connection is now being created.
- **Inbound:** An inbound session is connecting.
- **Disconnecting:** A session is disconnecting.
- **Disconnected:** The local computer has issued a disconnect, and is awaiting confirmation from the remote computer.

Network connections

Communications between two hosts on a large network often requires data to be sent through one or more routers. There can even be cases in which different paths are taken depending on traffic conditions and communications costs.

`Tracert` is a useful tool for troubleshooting communications problems on large networks (including the Internet) when routers are used. `Tracert` is a route-tracing utility used to determine the route that one host takes to reach another on a network. The `tracert` command can be used to determine where a packet has stopped on the network.

To do a `tracert` to `quicklearn.com`, the syntax of the command would be:

```
tracert quicklearn.com
```

MCSE TCP/IP ACE IT!

Have You Mastered?

Now it's time to review the concepts in this chapter and apply your knowledge. These questions will test your mastery of material covered in this chapter.

1. **Which utility would you use to monitor all of the network traffic coming into your server?**

    ☐ A. Netstat
    ☐ B. Performance Monitor
    ☐ C. Network Monitor
    ☐ D. Nbtstat

    C. Network monitor can be used to view all types of incoming network traffic on the server. See the "Network Monitor" section.

2. **Which utility would you use to view your routing table?**

    ☐ A. Netstat
    ☐ B. Performance Monitor
    ☐ C. Network Monitor
    ☐ D. Nbtstat

    A. The routing table can be viewed using the netstat -r command. See the "TCP/IP Connections and Statistics" section.

3. **Which utility would you use to view your name resolution cache?**

    ☐ A. Netstat
    ☐ B. Performance Monitor
    ☐ C. Network Monitor
    ☐ D. Nbtstat

   D. Nbtstat contains information concerning name resolution. See the "TCP/IP Connections and Statistics" section.

4. **Which utility would you use to view information about the amount of ICMP traffic coming to and from your server?**

    ☐ A. Netstat
    ☐ B. Performance Monitor
    ☐ C. Network Monitor
    ☐ D. Nbtstat

   B. Performance Monitor contains counters for the specific TCP/IP protocols. See the "Performance Monitor" section.

5. **What must be installed on your network before you can use the TCP/IP counters in Performance monitor?**

    ☐ A. SMS
    ☐ B. SNMP
    ☐ C. DNS
    ☐ D. WINS

   B. SNMP must be installed on the server before the TCP/IP counters are available in Performance monitor. See the "SMNP" section.

MCSE TCP/IP ACE IT!

Practice Your Skills

The exercises provide you with an opportunity to apply the knowledge you've gained in this chapter about TCP/IP performance monitoring and troubleshooting.

1. Monitoring network traffic on a remote subnet

EXERCISE You want to collect and view all network packets originating from the remote Windows NT computer. You will use Network Monitor on your computer to do this. What must be installed on the remote subnet so that you can do this?

ANALYSIS The Network Monitor agent must be installed on the remote subnet.

2. Diagnosing DHCP problems

EXERCISE Your Windows NT Workstation computer is not able to communicate with a host on a different subnet. How can you test to see if your computer was assigned a valid IP address by a DHCP Server? You have determined that DHCP has assigned your computer a valid IP address. How can you test whether or not the IP address for the default gateway is valid? You want to find out if your computer has the correct IP

14: TCP/IP PERFORMANCE MONITORING

address-to-computer name mapping for the host on the remote subnet. How can you view the computer name mappings on your computer?

ANALYSIS Use the `ipconfig.exe` utility to determine if your computer was assigned a valid IP address. Use the `ping` command along with the IP address of the default gateway to see if the IP address is valid. Use the `nbtstat.exe` utility to view computer name mappings.

3. Diagnosing communications problems when trying to connect to an FTP server

EXERCISE You are unsuccessful when you attempt to connect to an FTP server that is located on the Internet by typing `ftp ftp.quicklearn.com`. You want to determine how your request is being routed over the Internet. Which utility can you use to do this? You suspect your computer is not configured properly to resolve the host name of the FTP server. Which IP address, specified on your computer, should you verify? If your computer is unable to resolve the host name of the FTP server, what other method can you use to connect to the FTP server?

ANALYSIS Use `tracert.exe` to determine how your request is being routed. Verify the DNS server address to see if your computer is configured properly to resolve the hostname. Use the `ftp` command followed by the IP address of the FTP server to connect to the FTP server.

345

Practice Exam

1. Sharon is the administrator of a multiple domain NT network. There are three subnets that make up the network. Which entries does Sharon need to add to the LMHOSTS file to allow every Windows-based computer to browse every domain?

   - [x] A. One entry for the PDC in each remote domain; one entry for each domain controller in the local domain
   - [ ] B. One entry for a BDC in each remote domain; one entry for each domain controller in the local domain
   - [ ] C. One entry for the PDC in each remote domain; one entry for a BDC in the local domain
   - [ ] D. One entry for a BDC in each remote domain; one entry for a BDC in the local domain

2. What command would you use to view a list of all NetBIOS names currently cached on your Windows NT Workstation?

   - [x] A. `nbtstat`
   - [ ] B. `netstat`
   - [ ] C. `arp`
   - [ ] D. Network Monitor

3. Nick wants to create a backup DNS server to provide DNS database redundancy. What is the best way for Nick to do this?

   - [x] A. Create a secondary server.
   - [ ] B. Create a replication server.
   - [ ] C. Create a forwarder.
   - [ ] D. Create a caching-only server.

4. You have installed WINS servers on each of your four subnets. You want to ensure that WINS clients register their names with the local WINS server. How can you accomplish this?

   - [ ] A. Place a WINS proxy on each subnet.
   - [ ] B. Create an LMHOSTS file on each computer.
   - [ ] C. Install DHCP Relay Agents on the routers.
   - [x] D. Configure the WINS server address on each computer.

5. Charlotte wishes to browse the job listings located on her company's UNIX computer using her Windows 95 computer. Which will allow Charlotte to do this?

   - [ ] A. FTP
   - [x] B. Telnet
   - [ ] C. LPQ
   - [ ] D. Network Neighborhood

6. Sam is the administrator of an NT network and has just installed a UNIX computer on the network. He wants all of the WINS clients to be able to access the UNIX computer. Which of the following would allow this?

   - [ ] A. The hostname and IP address of the UNIX computer should be added as a client reservation on the DHCP server.

☐ B. The hostname and IP address of the UNIX computer should be added as a static mapping on the WINS server.
☐ C. The hostname and IP address of the WINS server should be added to the HOSTS file on the UNIX computer.
☐ D. A WINS proxy agent should be installed on the network.

7. What is the name resolution order used by a WINS client that has an LMHOSTS file configured as well?

☐ A. WINS server, local cache, broadcasting, LMHOSTS file
☐ B. Local cache, WINS server, broadcasting, LMHOSTS file
☐ C. Local cache, WINS server, LMHOSTS file, broadcasting
☐ D. WINS server, LMHOSTS file, local cache, broadcasting

8. You have recently added 25 new computers to your network, and you notice that communications seem to have slowed. What can you do to capture the necessary data to determine which computers are generating the most traffic?

☐ A. Run Network Monitor on each server.
☐ B. Run Performance Monitor on each server.
☐ C. Run Network Monitor on the server that has SNMP installed.
☐ D. Run Performance Monitor on each computer.

9. You wish to capture and decode TCP/IP packets on your company's NT server. Which utility provides this capability?

☐ A. Network Monitor
☐ B. Performance Monitor
☐ C. Performance Monitor with SNMP
☐ D. SNMP

MCSE TCP/IP ACE IT!

10. Which of the following allows you to view both IP and Ethernet statistics on an NT server? (Choose two)

    - [ ] A. ipconfig /all
    - [x] B. netstat
    - [x] C. Network Monitor
    - [ ] D. Nbtstat

11. Jacob is unable to access any of the devices located on his TCP/IP subnet using his Windows 95 computer. He can successfully ping 127.0.0.1. What is the most likely cause of his problems?

    - [ ] A. The computer has been configured with the incorrect gateway address.
    - [ ] B. The computer has been configured with the incorrect DHCP address.
    - [x] C. The computer has been configured with the incorrect subnet mask.
    - [ ] D. The computer has a duplicate IP address.

12. Rob has two subnets on his network connected by a router. If a DHCP server is installed on subnet A, what must be configured to allow computers on subnet B to receive IP addresses from the DHCP server on subnet A?

    - [x] A. A DHCP Relay Agent
    - [ ] B. A proxy
    - [ ] C. A WINS server
    - [ ] D. A DHCP server

13. Jennifer has added two additional network adapters to a computer on her WINS network. She wants to create a manual entry for the computer on the WINS server. What type of entry should she add?

    - [ ] A. Domain
    - [ ] B. Group
    - [x] C. Multihomed
    - [ ] D. Internet group

PRACTICE EXAM

14. You have recently reconfigured your network and created six new subnets. To connect the subnets, you have installed multihomed NT servers that will function as routers. Which of the following would allow the routing tables to be created with the least amount of effort on your part?

    ☐ A. Using the route utility
    ☒ B. Installing RIP for IP
    ☐ C. Creating an LMHOSTS file
    ☐ D. Creating a HOSTS file

15. You want your IP clients to broadcast for name resolution before contacting the WINS server. Which of the following nodes needs to be specified on the client computers?

    ☐ A. b-node
    ☐ B. p-node
    ☐ C. h-node
    ☐ D. m-node

16. You are able to ping a server located on a remote subnet. However, when you attempt to map a network drive to the server, you are unsuccessful. What is most likely the problem?

    ☐ A. The workstation is configured with an incorrect DNS server address.
    ☐ B. The workstation is configured with an incorrect gateway address.
    ☐ C. The server is configured with an incorrect DNS server address.
    ☐ D. The server is configured with an incorrect WINS server address.

351

17. Sara currently administers a network with a combination of Windows-based and UNIX computers. There is a printer connected to one of the UNIX computers, and the Windows-based clients need access to this printer. Which of the following steps would allow Windows-based clients to print to this print device? (Choose all that apply.)

    ☑ A. Install the TCP/IP printing service on an NT server.
    ☑ B. Configure a share for the printer.
    ☑ C. Map a printer port on the NT server to the IP address of the UNIX printer.
    ☐ D. Install TCP/IP printing service on the Windows 95 workstations.

18. You are planning a new TCP/IP network for your company. The network address you have been assigned is 199.72.132.0. You know that the network needs to support 12 subnets and the largest possible number of hosts on each subnet. Which subnet mask meets these requirements?

    ☐ A. 255.255.255.192
    ☐ B. 255.255.255.224
    ☑ C. 255.255.255.240
    ☐ D. 255.255.255.248

19. Chris administers a network with four subnets and a DHCP server on each subnet. He wants to provide redundancy on the network in case one of the DHCP servers fails. How can he do this?

    ☐ A. Create four DHCP scopes on each DHCP server.
    ☐ B. Create one DHCP scope on each DHCP server that contains valid IP addresses for each subnet.

352

PRACTICE EXAM

   C. Create two DHCP scopes on each DHCP server, one that has valid IP addresses for the local subnet, and another that has valid IP addresses for the remaining subnets.
   D. Create client reservations for each computer on each DHCP server.

20. Which resource record would you add to your DNS server for your domain's mail server?

   A. CNAME
   B. MX
   C. PTR
   D. WKS

21. Michael has configured his multihomed computer with a static router. However, it is not transferring data between the subnets. Which of the following may he have forgotten to do?

   A. Configure each adapter with a different subnet mask.
   B. Configure each adapter with the same subnet mask.
   C. Enable IP forwarding.
   D. Configure each adapter with the same IP address.

22. Becky is installing a new DNS server on her company's network to resolve hostnames on the Internet root name servers. What is the best way for Becky to configure her new DNS server?

   A. By using the boot file on the DNS server
   B. By using the cache.dns file on the DNS server
   C. By including the InterNIC IP address in the hosts file on the DNS server
   D. By including an entry for the InterNIC on the DNS server

MCSE TCP/IP ACE IT!

23. Todd administers a TCP/IP network that is composed of NT and UNIX computers. The NT computers use both DHCP and WINS. He recently installed a DNS server for hostname resolution and created an entry for each UNIX computer. What is the easiest way for him to manage hostname resolution?

- [ ] A. On the DNS server, enable WINS reverse lookup
- [x] B. On the DNS server, enable WINS resolution
- [ ] C. On each UNIX computer, create a HOSTS file with entries for each WINS server
- [ ] D. On each UNIX computer, create a HOSTS file with entries for each DNS server

24. Sue has not been able to connect to an NT server located on a remote subnet, but all other users can connect to the server. Using Network Monitor, she discovers that her computer sends an ARP request when she tries to access the server. What is the most likely cause of Sue's problems?

- [x] A. Her workstation has an incorrect subnet mask.
- [ ] B. Her workstation has a duplicate IP address.
- [ ] C. Her workstation has a duplicate hostname.
- [ ] D. The server has an incorrect subnet mask.

25. You are suddenly unable to connect to a computer located on a remote subnet. You know that IP is correctly installed on your computer. How can you check to verify that the router is working properly?

- [ ] A. Ping 127.0.0.1.
- [ ] B. Ping your local IP address.
- [ ] C. Ping the near side of the router.
- [x] D. Ping the far side of the router.

PRACTICE EXAM

26. Which command allows you to add entries to the routing tables on an NT server?

   - ☐ A. arp
   - ☐ B. netstat
   - ☑ C. route
   - ☐ D. nbtstat

27. Your company uses a RAS server to connect to an Internet Service Provider (ISP). Employees have remote access to the network using a PPTP connection through the ISP. A remote user calls to say that he is unable to connect to your network. What is the first step in troubleshooting the problem?

   - ☐ A. Reboot the RAS server.
   - ☐ B. Have the user attempt a PPP connection.
   - ☐ C. Have the user ping the server.
   - ☑ D. Have the user run a `tracert` to the server.

28. Jim's company has two offices, one located in Chicago, the other in Memphis. A WAN link connects the two sites. Each site has been configured with a WINS server. How should the servers be configured to replicate their databases to each other?

   - ☐ A. Configure the Directory Replicator Server service to replicate between the servers.
   - ☐ B. Configure each WINS server as a secondary WINS server of the other.
   - ☑ C. Configure each WINS server as both a push and pull partner of the other.
   - ☐ D. Configure each WINS server as a client of the other.

355

29. Your company has been assigned the network address of 136.84.0.0. You are responsible for planning the network, which currently has 42 subnets, but this will grow to 58 when a new location is opened. Which subnet mask allows for the current and future needs of the network?

   - [ ] A. 255.255.0.0
   - [ ] B. 255.255.255.0
   - [ ] C. 255.255.192.0
   - [x] D. 255.255.252.0

30. Your company has currently moved into a new building and you are responsible for configuring the new network. Each of the four floors will be on a separate subnet. The network address that you have been assigned is 199.72.134.0. Which subnet mask allows for the largest number of hosts on each subnet?

   - [ ] A. 255.255.255.192
   - [x] B. 255.255.255.224
   - [ ] C. 255.255.255.240
   - [ ] D. 255.255.255.248

31. Which file provides hostname-to-IP address mappings?

   - [ ] A. LMHOSTS
   - [ ] B. Cache.dns
   - [ ] C. Boot
   - [x] D. HOSTS

32. What must be supplied for an NT server to send trap messages to an SNMP trap destination? (Choose two.)

   - [ ] A. The SNMP management station's scope ID
   - [x] B. The SNMP management station's community
   - [x] C. The SNMP management station's IP address
   - [ ] D. The SNMP management station's hostname

PRACTICE EXAM

33. Which of the following provides capture and display filters? (Choose all that apply.)

    - ☑ A. Network Monitor
    - ☐ B. `tracert`
    - ☐ C. Performance Monitor
    - ☐ D. SNMP Trap Monitor

34. Your company has a UNIX server that contains all of the quarterly financial reports. Which utility would you use on a Windows 95 workstation to download these files?

    - ☐ A. Telnet
    - ☑ B. FTP
    - ☐ C. LPD
    - ☐ D. LPQ

35. When manually adding WINS entries for the UNIX workstations on your network, which entry type would you use?

    - ☐ A. Domain name
    - ☐ B. Group
    - ☐ C. Internet
    - ☑ D. Unique

36. UNIX computers using the LPR utility need access to a print device on an NT server. Which of the following should you do to allow them access? (Choose all that apply.)

    - ☑ A. Install the TCP/IP Printing service on the server.
    - ☐ B. Install the TCP/IP Printing service on the UNIX computer.
    - ☐ C. Assign an IP address to the printer.
    - ☑ D. Share the printer on the server.

MCSE TCP/IP ACE IT!

37. You want to create a static IP-Address-to-MAC-Address setting on your computer. Which utility do you use?

    - [ ] A. nbtstat
    - [ ] B. netstat
    - [x] C. arp
    - [ ] D. ping

38. Which command would you use to purge an NT server's NetBIOS name cache?

    - [x] A. nbtstat
    - [ ] B. netstat
    - [ ] C. arp
    - [ ] D. ping

39. You need to print a document to a UNIX print server on your network. What command would you use?

    - [ ] A. Telnet
    - [ ] B. FTP
    - [ ] C. LPQ
    - [x] D. LPR

40. Lucy's company has been assigned three Class C addresses: 199.72.4.0, 199.72.5.0, and 199.72.6.0. These addresses need to be combined to create one logical network to allow for all of the hosts on her company's network. Which subnet mask must she use?

    - [ ] A. 255.255.255.0
    - [x] B. 255.255.252.0
    - [ ] C. 255.255.255.252
    - [ ] D. 255.255.0.0

PRACTICE EXAM

41. Your company's primary domain controller (PDC) in the ACCOUNTING domain has failed, and the backup domain controller (BDC) with an IP address of 199.72.132.253 was promoted. How should you register ACCOUNTING in the LMHOSTS file on the client computers?

- [ ] A. `199.72.132.253 #dom:accounting`
- [ ] B. `199.72.132.253 bdc #dom:accounting`
- [ ] C. `199.72.132.253 bdc #pre:accounting`
- [x] D. `199.72.132.235 bdc #pre #dom:accounting`

42. Cathleen has recently installed a new NT network. The network consists of five subnets and one domain. A domain controller is located on each subnet. Cathleen wants the clients to be able to browse the entire network. Which service allows automatic updating of the browse list?

- [ ] A. DHCP
- [x] B. WINS
- [ ] C. DNS
- [ ] D. SNMP

43. What must you install on your NT server to view TCP/IP statistics for the server using Performance Monitor?

- [ ] A. RIP for IP
- [ ] B. Routing
- [x] C. SNMP
- [ ] D. TCP/IP counters

359

MCSE TCP/IP ACE IT!

44. Your network utilizes DHCP servers on each of its four subnets. Kelly has been transferred from the Order Entry division to Accounting. After moving her computer to a different subnet, Kelly is able to ping users on her subnet but cannot access anything on the remote subnets. What is most likely the problem?

- [ ] A. Her computer has an incorrect subnet mask.
- [x] B. Her computer has an incorrect default gateway setting.
- [ ] C. Her computer has an incorrect IP address.
- [ ] D. She was unable to get an IP address from the DHCP server.

45. Dan wants all of the UNIX and NT computers on his network to be able to access each other using hostnames. Which of the following should Dan use?

- [ ] A. WINS
- [x] B. DNS
- [ ] C. DHCP
- [ ] D. RIP

46. Karen wants all of the NT and Windows 95 computers on her network to be able to access each other using computer names. Which of the following should Karen use?

- [x] A. WINS
- [ ] B. DNS
- [ ] C. DHCP
- [ ] D. RIP

PRACTICE EXAM

47. You are unable to communicate with computers located on remote subnets. After reviewing the following information from the ipconfig utility, what is the problem?

```
Host Name . . . . . . . . . . . : NASH-PDC
DNS Servers . . . . . . . . . . :
Node Type . . . . . . . . . . .: hybrid
NetBIOS Scope ID . . . . . . . :
IP Routing Enabled . . . . . . : No
WINS Proxy Enabled . . . . . . : No
NetBIOS Resolution Uses DNS . : No
Ethernet Adapter . . . . . . . : SMCISA5
Description . . . . . . . . . : SMCISA5 Ethernet Adapter
Physical Address . . . . . . . : 00-00-C0-74-51-8F
DHCP Enabled . . . . . . . . .: No
IP Address . . . . . . . . . .: 199.72.132.05
Subnet Mask . . . . . . . . . : 255.255.255.252
Default Gateway . . . . . . . : 199.72.132.09
Primary WINS Server . . . . . : 199.72.132.130
Secondary WINS Server . . . . :
```

- [ ] A. The node type is incorrect.
- [ ] B. The subnet mask is incorrect.
- [ ] C. The host and the WINS server are on different subnets.
- [x] D. The host and the gateway are on different subnets.

48. You have recently installed Internet Information Server (IIS) on your NT server. Users may attempt to access the server using the hostname nash-pdc.usps.gov and nash.usps.gov. Which record type should she add on the DNS server to allow this?

- [ ] A. MX
- [x] B. CNAME
- [ ] C. MG
- [ ] D. MB

361

49. Your DHCP servers each have four scopes for subnet on your network. You have recently installed two WINS servers for name resolution. Which option type would you configure the WINS server addresses for all DHCP clients on the network?

☐ A. Client option
☐ B. Scope option
☑ C. Global option
☐ D. Internet option

50. Shelley's NT server is configured as a multihomed, static router. What utility should she use to add entries to the routing table?

☐ A. `ping`
☑ B. `route`
☐ C. `netstat`
☐ D. `nbtstat`

51. Your remote users would like to use their Internet connections to access the company's internal network. Which protocol must you use?

☐ A. PPP
☐ B. SLIP
☑ C. PPTP
☐ D. X.25

52. Abbie's company has recently installed an NT RAS server. One of the remote users calls to say that he cannot log on remotely using his SLIP connection. What is the problem?

☐ A. The server has an incorrect gateway setting.
☑ B. The server does not support SLIP.
☐ C. The remote computer has an incorrect IP address.
☐ D. The remote computer has an incorrect subnet mask.

PRACTICE EXAM

53. Mike is the administrator of an NT network and just added several new UNIX computers to the network. There are no DNS servers on the network. What is the best way for Mike to ensure proper hostname resolution on his network?

    ☐ A. Configure a WINS server.
    ☐ B. Install HOSTS files on each computer.
    ☐ C. Install LMHOSTS files on each computer.
    ☐ D. Configure DHCP Relay Agents on the network.

54. Suppose the following situation exists:

    Jeanie administers a Windows-based network with computers running TCP/IP on four subnets. She has installed a DHCP server on each subnet that will provide IP addresses to the devices on the network.

    Required result:

    Each DHCP server must be able to service other subnets if one of the other DHCP servers goes down.

    Optional desired results:

    1. DHCP should provide the WINS server addresses and the default gateway address to the clients.
    2. DHCP should always provide the same unique IP address to the servers on the network.

    Proposed solution:

    1. Configure four scopes on each DHCP server, one for each of the four subnets.
    2. Use a scope option to supply the default gateway address and a global option for the WINS server addresses.
    3. Create client reservations on the DHCP servers for each server on the network.

363

MCSE TCP/IP ACE IT!

Which results does the proposed solution produce?

- [ ] A. The proposed solution produces the required result and all of the optional desired results.
- [ ] B. The proposed solution produces the required result and one of the optional desired results.
- [ ] C. The proposed solution produces the required result, but does not produce any of the optional desired results.
- [x] D. The proposed solution does not produce the required result.

---

55. Suppose the following situation exists:

Jeanie administers a Windows-based network with computers running TCP/IP on four subnets. She has installed a DHCP server on each subnet that will provide IP addresses to the devices on the network.

Required result:

Each DHCP server must be able to service other subnets if one of the other DHCP servers goes down.

Optional desired results:

1. DHCP should provide the WINS server addresses and the default gateway address to the clients.
2. DHCP should always provide the same unique IP address to the servers on the network.

PRACTICE EXAM

Proposed solution:

1. Configure four scopes on each DHCP server, one for each of the four subnets.
2. Use a scope option to supply the default gateway address and a global option for the WINS server addresses.
3. Create client reservations on the DHCP servers for each server on the network.
4. Install DHCP Relay Agents on each of the subnets.

Which results does the proposed solution produce?

- [x] A. The proposed solution produces the required result and all of the optional desired results.
- [ ] B. The proposed solution produces the required result and one of the optional desired results.
- [ ] C. The proposed solution produces the required result, but does not produce any of the optional desired results.
- [ ] D. The proposed solution does not produce the desired result.

Exam Key

1. A
2. A
3. A
4. D
5. B
6. B
7. B
8. A
9. C
10. B
11. C
12. A
13. C
14. B
15. D
16. D
17. A, B, C
18. C
19. C
20. B
21. C
22. B
23. B
24. A
25. D
26. C
27. D
28. C
29. D
30. B
31. A
32. B and C
33. A
34. B
35. D
36. A and D
37. C
38. A
39. D
40. B
41. D
42. B
43. C
44. B
45. B
46. A
47. D
48. B
49. C
50. B
51. C
52. B
53. B
54. D
55. A

Exam Analysis

1. The LMHOSTS file should contain an entry for at least one domain controller of the remote domains. More could be added as needed. Each of the local domain controllers should have an entry in the file as well. All domain controllers should be flagged with the #pre and #dom keywords so they will be loaded into cache as domain controllers. For more information, see the "LMHOSTS File" section in Chapter 9.

2. Nbtstat is the utility used to view NetBIOS statistics. Netstat and Network Monitor allow viewing of other network statistics. Arp allows viewing of the IP-Address-to-MAC-Address mappings. For more information, see the "Troubleshooting TCP/IP" section in Chapter 14.

3. Secondary DNS servers provide a backup to the primary DNS server. Secondary servers receive zone information from the primary server. For zones that span multiple subnets, it is a good idea to place a secondary server on a different subnet than the primary server. This provides fault tolerance when one of the subnets fails. For more information, see the "Name Server Roles" section in Chapter 7.

4. Computers must be configured with the IP address of the WINS server before they can register with the server. WINS proxies are used to provide WINS name resolution to non-WINS clients. For more information, see the "Installing and Configuring WINS" section in Chapter 6.

5. Telnet is the utility that allows users to run programs remotely. FTP is used to transfer files from a remote computer. For more information, see the "Connectivity Utilities" section in Chapter 11.

6. Creating static mappings for the UNIX computers on the WINS server will allow WINS clients to use WINS for name resolution of the UNIX computers. A WINS proxy would enable the UNIX computers to use WINS for name resolution of other computers on the network. For more information, see the "Installing and Configuring WINS" section in Chapter 6.

7. WINS clients use h-node resolution. All resolution methods first search the local cache. H-node resolution will then attempt resolution on the WINS server. If unsuccessful, it broadcasts for resolution. If an LMHOSTS file is configured, it will be used after the broadcast attempt fails. For more information, see the "NetBIOS Name Resolution Methods" section in Chapter 9.

8. Network Monitor is capable of capturing the frames sent to and from the computer it is being run on. Running Network Monitor on each server would allow you to get an idea of all of the network traffic coming to the servers and being sent from the servers. For more information, see the "Monitoring TCP/IP Activity" section in Chapter 14.

9. Performance Monitor gains TCP/IP counters once SNMP has been installed on the server. These counters allow TCP/IP packets coming to the server to be captured and decoded. If SMS is installed on the server, Performance Monitor is then capable of using the counters on computers other than the server that is running it. For more information, see the "Monitoring TCP/IP Activity" section in Chapter 14.

10. `Netstat` and Network Monitor both allow viewing of IP and Ethernet statistics on an NT server. `Ipconfig` allows the viewing of IP configuration information. `Nbtstat` allows the viewing of

EXAM ANALYSIS

NetBIOS statistics. For more information, see the "TCP/IP Utilities" section in Chapter 14.

11. If Jacob is capable of pinging the loopback address (127.0.0.1), then IP is correctly installed on his computer. Being unable to communicate with computers on his subnet suggests an incorrect subnet mask. Incorrect gateway settings would prevent him from communicating with computers on remote subnets. For more information, see the "Troubleshooting TCP/IP" section in Chapter 14.

12. DHCP Relay Agents allow DHCP requests to be directed to DHCP servers on remote subnets. This allows one DHCP server to provide addresses for multiple subnets. For more information, see the "Using DHCP Across Multiple Subnets" section in Chapter 4.

13. Multihomed entries allow for computers with multiple IP addresses to be configured for WINS. These addresses can be assigned to multiple network adapters or a single adapter with several addresses. For more information, see the "Installing and Configuring WINS" section in Chapter 6.

14. RIP for IP allows for dynamic routing tables. Dynamic routing requires the least amount of administrative effort. Static routing requires the administrator to build and maintain the routing table manually. For more information, see the "Routing Protocols" section in Chapter 5.

15. M-node resolution broadcasts before checking the WINS server. H-node resolution is the opposite; it first checks the WINS server and then broadcasts for resolution. Both are a mixture of b-node resolution, which uses broadcast, and p-node resolution, which checks with a server. For more information, see the "NetBIOS Name Resolution Methods" section in Chapter 9.

16. Pinging a server uses either the IP address or the hostname. Network drives are mapped using computer names. If you are able to ping but unable to map a drive, it shows that there is a problem with the computer name resolution. This can be caused by an incorrect WINS server address entry in the IP configuration. For more information, see the "Troubleshooting TCP/IP" section in Chapter 14.

17. The server can be shared to the Windows-based clients using an NT server. The server must have the TCP/IP Printing service installed, a port on the server must be mapped to the printer, and the printer must be shared on the server. Once this is done, the Windows-based clients can connect the printer share and access the printer. For more information, see the "Microsoft TCP/IP Printing" section in Chapter 11.

18. The network address `192.72.132.0` is a Class C address with a default subnet mask of `255.255.255.0`. This would allow for one subnet and 254 hosts. The subnet mask of `255.255.255.240` allows for a maximum of 14 subnets, each with up to 14 hosts. For more information, see the "Subdividing a Network" section of Chapter 3.

19. Each subnet requires its own DHCP scope with addresses that are correct for the subnet. Creating only one scope with IP addresses for all of the subnets would result in clients receiving IP addresses that are invalid for their local subnet. For more information, see the "Using DHCP Across Multiple Subnets" section in Chapter 4.

20. MX records are used to specify mail servers. CNAME records are used to allow multiple hostnames for the same IP address. For more information, see the "DNS Configuration and Database Files" section in Chapter 7.

EXAM ANALYSIS

21. IP forwarding must be enabled for a multihomed computer to function as a static router. When dynamic routing is used, this option is not selected. For more information, see the "Routing Protocols" section of Chapter 5.

22. The cache.dns file is the file used to resolve Internet names. For more information, see the "Cache File" section in Chapter 7.

23. Enabling WINS lookup on the DNS server will allow the WINS clients to automatically be resolved by DNS. Todd would only need to add entries for the non-WINS, UNIX clients on the DNS server. For more information, see the "Installation and Configuration of Microsoft DNS Server" section of Chapter 7.

24. `Arp` broadcasts for resolution when the IP address of the destination is located on the local subnet. If `arp` is broadcasting for the IP address of a computer on a remote subnet, it suggests that the subnet mask on the sending computer is incorrect. This can cause the computer to believe that the destination is local and thus arp for resolution. For more information, see the "Remote IP Address Resolution" section in Chapter 8.

25. A successful ping to the far side of the router shows that the router is transferring data between subnets properly. For more information, see the "Troubleshooting TCP/IP" section in Chapter 14.

26. The `route` command is used to view and edit the routing table. `Netstat` enables you to view the routing table and other network statistics; it does not allow for adding or deleting entries to the routing table. `Nbtstat` provides NetBIOS statistics. The `arp` command is used to view and edit the arp cache. For more information, see the "TCP/IP Utilities" section in Chapter 14.

373

27. Tracert is the utility used to view the path of data across the network. It will list all of the routers that the data crosses, and the path can be tracked. This can help locate the point of failure in the data transmission. For more information, see the "TCP/IP Utilities" section in Chapter 14.

28. Configuring the WINS servers as push and pull partners ensures that the data is replicated after a certain number of changes and within a certain time frame. This allows the administrator to control the amount of WINS traffic across the WAN link. For more information, see the "Managing the WINS Server Database" section in Chapter 6.

29. The network address 136.84.0.0 is a Class B address with a default subnet mask of 255.255.0.0. This allows for a maximum of 65,532 hosts on one subnet. The subnet mask of 255.255.252.0 allows for a maximum of 62 subnets on the network, which will provide for the expected growth of the network. For more information, see the "Subdividing a Network" section in Chapter 3.

30. The network address of 199.72.132.0 is a Class C address with a default subnet mask of 255.255.255.0. This allows for 254 hosts on one subnet. The subnet mask of 255.255.255.224 allows for up to six subnets. For more information, see the "Subdividing a Network" section in Chapter 3.

31. The HOSTS file provides hostname-to-IP-Address mappings. The LMHOSTS file provides computer-name-to-IP-Address mappings. For more information, see the "Name Resolution Methods" section in Chapter 10.

32. For traps to be sent to a management station, the SNMP-enabled computer must be configured with the community ID and the IP address of the management station. SNMP traps can only be sent to computers that are members of the same community as the

EXAM ANALYSIS

sender. For more information, see the "Using and Managing SNMP" section in Chapter 12.

33. Network Monitor utilizes capture and display filters. Capture filters allow you to create a set of items for analysis; these can be protocols or computers. Display filters can filter data that has been collected based on source, destination, protocol, and other criteria to provide a more precise analysis. For more information, see the "Monitoring TCP/IP Activity" section in Chapter 14.

34. FTP is used to download files remotely. Telnet allows programs to be run remotely. For more information, see the "Connectivity Utilities" section in Chapter 11.

35. Unique entries are used to map one computer name to one IP address. This allows for static mappings of UNIX computers in the WINS database. This is useful because UNIX computers cannot be configured as WINS clients. For more information, see the "Installing and Configuring WINS" section in Chapter 6.

36. The LPR utility connects to a server shared through the LPD utility. Installing the TCP/IP Printing service on the server provides the LPD utility. The printer then simply needs to be shared for the UNIX client to access it. For more information, see the "Microsoft TCP/IP Printing" section in Chapter 11.

37. The `arp` utility can be used to view the IP-Address-to-MAC-address settings in the arp cache as well as to delete and add entries. For more information, see the "Address Resolution Protocol" section of Chapter 8.

38. `Nbtstat` is used to view NetBIOS statistics. It can also be used to clear the NetBIOS name cache. For more information, see the "Monitoring TCP/IP Activity" section in Chapter 14.

39. The LPR utility allows clients to print to any TCP/IP print device or to a UNIX print server on the network. For more information, see the "Microsoft TCP/IP Printing" section of Chapter 11.

40. Supernetting is used to combine Class C network addresses to allow for larger networks. The subnet mask of `255.255.252.0` is used because the only differing bits in the three network addresses are the last two bits of the third octet. This allows ten digits to be used for host IDs that will accommodate a larger network. For more information, see the "Supernetting" section of Chapter 3.

41. The `#pre` and `#dom` keywords specify that this is a domain controller and will load the entry into the name cache. For more information, see the "LMHOSTS" section of Chapter 9.

42. WINS is used for computer name resolution and also allows browsing across subnets. For more information, see the "How WINS Works" section of Chapter 6.

43. SNMP must be installed on the server before the TCP/IP counters are available in Performance Monitor. For more information, see the "Monitoring TCP/IP Activity" section in Chapter 14.

44. Settings specified on the client computer overwrite any options received from the DHCP server. If Kelly has a manual entry for the gateway setting, it would cause loss of communication with remote subnets when the computer is moved to another subnet. For more information, see the "DHCP Options" section in Chapter 4.

45. DNS servers maintain hostname-to-IP-Address mappings. Windows-based clients and UNIX computers all support the use of DNS servers on the network. For more information, see the "What Is DNS" section in Chapter 7.

EXAM ANALYSIS

46. WINS servers allow NT and Windows 95 computers to register their computer names and provide computer name resolution on the network. For more information, see the "How WINS Works" section of Chapter 6.

47. Comparing the subnet mask to the IP address of the computer and the IP address of the gateway reveals that they are located on different network addresses. This means that the computer is unable to access the gateway and cannot send data to remote subnets. For more information, see the "Subnet Addressing" section of Chapter 3.

48. CNAME records allow for multiple hostnames to be mapped to one IP address. For more information, see the "DNS Configuration and Database Files" section of Chapter 7.

49. WINS servers can be configured as global options because they are not subnet specific. For more information, see the "WINS Options" section in Chapter 6.

50. The route command allows entries to be added to the routing table when static routing is used. For more information, see the "Configuring NT Server as a Router" section in Chapter 5.

51. PPTP allows access to internal networks via the Internet. The RAS server must be configured for this connection protocol. For more information, see the "Remote Access Using TCP/IP" section of Chapter 11.

52. NT Server 4.0 cannot function as a SLIP server. It is only capable of acting as a SLIP client. The remote user should be using the PPP protocol to connect to the server. For more information, see the "Remote Access Using TCP/IP" section of Chapter 11.

53. HOSTS files should contain hostname-to-IP-Address mappings for all computers on the network and must be installed on each computer on the network. They allow for hostname resolution on both NT and UNIX computers when there are no DNS servers present. For more information, see the "Host Name Resolution Methods" section in Chapter 10.

54. The required result is not met because there is no fault tolerance on the network to provide IP addresses in the event that a DHCP server fails. Even though all of the optional results are met, this is not the correct solution. For more information, see Chapter 4.

55. This solution provides fault tolerance that satisfies the required result. All of the optional results are also met. This is an optimal solution. For more information, see Chapter 4.

Exam Revealed

1. **Which of the following can provide a summary of both IP statistics and Ethernet statistics on a Windows NT server? Choose all that apply.**

    A. Ipconfig /all
    B. Netstat
    C. Network Monitor
    D. Nbtstat

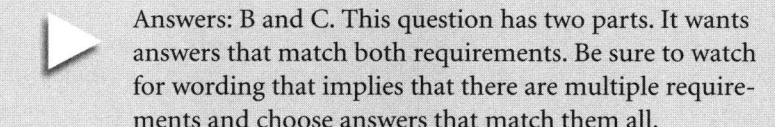

    > Answers: B and C. This question has two parts. It wants answers that match both requirements. Be sure to watch for wording that implies that there are multiple requirements and choose answers that match them all.

2. **You have recently reconfigured your network and created six new subnets. To connect the subnets, you have installed multihomed NT servers that will function as routers. Which of the following would allow the routing tables to be created with the least amount of effort on your part?**

    A. Using the route utility
    B. Installing RIP for IP
    C. Creating an `LMHOSTS` file
    D. Creating a `HOSTS` file

MCSE TCP/IP ACE IT!

> Answer: B. This question is looking for which option requires the LEAST amount of effort. Although several options may provide a solution, only the correct solution is the easiest.

---

3. Sara currently administers a network with a combination of Windows-based and UNIX computers. There is a printer connected to one of the UNIX computers, and the Windows-based clients need access to this printer. Which of the following steps would allow Windows-based clients to print to this print device? (Choose all that apply)

    A. Install the TCP/IP printing service on an NT server.
    B. Configure a share for the printer.
    C. Map a printer port on the NT server to the IP address of the UNIX printer.
    D. Install TCP/IP printing service on the Windows 95 workstations.

> Answers: A, B, and C. This question is looking for steps to complete a task. Be sure to include all of the steps that are necessary to answer the question completely.

---

4. You are planning a new TCP/IP network for your company. The network address you have been assigned is 199.72.132.0. You know that the network needs to support 12 subnets and have the largest possible number of hosts on each subnet. Which subnet mask meets these requirements?

    A. 255.255.255.192
    B. 255.255.255.224
    C. 255.255.255.240
    D. 255.255.255.248

EXAM REVEALED

> Answer: C. There will be a number of questions that require you to determine the correct subnet mask or network address. Be sure to be careful when converting from decimal to binary format and to use proper procedures for ANDING the subnet mask to the network address. Also remember that the host ID or network ID cannot consist of all 1s or 0s.

5. Sue has not been able to connect to an NT server located on a remote subnet; however, all other users can connect to the server. Using Network Monitor, she discovers that her computer sends an `arp` request when she tries to access the server. What is the most likely cause of Sue's problems?

    A. Her workstation has an incorrect subnet mask.
    B. Her workstation has a duplicate IP address.
    C. Her workstation has a duplicate hostname.
    D. The server has an incorrect subnet mask.

> Answer: A. Expect several questions like this on the test. You must understand how subnet masks, IP addresses, hostnames, and gateways function. A thorough understanding of the different IP statistics will also help you answer questions of this type.

6. Your company's primary domain controller (PDC) in the ACCOUNTING domain has failed and the backup domain controller (BDC) with an IP address of `199.72.132.253` was promoted. How should you register ACCOUNTING in the `LMHOSTS` file on the client computers?

    A. `199.72.132.253  #dom:accounting`
    B. `199.72.132.253  bdc  #dom:accounting`
    C. `199.72.132.253  bdc  #pre:accounting`
    D. `199.72.132.235  bdc  #pre #dom: accounting`

381

MCSE TCP/IP ACE IT!

> Answer: D. Be sure to pay close attention to the possible answers. They may appear very similar, but only one is correct. Take the extra time to read the question more than once. This can help you catch the small differences that you may miss.

---

7. Your network utilizes DHCP servers on each of its four subnets. Kelly has been transferred from the Order Entry division to Accounting. After moving her computer to a different subnet, Kelly is able to ping users on her subnet but cannot access anything on the remote subnets. What is most likely the problem?

   A. Her computer has an incorrect subnet mask.
   B. Her computer has an incorrect default gateway setting.
   C. Her computer has an incorrect IP address.
   D. She was unable to get an IP address from the DHCP server.

> Answer: B. You may assume that because DHCP is used on the network that all of the settings come from the DHCP server. However, remember that these settings can be overwritten on the client. Making incorrect assumptions on the test can cause a lot of heartache, so read the questions careful and only assume what is specified.

---

8. You are unable to communicate with computers located on remote subnets. After reviewing the following information from the `ipconfig` utility, what is the problem?

```
Host Name . . . . . . . . . . .: NASH-PDC
DNS Servers . . . . . . . . . .:
Node Type . . . . . . . . . . .: hybrid
NetBIOS Scope ID . . . . . . . :
IP Routing Enabled . . . . . : No
```

EXAM REVEALED

```
WINS Proxy Enabled . . . . . : No
NetBIOS Resolution Uses DNS .: No
Ethernet Adapter . . . . . . : SMCISA5
Description. . . . . . . . . : SMCISA5 Ethernet Adapter
Physical Address . . . . . . : 00-00-C0-74-51-8F
DHCP Enabled. . . . . . . . .: No
IP Address . . . . . . . . . : 199.72.132.05
Subnet Mask . . . . . . . . .: 255.255.255.252
Default Gateway . . . . . . .: 199.72.132.09
Primary WINS Server . . . . .: 199.72.132.130
Secondary WINS Server . . . .:
```

    A.   The node type is incorrect.
    B.   The subnet mask is incorrect.
    C.   The host and the WINS server are on different subnets.
    D.   The host and the gateway are on different subnets.

▶ Answer: D. You can expect at least one question like this on the exam. Be sure to pay careful attention to all of the options displayed. Convert the IP address, subnet mask, and gateway address to binary form and compare them carefully. These questions may take more time, but they provide the most real-world problem solving of any of the test questions.

---

9. Suppose the following situation exists:

Jeanie administers a Windows-based network with computers running TCP/IP on four subnets. She has installed a DHCP server on each subnet that will provide IP addresses to the devices on the network.

MCSE TCP/IP ACE IT!

Required result:

Each DHCP server must be able to service other subnets if one of the other DHCP servers goes down.

Optional desired results:

1. DHCP should provide the WINS server addresses and the default gateway address to the clients.
2. DHCP should always provide the same unique IP address to the servers on the network.

Proposed solution:

1. Configure four scopes on each DHCP server, one for each of the four subnets.
2. Use a scope option to supply the default gateway address and a global option for the WINS server addresses.
3. Create client reservations on the DHCP servers for each server on the network.

Which results does the proposed solution produce?

A. The proposed solution produces the required result and all of the optional desired results.
B. The proposed solution produces the required result and one of the optional desired results.
C. The proposed solution produces the required result, but does not produce any of the optional desired results.
D. The proposed solution does not produce the required result.

> Answer: D. Expect several of this type of question on the test. Check first to see if the required result is met. If it is not met, regardless of whether any of the optional requirements are met, the answer will be D.

10. Suppose the following situation exists:

Jeanie administers a Windows-based network with computers running TCP/IP on four subnets. She has installed a DHCP server on each subnet that will provide IP addresses to the devices on the network.

Required result:

Each DHCP server must be able to service other subnets if one of the other DHCP servers goes down.

Optional desired results:

1. DHCP should provide the WINS server addresses and the default gateway address to the clients.
2. DHCP should always provide the same unique IP address to the servers on the network.

Proposed solution:

1. Configure four scopes on each DHCP server, one for each of the four subnets.
2. Use a scope option to supply the default gateway address and a global option for the WINS server addresses.
3. Create client reservations on the DHCP servers for each server on the network.
4. Install DHCP Relay Agents on each of the subnets.

Which results does the proposed solution produce?

A. The proposed solution produces the required result and all of the optional desired results.
B. The proposed solution produces the required result and one of the optional desired results.
C. The proposed solution produces the required result, but does not produce any of the optional desired results.
D. The proposed solution does not produce the required result.

Answer: A. Expect to see the same situation with various solutions. Be careful with these questions. Tackle each question separately, even though they deal with the same situation. The answer to the previous question has no bearing on the answer to the current question: Either of them could work, not work, or partially work.

Glossary

A

acknowledgment (ACK) An acknowledgment is a packet that is returned to a sending host to acknowledge the receipt of data. Acknowledgments generate additional network traffic, diminishing the data transfer rate but increasing the reliability of the data being transferred. A receiving host sends an acknowledgment after a specified number of packets have been received or after a specified time interval has passed.

address An address is used to identify a node on a network and may also be used to specify routing information. With TCP/IP, each node on the network must be assigned a unique IP address, which is made up of the *network ID*, plus a unique *host ID* assigned by the network administrator. This address is typically represented in dotted decimal notation, with the decimal value of each octet separated by a period (for example, `172.25.16.51`).

address classes An address class is a predefined grouping of Internet addresses. Each class defines networks of a certain size. The range of numbers that can be assigned for the first octet in the IP address is based on the address class. Class A networks (values 1–126) are the largest, with more than 16 million hosts per network. Class B networks (128–191) have up to 65,534 hosts per network, and Class C networks (192–223) can have up to 254 hosts per network. *See also* octet.

Address Resolution Protocol (ARP) ARP is a protocol in the TCP/IP suite used to determine the physical address that is associated with a host's IP address.

Advanced Research Projects Agency Network (ARPANET) The ARPANET is the precursor to the Internet. The ARPANET was developed in the late 60s and early 70s by the U.S. Department of Defense as an experiment in wide area networking that would survive a nuclear war. ARPANET grew into the Internet with the help of the National Science Foundation in Washington, D.C., which began constructing the NSFNET (National Science Foundation Network).

application layer The application layer is defined at the top layer of the OSI model. Applications running on a network can communicate directly with lower-layer components or indirectly as requests that are intercepted by the network components themselves.

application programming interface (API) An API is a set of routines that an application programmer uses to request and carry out lower-level services performed by a computer's operating system. The API provides the program with a means of communicating with the operating system, by telling it which system-level task to perform and when.

B

backbone A backbone is a high-speed line or series of connections that forms a major pathway within a network. The term is relative, as a backbone in a small network will likely be much smaller than many nonbackbone lines in a large network.

bandwidth Bandwidth is how much data you can send through a connection. Bandwidth is usually measured in bits per second. A full page of text is about 16,000 bits. A fast modem can move about 15,000 bits in one second. Full-motion, full-screen video would require roughly 10,000,000 bits-per-second, depending on compression.

binary Binary is a base-2 number system, in which values are expressed as combinations of two digits, 0 and 1. For example, the binary value for 100 is 01100100.

bit (Binary DigIT) A binary digit is a single-digit number in base 2, in other words, either a 1 or a 0. It is the smallest unit of computerized data. Bandwidth is usually measured in bits per second. *See also* bandwidth.

Bootstrap Protocol (BOOTP) BOOTP is a TCP/IP network protocol, defined by RFC 951 and RFC 1542, used to configure systems. DHCP is an extension of BOOTP. *See also* DHCP.

bridge A bridge is a device used to connect multiple networks, subnets, or rings into one large logical network. A bridge maintains a table of hardware addresses and, based on this, forwards packets to a specific subnet, reducing traffic on other subnets. In a bridged network, there can be only one path to any destination (otherwise packets would circle the network, causing network storms). A bridge is more sophisticated than a repeater, but not as sophisticated as a router. *See also* packet, repeater, router, and subnet.

broadcast A broadcast is a message sent from a single computer and is distributed to all other devices on the same segment of the network as the sending computer.

brouter A brouter is a device that combines elements of a bridge and a router. Usually, a brouter acts as a router for one transport protocol (such as TCP/IP), sending packets of that format along detailed routes to their destinations. The brouter may also act as a bridge for all other types of packets (such as IPX), just passing them on, as long as they are not local to the LAN segment from which they originated. *See also* bridge, packet, and router.

browse list A browse list is kept by the master browser of all of the servers and domains on the network. This list is available to any workstation on the network requesting it. *See also* browsing.

browse master *See* master browser.

browser A browser is a client program (software) used to look at various kinds of network resources.

browsing Browsing is the process of viewing available network resources by looking through lists of folders, files, user accounts, groups, domains, or computers. Browsing allows users on a Windows

NT network to see what domains and computers are accessible from their local computer.

byte A byte is a set of bits that represent a single character. Usually there are 8 bits in a byte, sometimes more, depending on how the measurement is being made. *See also* bit.

C

cache A cache is a special memory location that stores the contents of frequently accessed information. TCP/IP hosts use caches to store information such as computer-name-to-IP address mappings and IP-address-to-physical-address mappings.

caching In DNS name resolution, caching refers to a local cache where information about the DNS domain name space is kept. Whenever a resolver request arrives, the local name server checks both its static information and the cache for the name-to-IP-address mapping. *See also* DNS and IP address.

checksum A checksum is a mathematical computation used to verify the accuracy of data in TCP/IP packets. *See also* packet and TCP/IP.

client A client is a software program used to contact and obtain data from a server software program on another computer. Each client program is designed to work with one or more specific kinds of server programs, and each server requires a specific kind of client. For example, a computer can be configured to be a DHCP client to obtain an IP address from a DHCP server.

community names A community name is a group of hosts that are running the SNMP service. The community name is placed in the SNMP packet when the trap is sent. Typically, all hosts belong to a community name called Public, which is the standard name for the common community of all hosts. *See also* packet, SNMP, and trap.

computer name A computer name is a unique name of up to 15 uppercase characters that identifies a computer to the network. The name cannot be the same as any other computer or domain name in the network.

connection A connection is a session or link between a client and a shared resource such as a printer or a shared directory on a server. Connections require a network card or modem.

D

daemon A daemon is a networking program that runs in the background on a TCP/IP server.

datagram A datagram is the basic unit of data transmission in TCP/IP terminology. It contains a source and destination address along with data. A datagram is a packet of data and other delivery information that is routed through a packet-switched network or transmitted on a local area network. *See also* packet.

datalink layer The datalink layer is an OSI model layer that is responsible for providing the error-free transfer of packets or frames from one computer to another over the physical layer. This allows the network layer to assume virtually error-free transmission over the network connection.

default gateway A default gateway (also known as a *router*) is the intermediate network device on the local network that has knowledge of the network IDs of the other networks in the internet, so it can forward the packets to other gateways until the packet is eventually delivered to a gateway connected to the specified destination. *See also* gateway, network ID, and packet.

device A device is any piece of equipment that can be attached to a network, for example, a computer, a printer, or any other peripheral equipment.

device driver A device driver is a program that enables a specific piece of hardware (device) to communicate with an operating system such as Windows NT. Although a device may be installed on your system,

Windows NT cannot recognize the device until you have installed and configured the appropriate driver. If a device is listed in the Hardware Compatibility List, a driver is usually included with Windows NT. Drivers are installed when you run the setup program (for a manufacturer's supplied driver) or by using Devices in the Control Panel.

DHCP   DHCP stands for *Dynamic Host Configuration Protocol*, which offers dynamic configuration of IP addresses and related information. DHCP provides safe, reliable, and simple TCP/IP network configuration, prevents address conflicts, and helps conserve the use of IP addresses through centralized management of address allocation. *See also* IP address.

DHCP relay agent   The DHCP relay agent is a component that is responsible for relaying DHCP and BOOTP broadcast messages between a DHCP server and a client across an IP router. *See also* BOOTP and DHCP.

dial-up networking   Dial-up networking refers to the client version of Windows NT *Remote Access Service* (RAS), enabling users to connect to remote networks.

direct routing   Direct routing is the transmission of a datagram from one host to another directly (without the need for a gateway).

directory database   A directory database is a database of security information, such as user account names and passwords, and the security policy settings. For Windows NT Workstation, the directory database is managed using User Manager. For a Windows NT Server domain, it is managed using User Manager for Domains. (Other Windows NT documents may refer to the directory database as the Security Accounts Manager (SAM) database.)

directory services   *See* Windows NT Directory Services.

DNS   *See* Domain Name System.

DNS name servers   DNS name servers are the servers containing information about a portion of the DNS database, which makes computer names available to client resolvers querying for name resolution across the internet. *See also* Domain Name System (DNS).

domain In Windows NT, a domain is a collection of computers, defined by the administrator of a Windows NT Server network, that share a common directory database. A domain provides access to the centralized user accounts and group accounts maintained by the domain administrator. Each domain has a unique name.

domain controller In a Windows NT Server domain, a domain controller refers to the computer running Windows NT Server that manages the Windows NT directory services. A domain controller manages all aspects of user-domain interactions, and uses information in the directory database to authenticate users logging on to domain accounts. One shared directory database is used to store security and user account information for the entire domain. A domain has one primary domain controller (PDC) and one or more backup domain controllers (BDCs).

domain name A domain name is the unique name that identifies an Internet site. Domain names always have two or more parts, separated by dots. The part on the left is the most specific, and the part on the right is the most general. A given machine may have more than one domain name, but a given domain name points to only one machine.

Domain Name System (DNS) DNS is sometimes referred to as the BIND service in BSD UNIX; the Domain Name System offers a static, hierarchical name service for TCP/IP hosts. The network administrator configures the DNS with a list of host names and IP addresses, enabling users of workstations configured to query the DNS to specify remote systems by host name rather than IP address. For example, a workstation configured to use DNS name resolution could use the command `ping remotehost` rather than `ping 172.25.16.51` if the mapping for the system named `remotehost` was contained in the DNS database. DNS domains should not be confused with Windows NT networking domains. *See also* IP address and ping.

dynamic routing Dynamic routing is used to automatically update the TCP/IP routing tables, reducing administrative overhead (but increasing traffic in large networks). *See also* routing table.

E

Ethernet Ethernet is a method of networking computers in a *local area network* (LAN). Ethernet will handle about 10,000,000 bits per second and can be used with almost any kind of computer.

F

Fiber Distributed Data Interface (FDDI) FDDI is a standard for transmitting data on optical fiber cables at a rate of around 100,000,000 bits per second (10 times as fast as Ethernet, about twice as fast as T-3).

file system A file system is the overall structure in which files are named, stored, and organized. NTFS and FAT are types of file systems.

File Transfer Protocol (FTP) FTP is a service supporting file transfers between local and remote systems that support the FTP protocol. FTP supports several commands that allow bidirectional transfer of binary and ASCII files between systems. The FTP Server service is part of the Internet Information Server (IIS). The FTP client is installed with TCP/IP connectivity utilities.

Finger Finger is an Internet software utility used to locate people on other Internet sites. Finger is also sometimes used to give access to non-personal information, but the most common use is to see if a person has an account at a particular Internet site.

firewall A firewall is a combination of hardware and software that separates a LAN into two or more parts for security purposes.

frame A frame is a data structure that is used by network devices to transmit data. Frames consist of the sender and destination addresses, data, and a checksum.

FTP *See* File Transfer Protocol.

GLOSSARY

fully qualified domain name (FQDN) An FQDN is part of the TCP/IP naming convention known as the Domain Name System. DNS computer names consist of two parts: host names with their domain names appended to them. For example, a host with host name `corpapps` and DNS domain name `sales.quicklearn.com` has an FQDN of `corpapps.sales.quicklearn.com`. (DNS domains should not be confused with Windows NT networking domains.) *See also* DNS.

G

gateway A gateway (also known as an IP router) is a device that is connected to multiple physical TCP/IP networks and capable of routing or delivering IP packets between them. A gateway translates between different transport protocols or data formats (for example IPX and IP) and is generally added to a network primarily for its translation ability. *See also* IP address and IP router.

H

h-node h-node is a NetBIOS implementation that uses the p-node protocol first, then the b-node protocol if the name service is unavailable. For registration, it uses the b-node protocol, and then the p-node protocol.

hop A hop refers to the next router. In IP routing, packets are always forwarded one router at a time. Packets often hop from router to router before reaching their destination. *See also* IP address, packet, and router.

host A host is a uniquely addressable device that is attached to the network. A host can be a workstation, server, router, network printer, or any other device that connects to the network using a network interface card.

host ID A host ID is the portion of the IP address that identifies a computer within a particular network ID. *See also* IP address and network ID.

395

host name A host name is the name of a device on a network. For a device on a Windows or Windows NT network, this can be the same as the computer name, but it may not be. The host name must be in the host table or be known by a DNS server for that host to be found by another computer attempting to communicate with it. *See also* DNS and host table.

host table A host table is maintained in the HOSTS and LMHOSTS files, which contain mappings of known IP addresses mapped to host names.

HOSTS file A HOSTS file is a local text file in the same format as the 4.3 Berkeley Staandard Distribution (BSD) UNIX `\etc\hosts` file. This file maps host names to IP addresses. In Windows NT, this file is stored in the `\systemroot\System32\Drivers\Etc` directory. *See also* IP address.

HyperText Markup Language (HTML) HTML is the coding language used to create hypertext documents for use on the World Wide Web. HTML looks a lot like old-fashioned typesetting code, where you surround a block of text with codes that indicate how it should appear. Additionally, in HTML you can specify that a block of text, or a word, is linked to another file on the Internet. HTML files are meant to be viewed using a World Wide Web client program, such as Netscape Navigator or Internet Explorer.

I

ICMP *See* Internet Control Message Protocol.

IETF *See* Internet Engineering Task Force.

Indirect routing Indirect routing is the transmission of a datagram from one host to another that is located on a different network. Indirect routing forces the sender to pass the datagram to a router for delivery.

Integrated Services Digital Network (ISDN) ISDN is a type of phone line used to enhance wide area network (WAN) speeds. ISDN lines can

GLOSSARY

transmit at speeds of 64 or 128 kilobits per second, as opposed to standard phone lines, which typically transmit at only 9,600 bits per second (bps). An ISDN line must be installed by the phone company at both the server site and the remote site.

internet An internet (lowercase *i*) is a collection of two or more private networks. Any time you connect two or more networks together, you have an internet — as in inter-national or inter-state.

Internet The Internet (uppercase *I*) is the vast collection of interconnected networks that all use the TCP/IP protocols and that evolved from the ARPANET of the late 60s and early 70s. The Internet now connects roughly tens of thousands of independent networks into a vast global network.

Internet Control Message Protocol (ICMP) The *Internet Control Message Protocol* (ICMP) provides a mechanism for reporting errors due to datagram delivery problems. A connectionless system means that datagrams are delivered without any coordination between the originating and destination workstations. Although ICMP does not enable IP to function as a reliable protocol, it does report some errors that occur when IP actions fail. If, for example, the time-to-live (TTL) counter expires due to network congestion or the unavailability of the destination workstation, IP fails to deliver the datagram, a failure that will generate an ICMP message. ICMP is a standard component in all TCP/IP implementations. *See also* ping.

Internet engineering task force (IETF) The IETF is a consortium that introduces procedures for new technology on the Internet. IETF specifications are released in documents called Requests for Comments (RFCs). *See also* RFC.

Internet Group Management Protocol (IGMP) IGMP provides routers with the identifications of multicast groups that are active on their attached networks. This information is propagated to other routers to enable multicasting support throughout the network. IGMP messages are delivered in IP datagrams, hence delivery of IGMP messages is unreliable.

Internet group name An Internet group name is a name that is known by a DNS server that includes a list of the specific addresses of systems that have registered the name. *See also* DNS.

397

Internet Network Information Center (InterNIC) The InterNIC is the organization that is responsible for, among other things, managing the registration of IP network numbers and domain names for organizations who access the Internet.

Internet Protocol (IP) The Internet Protocol is the messenger protocol of TCP/IP that is responsible for addressing and sending TCP packets over the network. IP provides a best-effort, connectionless delivery system that does not guarantee that packets arrive at their destination or that they are received in the sequence in which they were sent. *See also* packet and TCP/IP.

Internet router An Internet router is a device that connects networks and directs network information to other networks, usually choosing the most efficient route through other routers. *See also* router.

Internet service provider (ISP) An ISP is an organization that provides access to the Internet in some form, usually for money.

Internet Society (ISOC) The ISOC is an organization that was formed to promote a global information exchange of networking technologies and Internet applications. The ISOC is divided into other functional groups that are responsible for technical issues and developing standards.

internetworks Internetworks are networks that connect local-area networks (LANs) together.

intranet A intranet is a private network inside a company or organization that uses the same kinds of software that you would find on the public Internet, but that is for internal use only.

IP *See* Internet Protocol.

IP address An IP address is used to identify a specific host on a network and to specify routing information. Each host on the network must be assigned a unique IP address, which is made up of the *network ID*, plus a unique *host ID* assigned by the network administrator. This address is typically represented in dotted decimal notation, with the decimal value of each octet separated by a period (for example, 172.25.16.1). In Windows NT, the IP address can be configured statically on the client or configured dynamically through DHCP. *See also* DHCP and octet.

IP header Each IP datagram has an IP header, which is a sequence of bits that serves to label the datagram and controls how the datagram is managed.

IP router An IP router is a system connected to multiple physical TCP/IP networks that can route or deliver IP packets between the networks. *See also* packet, routing, and TCP/IP.

K

kilobyte A thousand bytes. Actually, it is usually 1,024 (2^{10}) bytes.

L

line printer daemon (LPD) An LPD service on the print server receives documents (print jobs) from line printer remote (LPR) utilities running on client systems.

LMHOSTS file An LMHOSTS file is a local text file that maps IP addresses to the computer names of Windows NT networking computers outside the local subnet. In Windows NT, this file is stored in the *systemroot*\System32\Drivers\Etc directory.

LPD *See* line printer daemon.

M

MAC *See* media access control.

MAC address A MAC address is a unique 48-bit number assigned to the network interface card (NIC) by the manufacturer.

management information base (MIB) A MIB is a set of objects that represent various types of information about a device, used by SNMP to manage devices. Because different network-management services are used for different types of devices or protocols, each service has its own set of objects. The entire set of objects that any service or protocol uses is referred to as its MIB. *See also* SNMP.

master browser A master browser is a network server service that keeps a browse list of all the servers and domains on the network. Also referred to as browse master. *See also* browser and Windows NT browser system.

master domain In the master domain model, the master domain is the domain that is trusted by all other domains on the network and acts as the central administrative unit for user and group accounts.

media access control (MAC) Media access control is the layer in the network architecture that deals with network access and collision detection.

MIB *See* management information base.

m-node An m-node is a NetBIOS implementation that uses the b-node protocol first, then the p-node protocol if the broadcast fails to resolve a name to an IP address. *See also* IP address, NetBIOS, and p-node.

multicast datagrams An IP multicast datagram is the transmission of an IP datagram to a host group (a set of 0 or more hosts identified by a single IP destination address). An IP datagram sent to one host is called a unicast datagram. An IP datagram sent to all hosts is called a broadcast datagram. *See also* broadcast datagram, host, and IP address.

multihomed computer A multihomed computer is a system that has multiple network cards, or that has been configured with multiple IP addresses for a single network interface card. *See also* interface card, IP address, and network.

N

NetBIOS See network basic input/output system.

NetBIOS over TCP/IP (NetBT) NetBT is the session-layer network service that performs name-to-IP address mapping for name resolution. *See also* IP address, name resolution service, NetBIOS, and TCP/IP.

network adapter A network adapter is an expansion card or other device used to connect a computer to a local area network (LAN). Also called a network adapter; network adapter card; adapter card; network interface card (NIC).

network basic input/output system (NetBIOS) NetBIOS is an application program interface (API) and a protocol that can be used by application programs on a local area network. NetBIOS provides application programs with a uniform set of commands for requesting the lower-level services required to conduct sessions between nodes on a network and to transmit information back and forth. *See also* API.

network device interface specification (NDIS) NDIS provides an interface between the transport protocols and the network adapter drivers (the network adapter driver is the software interface between the protocol and the network adapter). For outgoing messages, protocols make calls to NDIS whenever access to the network adapter is necessary. When the network adapter receives incoming messages, the network adapter driver makes a call to NDIS so that the message can be processed by the transport protocols. The network driver is provided by the vendor of the network adapter and must conform to the NDIS specification. The benefit of NDIS to a manufacturer of network adapters is that the amount of code and effort necessary to support the adapter under Windows NT is minimal. The NDIS specification provides for multiple protocols and multiple network adapters to exist in a computer.

network ID The network ID is the portion of the IP address that identifies a group of computers and devices located on the same logical network.

network interface card (NIC) *See* network card.

network layer The network layer is responsible for addressing messages and translating logical addresses and names into physical addresses. This layer also controls the operation of the subnet by determining the route to take from the source to the destination computer. Protocols that run at the network layer determine which path the data should take based on network conditions, priority of service, and other factors. It also manages traffic problems such as switching, routing, and controlling the congestion of data packets on the network.

network protocol A network protocol is the software that enables computers to communicate over a network. TCP/IP is a network protocol used on the Internet. *See also* TCP/IP.

O

octet An octet refers to eight bits or one byte. IP addresses, for example, are typically represented in dotted decimal notation, that is, with the decimal value of each octet of the address separated by a period. *See also* IP address.

Open System Interconnect (OSI) The OSI model describes a network architecture that breaks up the functions of moving data from one point to another into seven different tasks. This model was designed by the *International Standards Organization* (ISO) as a method of standardization of various protocols required for network communications. The idea is to break out each function of communication and assign it a label. This permits protocols to be broken into modular components with interfaces that communicate with the upper and lower layer. Each layer is shielded from the details of how the other layers are implemented.

GLOSSARY

P

packet A packet is a transmission unit of fixed maximum size that consists of binary information representing both data and a header containing an ID number, source and destination addresses, and error-control data.

packet header A packet header is the part of a packet that contains an identification number, source and destination addresses, and — sometimes — error-control data. *See also* packet.

packet switching Packet switching is the method used to move data around on the Internet. In packet switching, all the data coming out of a machine is broken up into chunks, and each chunk has the address of where it came from and where it is going.

physical address A physical address is a unique number that is normally encoded into the hardware of a networking interface device by the manufacturer.

physical layer The physical layer is the lowest layer of the OSI model. This layer generates the physical pulses, electrical currents, and optical pulses involved in moving data across the network media and to the network interface card. Information at this layer is represented as bits by identifying the pulse duration and timing of the signals on the media. Data encoding methods are used at the physical layer to represent bit patterns for purposes such as bit and frame synchronization and as a delimiter (a way of determining the separation point between frames).

ping `Ping` is a command used to verify connections to one or more remote hosts. The `ping` utility uses the ICMP echo request and echo reply packets to determine whether a particular IP system on a network is functional. The `ping` utility is useful for diagnosing IP network or router failures. *See also* ICMP and router.

p-node p-node is a NetBIOS implementation that uses point-to-point communications with a name server to resolve names as IP addresses. *See also* h-node and IP address.

Point-to-Point Protocol (PPP) PPP is a set of industry-standard framing and authentication protocols that are part of Windows NT RAS to ensure interoperability with third-party remote access software. PPP negotiates configuration parameters for multiple layers of the OSI model. *See also* OSI.

Point-to-Point Tunneling Protocol (PPTP) PPTP is a new networking technology that supports multiprotocol *virtual private networks* (VPNs), enabling remote users to access corporate networks securely across the Internet by dialing into an *Internet service provider* (ISP) or by connecting directly to the Internet.

port A port is a place where information goes into or out of a computer, or both, e.g., the serial port on a personal computer is where a modem would be connected. On the Internet, port often refers to a number that is part of a URL, appearing after a colon (:) right after the domain name. Every service on an Internet server listens on a particular port number on that server. Most services have standard port numbers; for example, Web servers normally listen on port 80.

presentation layer The presentation layer determines the method used to exchange data between networked computers. It can be called the network's translator. At the sending computer, this layer translates data from a format sent down from the application layer into a commonly recognized, intermediary format. The presentation layer also manages network security issues by providing services such as data encryption. It also provides rules for data transfers and provides data compression to reduce the number of bits that need to be transmitted. Microsoft implements a protocol called Server Messages Blocks (SMBs) for presentation layer communications.

primary domain controller (PDC) In a Windows NT Server domain, a PDC is the computer running Windows NT Server that authenticates domain logons and maintains the directory database for a domain. The PDC tracks changes made to accounts of all computers on a domain. It is the only computer to receive these changes directly. A domain has only one PDC.

print spooler A print spooler is a collection of *dynamic link libraries* (DLLs) that receive, process, schedule, and distribute documents.

printer In Windows NT terminology, a printer refers to the software interface between the operating system and the print device. The printer defines where the document will go before it reaches the print device (to a local port, to a file, or to a remote print share), when it will go, and various other aspects of the printing process.

printer driver A printer driver is the program that converts graphics commands into a specific printer language, such as PostScript or PCL.

printing device In Windows NT terminology, a printing device refers to the physical printer.

protocol A protocol is a set of rules and conventions for sending information over a network. These rules govern the content, format, timing, sequencing, and error control of messages exchanged among network devices.

protocol driver A protocol driver is a network device driver that implements a protocol, communicating between Windows NT Server and one or more network adapter card drivers.

protocol stack A protocol stack is the implementation of a specific protocol family (such as TCP/IP) in a computer or other device on the network.

proxy A proxy is a computer that listens to name query broadcasts and responds for those names not on the local subnet. The proxy communicates with the name server to resolve names and then caches them for a time period. *See also* caching, DNS, and subnet.

pull partner A pull partner is a WINS server that pulls in replicas from its push partner by requesting it and then accepting the pushed replicas. *See also* WINS.

push partner A push partner is a WINS server that sends replicas to its pull partner upon receiving a request from it. *See also* WINS.

Q

queue In Windows NT terminology, a queue refers to a group of documents waiting to be printed. (In NetWare and OS/2 environments, queues are the primary software interface between the application and print device; users submit documents to a queue. However, with Windows NT, the printer is that interface — the document is sent to a printer, not a queue.)

R

RAS *See* Remote access service.

remote access service (RAS) RAS is a service that provides remote networking for telecommuters, mobile workers, and system administrators who monitor and manage servers at multiple branch offices. Users with RAS on a Windows NT computer can dial in to remotely access their networks for services such as file and printer sharing, electronic mail, scheduling, and SQL database access.

repeaters The most basic LAN connection device, repeaters strengthen the physical transmission signal. A repeater simply takes the electrical signals that reach it and then regenerates them to full strength before passing them on. Repeaters generally extend a single network (rather than link two networks).

requests for comments (RFCs) RFCs are published documents that describe official Internet standards. An RFC is discussed for a while — often a long while — on the network itself, where anyone can express an opinion. At this point, the working documents are assigned an RFC number and the RFC is classified as a *proposed standard*. After suitable time for review and testing, the proposed standard may be advanced to a *draft standard* and finally to an official *Internet standard*. Because the process of reviewing and advancing an RFC is complex and formal, it is likely that the proposed standard may have spent some time as an *inter-*

net draft. Internet drafts are revised more informally and may go through several generations before the concept is thought ready for the formal standards process.

resolvers Resolvers are DNS clients that query DNS servers for name resolution on networks. *See also* DNS.

RIP *See* Routing Information Protocol.

router In the Windows NT environment, a router helps LANs and WANs achieve interoperability and connectivity and can link LANs that have different network topologies (such as Ethernet and Token Ring). Routers match packet headers to a LAN segment and choose the best path for the packet, optimizing network performance.

routing Routing is the process of addressing and sending a message from one device to another. However, normally when the term routing is used, it refers to the mechanisms used to deliver a message to a device that exists on a remote network. Communications protocols must include information that allows two devices on different networks to communicate with one another.

Routing Information Protocol (RIP) RIP enables a router to exchange routing information with a neighboring router. *See also* routing.

routing table A routing table controls the decisions made by computers running TCP/IP. Routing tables are built automatically by Windows NT based on the IP configuration of your computer. *See also* dynamic routing, table routing, static routing, and TCP/IP.

S

Server Message Block (SMB) SMB is a file sharing protocol designed to allow systems to transparently access files that reside on remote systems.

server service A server service provides the ability for a computer to provide shared resources to other clients. A server service is composed of two parts. The server is the service that is used to manage incoming requests for resources from other computers across the network. A file system driver handles the interaction with various file system devices to satisfy file and print requests from a client.

session layer The session layer allows two applications on different computers to establish, use, and end a connection, called a *session*. This layer performs name recognition and includes functions that allow two applications to communicate over the network. Microsoft provides the industry standard NetBIOS interface for managing sessions between Windows-based computers. NetBIOS services provide virtual-circuit session functions that applications can use to manage connections between two computers.

Simple Network Management Protocol (SNMP) SNMP is a set of standards for communication with devices connected to a TCP/IP network. Examples of these devices include routers, hubs, and switches. A device is said to be SNMP compatible if it can be monitored and/or controlled using SNMP messages.

SNMP agent An SNMP agent is a software program that processes manager requests for data by retrieving data from managed objects on the computer. The agent program is part of the SNMP service running under Windows NT.

SNMP manager An SNMP manager is a software program that sends requests for data to other computers on the network. Typically, the manager includes a *user interface* (UI) for displaying status and data retrieved from the network computers and devices.

socket A socket is a bidirectional pipe for incoming and outgoing data between networked computers. The Windows Sockets API is a networking API used by programmers creating TCP/IP-based sockets applications. *See also* API.

GLOSSARY

Sockets Windows Sockets is a Windows implementation of the widely used UC Berkeley sockets API. Microsoft TCP/IP, NWLink, and AppleTalk protocols use this interface. Sockets interfaces between programs and the transport protocol and works as a bidirectional pipe for incoming and outgoing data.

static routing Static routing is a method of routing that is limited to fixed routing tables, as opposed to dynamically updated routing tables. *See also* dynamic routing and routing table.

subnet A subnet is a portion of a network, which may be a physically independent network segment, which shares a network address with other portions of the network and is distinguished by a subnet number. A subnet is to a network what a network is to an internet.

subnet mask A subnet mask is a 32-bit value that enables the recipient of IP packets to distinguish the network ID portion of the IP address from the host ID. *See also* IP address and packet.

T

TCP *See* Transmission Control Protocol.

TDI *See* transport driver interface.

Telnet Telnet is the command and program used to log in from one Internet site to another. The telnet command/program gets you to the login prompt of another host.

terminal A terminal is a device that allows you to send commands to a computer somewhere else. At a minimum, this usually means a keyboard and a display screen and some simple circuitry. Usually you will use terminal software in a personal computer; the software pretends to be (emulates) a physical terminal and allows you to type commands to a computer somewhere else.

terminal server A terminal server is a special-purpose computer that has places to plug in many modems on one side and a connection to a LAN or host machine on the other side. Thus, the terminal server does the work of answering the calls and passes the connections on to the appropriate node. Most terminal servers can provide PPP or SLIP services if connected to the Internet.

Transmission Control Protocol/Internet Protocol (TCP/IP) TCP/IP is a set of networking protocols that provides communications across interconnected networks made up of computers with diverse hardware architectures and various operating systems. TCP/IP includes standards for how computers communicate and conventions for connecting networks and routing traffic.

transport driver interface (TDI) The *transport driver interface* (TDI) boundary layer provides a common interface between transport protocols and client services. TDI describes a set of functions that transport drivers and clients use to communicate with each other. Network client services such as the redirector or server are examples of client services provided on Windows NT computers. The redirector and server call TDI functions to communicate with network protocols instead of having to be bound directly to a specific transport protocol.

transport layer The transport layer manages reliable message transfers between hosts using flow control and synchronization fields. This layer repackages messages — dividing long messages into several packets and collecting small messages together in one packet — to provide for their efficient transmission over the network.

trap In SNMP, a trap is a discrete block of data that indicates that the request failed authentication. The SNMP service can send a trap when it receives a request for information that does not contain the correct community name and that does not match an accepted host name for the service. Trap destinations are the names or IP addresses of hosts to which the SNMP service is to send traps with community names. *See also* IP address and SNMP.

GLOSSARY

U

UDP *See* User Datagram Protocol.

uniform resource locator (URL) A URL is the standard way to give the address of any resource on the Internet that is part of the World Wide Web.

UNIX UNIX is a computer operating system (the basic software running on a computer, underneath things like word processors and spreadsheets). UNIX is designed to be used by many people at the same time (it is multiuser) and has TCP/IP built in. It is the most common operating system for servers on the Internet.

User Datagram Protocol (UDP) UDP is a TCP complement that offers a connectionless datagram service that guarantees neither delivery nor correct sequencing of delivered packets (much like IP). *See also* datagram, IP, and packet.

W

wide area network (WAN) A WAN is any internet or network that covers an area larger than a single building or campus.

Windows Internet Name Service (WINS) WINS is a name resolution service that resolves Windows networking computer names to IP addresses in a routed environment. A WINS server handles name registrations, queries, and releases. *See also* IP address and routing.

Windows NT Server Directory Services The Windows NT Directory Services is a Windows NT protected subsystem that maintain the directory database and provides an application programming interface (API) for accessing the database. *See also* API and directory database.

411

Windows Sockets The Windows Sockets specification provides an API to which application developers can write TCP/IP programs. Windows Sockets specifies a programming interface based on the "socket" interface from the University of California at Berkeley. Windows Sockets applications (also known as Sockets-based applications) eliminate the need for NetBIOS to communicate between hosts. Windows Sockets APIs include functions for sending and receiving data on a network. They include a set of extensions designed to take advantage of the message-driven nature of Microsoft Windows. Applications developed to the Windows Sockets specification form a socket between two ports on different hosts to enable communications. Sockets-based applications can use a host name or an IP address for communicating with a remote host. Some examples of sockets-based utilities and applications include `ping`, FTP, and World Wide Web (WWW) browsers.

Workstation Service Windows NT computers include a component called the Workstation Service, which also resides just above the TDI. The main function of the Workstation Service is to manage requests for local files and outgoing connections to another computer. The Workstation Service consists of two components. The user-mode interface passes network commands down to the redirector. These commands are initiated from Windows NT Explorer or from a command line using commands such as `Net Use`. The redirector is a file system driver that interacts with the lower-level network drivers by means of the TDI interface.

World Wide Web (WWW) WWW has two meanings: First, loosely used, it is the whole constellation of resources that can be accessed using Gopher, FTP, HTTP, telnet, USENET, WAIS, and some other tools. Second, it is the universe of hypertext servers (HTTP servers) which are the servers that enable text, graphics, sound files, and so on to be mixed together.

Index

@ (at sign), 168
\ (backslash), 256
" (double quotes), 222
\ (forward slash), 180, 256
- (hyphen), 180, 235, 305
. (period), 157, 169, 170, 176, 235, 256, 305, 308
(pound sign), 237
? (question mark), 258
; (semicolon), 166, 168
#BEGIN_ALTERNATE keyword, 221
#DOM keyword, 140, 221
#DOM tag, 268
#END_ALTERNATE keyword, 222
#INCLUDE keyword, 221, 222
#PRE keyword, 221, 222
#PRE tag, 268

A

-a field, 195
-a parameter, 223, 256, 327, 339
-A parameter, 223, 339
A (address) records, 168–169, 172, 175, 176
Accept SNMP Service Packets From Any Host option, 287
Accepted Community Names option, 287
Accepting state, 225, 341
ACKs (acknowledgements), 21
adapters, 307, 312, 338
Add Host dialog box, 174
administrative privileges, 304
Administrative Tools folder, 172
Administrative Tools menu, 136
agent parameter, 290
algorithms
  distance-vector, implemented by RIP, 112–114
  error control, 6
  OSI model and, 7
  new RFCs for, 325
alias (CNAME) records, 175
AND computations, 52
APIs (application program interfaces)
  application layer and, 14
  NetBIOS, 24, 213
AppleTalk, 279
application layer, 7–8, 11–12, 14–16, 23
ARP (Address Resolution Protocol). See also arp utility
  basic description of, 13, 19, 187, 191–196
  cache, 193–194, 197–201, 203, 238, 338
  entries, invalid, 203
  entries, static, 194–195
  hardware address resolution methods, 196–200
  host name resolution and, 238, 240
  IP routing and, 103–104
  NetBIOS name resolution and, 217
  problems, troubleshooting, 202–203, 336
  request frame, 191–192
arp utility, 195–196, 203
ArpCacheLife parameter, 194
AS (autonomous system), 111
ASCII (American Standard Code for Information Interchange), 257, 258, 332
ascii command, 257
Associated state, 224, 340
automatic addressing, 302

B

-b parameter, 256
b-node method/node type, 132, 216, 217–218, 220, 241
backup browser role, 264
backup domain controller, 268
Backup On Termination option, 146
backups
  directories for, 144, 146
  for the WINS database, 144–146
bandwidth, of links, 114
banner pages, 263
binary command, 257
binary format
  converting, to decimal format, 34–35
  converting decimal format to, 51
BIND (Berkeley Internet Name Domain) servers, 164–166, 171, 172
Bindings dialog box, 307

413

INDEX

BIOS (Basic Input/Output System), 309. *See also* I/O (Input/Output)
bitwise AND computations, 52
BOOT file, 165–166, 168
Boot Method property page, 173
BOOT.BAK, 173
BOOTP forwarding, 80
browse lists. *See also* browsing
   collecting, 265–266
   distributing, 266
   passing, 128
browsing. *See also* browse lists
   basic description of, 264–268
   how it works, 265–267
   servicing client browser requests, 266–267
bye command, 258
bytes, 34, 86

C

-c parameter, 223, 339
caching
   ARP and, 193–194, 197–201, 203, 238, 338
   DNS and, 162–164, 169, 170, 174
   -only servers, 162–163
Capture Summary window, 331–332
carriage returns, 258
case-sensitivity, of host names, 235
-CClass parameter, 263
cd command, 257
checkpoint files, 144
checksums, 21
Cisco Systems, 113
Class A addresses, 36–39, 48, 53, 56–58, 113
Class B addresses, 37–39, 48, 53, 56, 58, 61, 103, 113, 337
Class C addresses, 38, 39, 53, 56, 59
client(s)
   browser requests, 266–267

comments, 91
DHCP options for, 89–90
names, 91
non-WINS, 139–140
options, for scopes, 77–78
reservations, creating, 90–91
static entries for, 139–140
WINS, 126–127, 133–134
CNAME (canonical name) records, 168
.com domains, 158
COM ports, 260
command lines, length of, 180
command parameter, 254
commands (listed by name)
   /all command, 131, 339
   ascii command, 257
   binary command, 257
   bye command, 258
   cd command, 257
   ftp command, 199
   get command, 258
   lcd command, 258
   lpq command, 263
   lpr command, 262
   ls command, 258
   nbtstat command, 129, 223–225, 339, 340
   open command, 258
   ping command, 203, 235–236, 335–336
   quit command, 258
   /release command, 86, 92
   /renew command, 81–82, 92
   route command, 115–116
   rshd command, 255–256
comments, 91, 168
community names, 287
community parameter, 290
components,
   adding/removing, 307
Computer Browser service, 264–268
computer names (NetBIOS names)
   assigning, 214–215
   character restrictions for, 305
   duplicate, preventing of, 128, 129
   restrictions on, 220
configuration (TCP/IP)
   basic description of, 297–320

problems, troubleshooting, 309–313, 318, 333–334
testing, 311–313, 316–317
computer roles, 264–265
Connected state, 224, 340
Connecting state, 225, 341
connectivity
   basic description of, 247–274
   utilities, 253–259
Contact option, 288
Control Panel
   Network applet, 87
   Network option, 307
   Services icon, 116
converting
   addresses, 34–35
   from binary format to decimal format, 34–35
   from decimal format to binary format, 51
EOL characters, 258
copying files
   from FTP servers, 272
   from UNIX computers, 272
country codes, for domain names, 159
CPUs (central processing units), 133, 325, 330
Create PTR Record option, 174
cyclical redundancy check (CRC) field, 10

D

-d field, 195
-d parameter, 257, 263
daemons
   basic description of, 253
   LPD (line printer daemon), 252, 260–262
   Telnet, 254
data transfer utility, 255–259
Database Backup Path option, 146
datagrams, 22, 199, 200
   basic description of, 17
   IP address resolution and, 198

414

INDEX

IP routing and, 103, 112–113
RIP and, 112–113
SNMP service and, 281
datalink layer, 8, 9–12, 23
DDLs (Dynamic Link Libraries), 331
dead gateway detection, 108–109
decimal format
  converting binary format to, 34–35
  converting, to binary format, 51
DECVT52 emulation, 254
DECVT100 emulation, 254
delay due to links, 114
Delete Owner option, 142
destination parameter, 259
destination unreachable message, 20
Detail pane, 332
device drivers, 259
Device Manager, 309
DHCP. *See* Dynamic Configuration Host Protocol
DHCP Manager (Microsoft)
  basic description of, 75
  client reservations and, 90–91
  list of services in, 87
  options, 89
DHCP Server (Microsoft), 74–75, 85–89
  basic description of, 75
  installing, 86–87
  lease renewal and, 86
  options, 89
  subnet masks and, 87–88
DHCPACK message/packet, 81
DHCP/BOOTP relay agent, 84–85
DHCPDISCOVER message/packet, 79–80, 84
DHCPOFFER message/packet, 80–81, 84
DHCPREQUEST message/packet, 81, 82, 91, 92

Diagnostics (Windows NT), 309
dial-up connections, 16–17, 112
directories
  changing, with the cd command, 257
  current, indicating, with a period, 256
  storing the HOSTS file in, 237, 238, 338
Disconnected state, 225, 341
Disconnecting state, 225, 341
Display Options-Owner option, 141
Display Options-Sort Order option, 142
distance-vector algorithms, 112–114
distance-vector routing protocols, 111
DNS (Domain Name Service), 235–236, 238–240, 333
  application layer and, 14–15
  basic description of, 153–186, 303
  configuration files, 164–170
  database files, 164–170
  DHCP and, 74, 78–79, 89
  files, porting, 173
  NetBIOS name resolution and, 220
  problems, troubleshooting, 179–180
  specifications, 157
  TCP/IP installation and, 303, 305–309
  WINS and, 132
DNS Manager, 172–175
DNS Server (Microsoft), 164–166, 169
  configuring, 171–180
  installing, 171–180
DOD (Department of Defense), 282
domain(s). *See also* domain names
  basic description of, 158–159
  DNS versus Windows NT, 239
  geographical, 158–159
  organizational, 158–159

reverse, 158–159
root, 158, 160
domain controllers, promotion of, 268
domain master browser role, 264, 267, 268
domain names. *See also* DNS (Domain Name Service); domains
  DHCP and, 78–79
  fully qualified (FQDNs), 176, 235, 240, 305–306, 308
  registering, with InterNIC, 170
  static mappings and, 140
domain suffix search orders, 306
DOS (Disk Operating System), 81, 257
dotted decimal notation, 34–35, 56, 195, 209
Dynamic Configuration Host Protocol (DHCP). *See also* DHCP Manager (Microsoft); DHCP Server (Microsoft)
  basic description of, 69–98
  clients, 75–76
  components, 75
  configuring, 81, 86–92
  how it works, 73–82
  initialization phases, 79–91
  installing, 82–92
  monitoring, 329
  NetBIOS name resolution and, 218, 220
  options, 77–79, 87–89
  relay agents, 84–85
  server failures, 85
  servers, determining the required number of, 85–86
  servers, multiple, 83–84
  SNMP service and, 283–286, 288, 289
  TCP/IP installation and, 301–310
  traffic considerations for, 85–86
  WINS and, 133, 136, 140

415

INDEX

E

-e parameter, 327
echo packets, 117
echo replies, 311–313
echo requests, 20, 311–313
.edu domains, 158
Enable Automatic DHCP Configuration checkbox, 87
Enable IP Forwarding checkbox, 117
EnableRegistryBoot Registry key, 173
EOL (end-of-line) characters, 258
error(s)
 control, basic description of, 6
 duplicate address, 201–202
 "Request timed out," 203
 TCP and, 20
escape characters, 180, 256
Ethernet
 frames, 9–10
 IP address resolution and, 191, 193
 network interface layer and, 15
 statistics, monitoring, 327
Ethernet II, 15
event logs, 201–202, 336
Event Viewer, 335, 336
exclusive mode, 162
expiration dates/times, 141, 178
Expire Time option, 178
Explorer (Windows NT), 25, 251, 312
exterior routing protocols, 110–111
extinction intervals, 138, 145
Extinction Interval option, 145
Extinction Timeout option, 145

F

fields
 -a field, 195
 arp utility, 195–196
 cyclical redundancy check (CRC) field, 10
 -d field, 195
 data fields, 9–10
 -N field, 196
 -s field, 195
 type fields, 9–10
file extensions, 166
File Manager, 251
file system drivers, 26
filename parameter, 263
files. *See also* files (listed by name)
 checkpoint files, 144
 copying, 272
 import files, 140
 PostScript files, 263
files (listed by name)
 BOOT file, 165–166, 168
 HOSTS file, 132, 220, 236–238, 240, 338, 340
 LMHOSTS file, 126, 132, 137, 140, 216, 218, 220–222, 236, 238–241, 267–268, 304, 313, 339
 NETWORKS file, 106
filters, 330–331, 329
flow control, 5–6, 10, 20
font cartridges, 259
forwarders, 161–162, 179
FQDNs (fully qualified domain names), 176, 235, 240, 305–306, 308
frames, basic description of, 9. *See also* packets
FTP (File Transfer Protocol), 17–18, 159, 284, 329
 accessing help for, 258
 application layer and, 14–15
 basic description of, 255, 257–258
 host name resolution and, 235–236
 internetworks and, 251–252, 257–258, 272–273
 OSI model and, 7
 servers, copying files from, 272–273
 SNMP service and, 289
 TCP/IP installation and, 313
ftp command, 199

G

-g parameter, 257
gateway(s). *See also* routers
 basic description of, 6–7, 17, 102, 107
 default, 103, 106, 198, 199, 302, 303, 312
 detection, dead, 108–109
 DHCP and, 79–90
 IP address resolution and, 198, 199
 print, 259, 261
 TCP/IP installation and, 302, 303, 312
General tab, 176
geographical domains, 158–159
get command, 258
get operation, 280, 281
get-next operation, 280
global options, 77–78, 89–90
Gopher
 internetworks and, 251
 SNMP service and, 284
Graph pane, 331
graphics, HTTP support for, 259
group conflict statistics, 139
group names, 215
group registration statistics, 139
group renewal statistics, 139
group static mappings, 139–140

416

INDEX

H

-h parameter, 256
h-node node type/method, 131, 217, 219–220
handshaking, 20
hangs, 201
hardware
　addresses, 32, 191, 192, 193, 195–202
　CPUs (central processing units), 133, 325, 330
　performance, monitoring, 325–326
　problems, troubleshooting, 333–334
headers, protocol, 8–9
Hewlett Packard, 280
Hex pane, 332
HKEY_PERFORMANCE_DA TA Registry key, 289
host(s). *See also* host IDs; host names
　configuring, 18
　delivery of datagrams to, 17
　IP routing and, 102–108
　local, 102, 196, 197–198
　multihomed, 102, 116–117, 140, 303
　verifying communications between, 203
host IDs
　assigning, 39–40
　basic description of, 36–40, 49–50
　grouping host computers by, 40
　guidelines for, 40
　range of, determining, 61–62
　required number of, determining, 55
　subdividing networks and, 54–62
　subnet addressing and, 48, 49–50, 55, 61–62
host name(s). *See also* host name resolution
　basic description of, 235–236
　character restrictions for, 305

mapping, with A records, 168, 175
　problems, troubleshooting, 334, 338
host name resolution, 334, 338. *See also* host names
　basic description of, 231–245
　methods, 236–241
host parameter, 254, 259
hostname parameter, 257
HOSTS file, 132, 220, 236–238, 240, 338, 340
HTTP (HyperText Transfer Protocol)
　basic description of, 255, 259
　SNMP service and, 284
hybrid node type, 131

I

-i parameter, 257, 258
IANA (Internet Assigned Numbers Authority), 18
ICMP (Internet Control Message Protocol), 117, 311–313
　basic description of, 13, 15–22
　SNMP service and, 289
　statistics, monitoring, 326–327, 328
Idle state, 224, 341
IEEE (Institute of Electrical and Electronics Engineers), 15, 32
IETF (Internet Engineering Task Force), 53
IGMP (Internet Group Management Protocol), 13, 20
IGP (Interior Gateway Protocol), 110–111
IGRP (Interior Gateway Routing Protocol), 112–114
import files, 140
In column, 224, 340

Inbound state, 225, 341
In/Out column, 224
installation
　DHCP, 82–86
　DNS, 170–171
　Microsoft DNS Server, 171–180
　SNMP service, 286–288
　TCP/IP, 297–320
　WINS, 132–137
interactive mode, 180
interdomain routing protocols, 111
interfaces, basic description of, 107
interior routing protocols, 110–111
Internet
　basic description of, 48
　layer, 7–8, 12, 16–20, 191
Internet Explorer browser, 259
Internet Information Server (IIS), 286
Internet MIB-II, 283
internetwork(s)
　basic description of, 247–274
　browsing, 264–268
　private, 53–54
　use of the term, 48
　WINS and, 134–135
InterNIC, 36, 113
　assignment of domain names by, 158–159, 170
　Class C addresses allocated by, 54
　obtaining an IP address from, 38
Interval parameter, 223
inverse queries, 163
I/O (Input/Output)
　addresses, 309
　calls, redirectors and, 25
In/Out column, 340
IP (Internet Protocol). *See also* IP addresses; IP address resolution; IP routing
　basic description of, 13, 17–22
　printers, configuring, 261
　SNMP service and, 289
　statistics, monitoring, 326–327, 328

417

INDEX

IP address(es). *See also* IP
(Internet Protocol); IP
address resolution; IP
routing
assigning, 33–34, 39,
301–303, 307, 308
basic description of, 5, 29–44
Class A addresses, 36–39,
48, 53, 56, 57–58, 113
Class B addresses, 37–38, 39,
48, 53, 56, 58, 61, 103,
337
Class C addresses, 38, 39, 53,
56, 59
client reservations and, 91
configuration of, 86–87,
91–92
contents of, 34
determination of packet
destinations by, 52
DNS and, 157, 163,
166–168, 169
duplicate, 201–202
excluding, 88
host name resolution and,
238–241
NetBIOS name resolution
and, 215, 217–218
obtaining, 38
partitioning, 49–50
pools, 87–88
problems, troubleshooting,
336–338
range of, determining, 61–62
WINS and, 127–142
IP address resolution. *See also*
ARP (Address
Resolution Protocol)
basic description of, 187–208
problems, troubleshooting,
193, 202–203
IP routing
basic description of, 99–122
dead gateway detection and,
108–109
direct/indirect, 103–104
dynamic, 109, 110, 116–117
enabling, 114–117
how it works, 103–104
protocols, 109–114
tables, 105–108
ipconfig utility, 91–92, 203,
309–310, 334–335, 337

/all command, 131, 339
/release command, 86, 92
/renew command, 81–82, 92
IRQs (interrupt request
numbers), 309
ISO (International Standards
Organization), 159, 282
ISPs (Internet Service
Providers), 16, 170
iterative queries, 163

J

J50.#####.log, 144
J50.chk, 144
J50.log, 144, 145
-JJobname parameter, 263

L

-l parameter, 263
LAN Manager, 283, 286, 288
LAN Manager MIB-II, 283
LANs (Local Area Networks)
browsing and, 264, 266–267
NetBIOS name resolution
and, 219
-to-LAN routing, 114–117
layers
application layer, 7–8,
11–12, 14–16, 23
basic description of, 7
datalink layer, 8, 9–12, 23
Network Interface layer, 12,
13, 16
network layer, 7–8, 10–12, 23
physical layer, 9, 11, 12, 23
presentation layer, 8, 11–12,
23
session layer, 8, 10–12, 23
transport layer, 7–8, 10–12,
14, 16, 20–23
lcd command, 258
lease acquisition, 86
lease renewal, 81–82, 86

lease time, 77–78, 88
line printer port monitor, 262
link-state routing protocols, 111
Listening state, 224, 340
LMHOSTS file, 126, 132, 137,
140, 216, 218, 220–222,
236, 238–241, 267–268,
304, 313, 339
load balancing, 161
local hosts
basic description of, 102
IP address resolution and,
196, 197–198
Local Name column, 224, 340
local subnet addresses, 108
Location option, 288
log(s)
event logs, 201–202, 336
options for, 145–146
system logs, 335, 336
Log Detailed Events option, 146
Logging Enabled option, 145
logical addresses, 10
loopback addresses, 108, 312
loopback drivers, 312
loops, reducing the effects of,
with RIP, 112–113
LPD (line printer daemon)
utility, 252, 260–262
lpq (line printer query) utility,
263
lpq command, 263
LPQ (line printer queue)
utility, 252
LPR (line printer) utility,
260–263
lpr command, 262
LPR port print monitor, 262
lpr.exe, 261
ls command, 258

M

m-node method/node type,
217, 219
MAC (media access control)
addresses, 32
manual addressing, 301

418

INDEX

mapping(s)
 information for, in the
  WINS database,
  141–142
 static, 139–140
 tables, 144
Mappings column, 141
master browser role, 264, 266,
 267, 268
master name servers, 161
metrics
 basic description of, 107
 IP routing and, 107
MIBfilename parameter, 289
MIBIndex parameter, 289–290
MIBPrefix parameter, 289–290
MIBs (Management
 Information Bases),
 281–284, 286, 288–290
microprocessors, 133, 325, 330
Microsoft Knowledge Base, 333
Microsoft TCP/IP Printing
 service, 261
Microsoft TCP/IP Properties
 dialog box, 305, 309, 312
Microsoft TechNet, 333
Migrate On/Off option, 146
multicast addresses, 108
multihomed hosts, 102,
 116–117
 static mappings and, 140
 TCP/IP installation and, 303
multiple domains, 171
MX (mail exchanger) records,
 168, 175

N

-N field, 196
-n parameter, 223, 254, 257,
 327, 339
name queries, 131–132
name refresh
 requests/responses, 130
name releases, 130–132
name renewal
 intervals, altering, 130
 WINS and, 130–132
name servers, 167, 168

basic description of, 157,
 160–163
 making queries to, name
  resolution methods for,
  163
 NBNS (NetBIOS Name
  Server), 78–79, 219
named objects
 basic description of, 4–5
 examples of, 4
 NBNS (NetBIOS Name
  Server), 78–79, 219
NBT node type, 78–79
nbtstat command, 129,
 223–225, 339, 340
NDIS (Network Device
 Interface Specification),
 23–24, 235, 330
negative name registration
 responses, 216
NetBEUI, 15
NetBIOS. *See also* NetBIOS
 (computer) names
 API, 24, 213
 application layer and, 15
 basic description of, 11, 213
 name cache, 220
 name registration, 129,
  134–135, 214–216
 name release, 215, 216
 name renewal, 130–131
 name resolution, 131–132,
  209–230, 240, 334,
  339–341
 naming services, 213–216
 problems, troubleshooting,
  334, 339–341
 scopes, 74, 77, 78–79, 89
 TCP/IP installation and,
  302–305, 308, 313
 WINS and, 123, 126, 129,
  134–135, 136
NetBIOS (computer) names
 assigning, 214–215
 character restrictions for,
  305
 duplicate, preventing of,
  128, 129
 restrictions on, 220
NetBIOS Scope ID option, 89
NetBT (NetBIOS over
 TCP/IP), 213, 214

basic description of, 23, 24,
 213
 name resolution modes,
  216–220
 WINS and, 131–132
netmasks, 106–107
Netscape Navigator browser,
 259
Netstat utility, 326–327
network adapters, 307, 312, 338
Network applet, 87
Network Client for MS-DOS
 (Microsoft), 134
network IDs, 36–38, 40–42
 basic description of, 49–51
 guidelines for, 42
 required number of,
  determining, 55
 subdividing networks and,
  54–62
Network Interface layer, 12, 13,
 16
network layer, 7–8, 10–12, 23
Network Monitor (Microsoft),
 203, 329–332
Network Monitor Agent, 332
Network option, 307
NETWORKS file, 106
New record option, 175
NFS (Network File System), 251
non-browser role, 264–265
nonexclusive mode, 162
noninteractive mode, 180
nonprinting characters, 222
Notify tab, 176
NS records, 168, 169, 172, 175
nslookup
 basic description of, 179–180
 command reference, 180

O

-o option parameter, 263
ObjectName parameter,
 289–290
objects, 4–5, 283–284
octets, 34, 37, 38
oid parameter, 291
OIDs (object-identifiers), 283

419

INDEX

Only Accept SNMP service Packets From These Hosts option, 287
open command, 258
Open View (Hewlett Packard), 280
options
 Accept SNMP Service Packets From Any Host option, 287
 Accepted Community Names option, 287
 Backup On Termination option, 146
 Contact option, 288
 Create PTR Record option, 174
 Database Backup Path option, 146
 Delete Owner option, 142
 Display Options-Owner option, 141
 Display Options-Sort Order option, 142
 Expire Time option, 178
 Extinction Interval option, 145
 Extinction Timeout option, 145
 global options, 77–78, 89–90
 Location option, 288
 Log Detailed Events option, 146
 Logging Enabled option, 145
 Migrate On/Off option, 146
 NetBIOS Scope ID option, 89
 Network option, 307
 New record option, 175
 Only Accept SNMP service Packets From These Hosts option, 287
 Renewal Interval option, 145
 Replicate Only With Partners option, 146
 Send Authentication Trap option, 287
 Service:Applications option, 288

Service:Datalink/Subnetwork option, 288
Service:End-toEnd option, 288
Service:Internet option, 288
Service:Physical option, 288
Set Filter option, 142
Show Automatically Created Zone option, 174
Starting Version Count option, 146
Verify Interval option, 145
organizational domains, 158–159
OSI (Open Systems Interconnect) model
 application layer, 7–8, 11–12, 14–16, 23
 basic description of, 7–12
 datalink layer, 8, 9–12, 23
 Internet layer, 7–8, 12, 16–20, 191
 layered protocols, 9–12
 network layer, 7–8, 10–12, 23
 physical layer, 9, 11, 12, 23
 presentation layer, 8, 11–12, 23
 session layer, 8, 10–12, 23
 SNMP service and, 279
 transport layer, 7–8, 10–12, 14, 16, 20–23
OSPF (Open Shortest Path First Protocol), 112, 113
Out column, 224, 340
Outbound state, 225, 341

P

-p parameter, 327
packet(s)
 basic description of, 9
 destinations, determination of, 52
 DHCP and, 79–80
 IP address resolution and, 191–192
 monitoring, 329

routers and, 102
TCP/IP installation and, 302
paper trays, 259
parameter(s)
 -a parameter, 223, 256, 327, 339
 -A parameter, 223, 339
 agent parameter, 290
 ArpCacheLife parameter, 194
 -b parameter, 256
 -c parameter, 223, 339
 -CClass parameter, 263
 command parameter, 254
 community parameter, 290
 -d parameter, 257, 263
 destination parameter, 259
 -e parameter, 327
 filename parameter, 263
 -g parameter, 257
 -h parameter, 256
 host parameter, 254, 259
 hostname parameter, 257
 -i parameter, 257, 258
 Interval parameter, 223
 -JJobname parameter, 263
 -l parameter, 263
 MIBfilename parameter, 289
 MIBIndex parameter, 289–290
 MIBPrefix parameter, 289–290
 -n parameter, 223, 254, 257, 327, 339
 -o option parameter, 263
 ObjectName parameter, 289–290
 oid parameter, 291
 -p parameter, 327
 -PPrinter parameter, 263
 put parameter, 259
 -r parameter, 223, 256, 327, 339
 -R parameter, 223, 339
 -s parameter, 223, 257, 327, 339
 -S parameter, 223, 339
 source parameter, 256, 259
 -SServer parameter, 263
 trap parameter, 290
 -v parameter, 257
 walk parameter, 290

420

INDEX

-x parameter, 263
passwords, 252, 254
PERF2MIB.EXE, 289–290
performance monitoring, 321–346
Phase 1 (DHCP Lease Request), 79
Phase 1 (IP Lease Renewal), 82
Phase 2 (DHCP Lease Offer), 79
Phase 2 (IP Lease Acknowledgement), 80–81, 82
Phase 3 (DHCP Lease Select), 79
Phase 4 (DHCP Lease Acknowledgment), 79
physical addresses
 ARP and, 19
 basic description of, 5, 32
 IP addresses versus, 33–34
 network layer and, 10
physical layer, 9, 11, 12, 23
ping command, 203, 235–236, 335–336
ping utility, 203, 237, 311–313, 333–337
p-node node type, 216, 218–219
Point-to-Point Protocol (PPP), 16–17
polling-based method, 279
port(s)
 COM ports, 260
 monitors, 261, 262
 used by the Sockets interface, 18
PostScript files, 263
potential browser role, 264
pound sign (#), 237
PPP (Point-to-Point Protocol), 16–17
-PPrinter parameter, 263
PPTP (Point-to-Point Tunneling Protocol), 16
presentation layer, 8, 11–12, 23
primary domain controller, 268
primary name servers, 160
print gateways, 259, 261
printers. *See also* printing
 configuring, 261
 connecting, methods for, 260–261

network interface, 260
OSI model and, 11
SNMP service and, 279
use of the term, 259
printing. *See also* printers
 devices, 259
 table entries, 115–116
 TCP/IP, 259–263
 utilities, 262–263
processors, 133, 325, 330
promiscuous mode, 330
protocols. *See also* ARP (Address Resolution Protocol); DHCP (Dynamic Configuration Host Protocol); FTP (File Transfer Protocol); IP (Internet Protocol); TCP/IP (Transmission Control Protocol/Internet Protocol)
 HTTP (HyperText Transfer Protocol), 255, 259, 284
 ICMP (Internet Control Message Protocol), 13, 15–22, 117, 289, 311–313, 326–327, 328
 IGMP (Internet Group Management Protocol), 13, 20
 IGP (Interior Gateway Protocol), 110–111
 IGRP (Interior Gateway Routing Protocol), 112–114
 OSPF (Open Shortest Path First Protocol), 112, 113
 Point-to-Point Protocol (PPP), 16–17
 PPTP (Point-to-Point Tunneling Protocol), 16
 RIP (Routing Information Protocol), 112–117
 SLIP (Serial Line Internet Protocol), 16–17
 SNMP (Simple Network Management Protocol), 7, 14–15, 327–328
 TCP (Transmission Control Protocol), 14, 15–22, 254, 289, 326–327
 TFTP (Trivial File Transfer Protocol), 253, 255, 258

UDP (User Datagram Protocol), 14–22, 73, 258, 281, 289, 326–327, 328
PTR (pointer) records, 169, 175
pull partners, 142–144
push partners, 142–144
put parameter, 259

Q

queries
 inverse (reverse lookups), 163, 169–170, 174
 statistics for, 137
quit command, 258

R

-r parameter, 223, 256, 327, 339
-R parameter, 223, 339
RAM (random-access memory), 325
RCP (remote copy) utility, 252, 255–256
rebinding time, 78
recho replies, 20
Reconnecting state, 225
Reconnection state, 341
recursive queries, 163
redirectors, 25
redundancy, 161
refresh values, 167, 178
Registry
 ArpCacheLife parameter, 194
 EnableRegistryBoot key, 173
 HKEY_PERFORMANCE_DATA key, 289
 IP address resolution and, 194
 MIBs and, 281
 saving DHCP configurations in, 81
 SNMP service and, 281, 289

421

INDEX

reliability of links, 114
remote execution utilities, 253–255
remote host(s)
  basic description of, 102
  column, 224, 340
  IP address resolution and, 196, 198–199
Renewal Interval option, 145
renewal time, 78, 145
Replicate Only With Partners option, 146
replication
  options, 146
  times, 137
  triggers, 144
resolvers, 157
resource records, 166–168, 175
resource sharing, 11
retry values, 167, 178
reverse domains, 158–159
reverse lookups (inverse queries), 163, 169–170, 174
REXEC (remote execution) utility, 252, 253–254
RFCs (Requests for Comment)
  no. 950, 50–51
  no. 1002, 24, 89
  no. 1001, 24, 89
  no. 1034, 157
  no. 1035, 157
  no. 1155, 279
  no. 1157, 279
  no. 1179, 260, 261
  no. 1213, 279, 282
  no. 1542, 84
  no. 1700, 18
RIP (Routing Information Protocol)
  basic description of, 112–114
  enabling routing over IP using, 114–117
  OSPF and, 113
  version 1 (RIPv1), 113
RIP for Internet Protocol service, 116
root domains, 158, 160
route command, 115–116

router(s). *See also* gateways; IP routing
  ARP and, 198, 199
  basic description of, 6–12, 17
  DHCP and, 78–79, 86
  host name resolution and, 238
  NetBIOS name resolution and, 219
  network IDs and, 41
  SNMP service and, 279
  subnet addressing and, 48, 55
  TCP/IP installation and, 301
Routing tab, 117
RSH utility, 252, 253–255
rshd command, 255–256

S

-s field, 195
-s parameter, 223, 257, 327, 339
-S parameter, 223, 339
saving DHCP configurations, 81
scavenging times, 138
scope(s)
  basic description of, 76–77
  configuring, 83, 84, 87–89
  creating, 86
  IDs, 304–305, 313
  local, 84
  options, 77–78, 89–90, 109
  reducing DHCP traffic and, 86
secondary name servers, 160–161
second-level domains, 159
security
  configuring, for the SNMP service, 287
  passwords, 252, 254
Security tab, 287
semicolon (;), 166, 168
Send Authentication Trap option, 287

serial numbers, 178
Service:Applications option, 288
Service:Datalink/Subnetwork option, 288
Service:End-to-End option, 288
Service:Internet option, 288
Service:Physical option, 288
Services icon, 116
session layer, 8, 10–12, 23
Session Statistics pane, 331
Set Filter option, 142
set operation, 280
Show Automatically Created Zone option, 174
Show Database window, 141–142
single domains, 170–171
slaves, 161–162, 179
SLIP (Serial Line Internet Protocol), 16–17
SMBs (Server Message Blocks), 11, 25, 251
SMS (Microsoft Systems Management Server), 329
SNMP (Simple Network Management Protocol), 7, 14–15, 327–328
SNMP Properties dialog box, 287–288
SNMP service, 284, 328
  agents, 279, 280, 281, 285, 286, 288
  basic description of, 279–296
  manager, 279–282
  preparation quiz, 277–278
  problems, troubleshooting, 295
  review quiz, 292–293
  skill practice, 294–295
SOA (start of authority) records, 167–168, 172, 175, 176
SOA Record tab, 176
Sockets (Microsoft), 14, 18–19, 24–25, 334
sort order, for mapping, 142
sound, HTTP support for, 259
source parameter, 256, 259

422

INDEX

source quench, 19–20
-Sserver parameter, 263
Starting Version Count option, 146
State column, 224, 340
static mapping, 139–140
static routing, 109–110, 114–116
Station Statistics pane, 331
statistics
  monitoring, 326–327, 330
  WINS, 137–138
subnet(s), 86, 198, 220, 222. *See also* subnet masks
  addressing, 45–68
  ARPing across, 192
  basic description of, 37, 48, 50–51
  dividing your network into, 54–62
  host name resolution and, 238, 241
  IDs, 49–50
  IP routing and, 102, 103, 104, 107–108
  problems with, troubleshooting, 333–334
  range of host IDs for, determining, 61–62
  remote, locating computers on, 128
  rules, 50–51
subnet mask(s), 81, 87–88, 113, 301–302. *See also* subnets
  basic description of, 50–53
  custom, defining, 56–57
  DHCP and, 74
  invalid, 202–203
  IP routing and, 106–107, 113
  selecting appropriate, 57–58
  subdividing networks and, 54–62
Summary pane, 332
Sun Microsystems, 163, 280
SunNet Manager (Sun Microsystems), 280
SunOS operating system, 263
supernetting, 54
synchronization
  basic description of, 5–6

transport layer and, 10
system logs, 335, 336

T

tables
  address translation, used by ARP, 195
  dynamic, 109
  printing/managing entries from, 115–116
  routing, 105–110
  WINS, 144
TCP (Transmission Control Protocol)
  basic description of, 14, 15–22
  datagrams and, 17
  SNMP service and, 289
  statistics, monitoring, 326–327
  Telnet connectivity and, 254
TCP/IP (Transmission Control Protocol/Internet Protocol). *See also* TCP/IP configuration
  model, 12–15
  review questions, 3
  review quiz, 27–28
  as a suite of protocols, 7
TCP/IP configuration
  basic description of, 297–320
  preparation quiz, 229–300
  problems, troubleshooting, 309–313, 318, 333–334
  review quiz, 314–315
  skill practice, 316–319
  testing, 311–313, 316–317
TCP/IP Properties dialog box, 109, 117
TDI (Transport Driver Interface), 23, 24, 25
Telnet, 7, 14–15, 251–255, 313
TFTP (Trivial File Transfer Protocol), 253, 255, 258
Token Ring networks, 15, 191
top-level domains, 158–159

Total Statistics pane, 331
tracert utility, 117, 341
traffic, network, 85–86, 128, 326
trailers, 8
transport layer, 7–8, 10–12, 14, 16, 20–23
trap parameter, 290
traps, 279, 281, 285–287, 290–291
Traps tab, 287
troubleshooting
  ARP, 202–203, 336
  basic description of, 321–324
  DNS, 179–180
  hardware problems, 333–334
  host names, 334, 338
  IP addresses, 193, 202–203, 336–338
  NetBIOS, 334, 339–341
  preparation quiz, 323–324
  review quiz, 342–344
  skill practice, 345
  SNMP service, 295
  subnets, 333–334
  TCP/IP configuration, 309–313, 318, 333–334
TTL (time-to-live) counters, 19, 112, 117, 129–130
  DNS and, 164, 167, 176, 178
  IP address resolution and, 194
TTY emulation, 254
type fields, 9–10

U

UDP (User Datagram Protocol), 73, 258
  basic description of, 14–22
  SNMP service and, 281, 289
  statistics, monitoring, 326–327, 328
UNC (Universal Naming Convention), 221
unique conflicts statistics, 138

423

INDEX

unique identifiers, 91
unique names, 215
unique registration statistics, 138
unique renewal statistics, 138
unique static mappings, 139–140
UNIX, 237, 253–254, 261
  carriage returns, converting EOL characters to, 258
  computers, copying files from, 272
  printers, 247
  SMBs and, 251
  using a backslash in, 256
updates, 137, 143
user-mode interface, 25
utilities
  arp utility, 195–196, 203
  data transfer utility, 255–259
  ipconfig utility, 81–82, 86, 91–92, 131, 203, 309–310, 334–335, 337, 339
  LPD (line printer daemon) utility, 252, 260–262
  lpq (line printer query) utility, 263
  LPQ (line printer queue) utility, 252
  LPR (line printer) utility, 260–263
  Netstat utility, 326–327
  ping utility, 203, 237, 311–313, 333–337
  RCP (remote copy) utility, 252, 255–256
  REXEC (remote execution) utility, 252, 253–254
  RSH utility, 252, 253–255
  tracert utility, 117, 341
  winipcfg utility, 91, 309–310

V

-v parameter, 257
Verify Interval option, 145

version IDs, 141, 142
video, HTTP support for, 259
VPNs (Virtual Private Networks), 16

W

walk parameter, 290
WANs (Wide Area Networks), 16, 18, 38, 55, 114
well-known port numbers, 18
wildcard characters, 256
Windows 95 (Microsoft)
  browsing and, 266
  TCP/IP installation and, 301, 306–339
  saving DHCP configurations in, 81
  WINS and, 134
Windows for Workgroups (Microsoft), 86, 134, 266
Windows NT (Microsoft), 201, 213–214
  configuring, as an IP router, 114–117
  DHCP and, 86
  Diagnostics, 309
  domains, versus DNS domains, 239
  network architecture, components of, 22–26
  printing and, 261, 262
  saving DHCP configurations in, 81
  TCP/IP installation and, 301, 304–306
  utilities, list of, 251–253
Windows NT Server (Microsoft), 113, 116–117, 266, 286
  configuring, 127, 171–172
  Resource Kit, 289, 290
  WINS and, 127, 133–134, 135–140
Windows NT Workstation (Microsoft), 134, 266, 286

Windows Sockets (Microsoft), 14, 18–19, 24–25, 334
winipcfg utility, 91, 309–310
WINS (Windows Internet Naming Service)
  basic description of, 123–152
  benefits of using, 128
  browsing and, 267–268
  configuring, 135–140
  database, backups for, 144–145
  database, configuration options for, 145
  database, managing, 141–152
  database, replication of, 142–144
  DHCP and, 74, 78–79, 89
  installation, 132–137
  integration of, with Microsoft DNS Server, 171
  monitoring, 329, 339
  name registration, 128–129
  name resolution and, 215–221, 237–238, 240–241
  preparation quiz, 125
  review quiz, 147–148
  running, with multiple processors, 133
  server/client requirements, 133–134
  skill practice, 149–152
  SNMP service and, 283–286, 288–289
  statistics, 137–138
  TCP/IP installation and, 302–304, 308, 310, 312
  WINS Manager, 123, 136–137, 139–152
Wins.mdb, 144
winstmp.mdb, 144
Workstation Service, 23, 24
world readable files, 258
World Wide Web
  internetworks and, 251
  HTTP and, 259

424

INDEX

X

-x parameter, 263
X.25 networks, 191

Z

zone(s)
    basic description of, 159–160
    creating, 174
    files, 166–168, 173
    hidden, 174
    name server roles and, 160–161
    properties, configuring, 176–179
    transfers, 160–163, 170, 179
Zone Properties dialog box, 176–177

my2cents.idgbooks.com

Register This Book — And Win!

Visit **http://my2cents.idgbooks.com** to register this book and we'll automatically enter you in our fantastic monthly prize giveaway. It's also your opportunity to give us feedback: let us know what you thought of this book and how you would like to see other topics covered.

Discover IDG Books Online!

The IDG Books Online Web site is your online resource for tackling technology — at home and at the office. Frequently updated, the IDG Books Online Web site features exclusive software, insider information, online books, and live events!

10 Productive & Career-Enhancing Things You Can Do at www.idgbooks.com

1. Nab source code for your own programming projects.
2. Download software.
3. Read Web exclusives: special articles and book excerpts by IDG Books Worldwide authors.
4. Take advantage of resources to help you advance your career as a Novell or Microsoft professional.
5. Buy IDG Books Worldwide titles or find a convenient bookstore that carries them.
6. Register your book and win a prize.
7. Chat live online with authors.
8. Sign up for regular e-mail updates about our latest books.
9. Suggest a book you'd like to read or write.
10. Give us your 2¢ about our books and about our Web site.

You say you're not on the Web yet? It's easy to get started with IDG Books' *Discover the Internet*, available at local retailers everywhere.